Integrating Macs® into Windows® Networks

WITHDRAWN
UTSA LIBRARIES

About the Author

Guy Hart-Davis is the author of more than 50 computer books about Mac OS X, iPods and iPhones, Windows, and other topics. His recent books include *Mac OS X System Administration* and *AppleScript: A Beginner's Guide.*

About the Technical Editor

Dwight Spivey has written several books about Macs, Mac OS X, Microsoft Office, and the iPod touch and iPhone. He is an engineer for Konica Minolta, which entails the integration of Macs and Windows-based PCs on a daily basis.

Integrating Macs® into Windows® Networks

GUY **HART-DAVIS**

New York   Chicago   San Francisco
Lisbon   London   Madrid   Mexico City   Milan
New Delhi   San Juan   Seoul   Singapore   Sydney   Toronto

The McGraw·Hill Companies

Cataloging-in-Publication Data is on file with the Library of Congress

McGraw-Hill books are available at special quantity discounts to use as premiums and sales promotions, or for use in corporate training programs. To contact a representative, please e-mail us at bulksales@mcgraw-hill.com.

Integrating Macs® into Windows® Networks

1234567890   DOC DOC   109876543210

ISBN   978-0-07-171302-3
MHID   0-07-171302-6

Sponsoring Editor Jane K. Brownlow	**Copy Editor** Bart Reed	**Illustration** Glyph International
Editorial Supervisor Patty Mon	**Proofreader** Elise Oranges	**Art Director, Cover** Jeff Weeks
Project Manager Vasundhara Sawhney, Glyph International	**Indexer** James Minkin	**Cover Designer** Jeff Weeks
Acquisitions Coordinator Joya Anthony	**Production Supervisor** Jean Bodeaux	
Technical Editor Dwight Spivey	**Composition** Glyph International	

This book is dedicated to Rhonda and Teddy.

At a Glance

Contents

Acknowledgments

My thanks go to the following people for making this book happen:

- Jane Brownlow, for getting the book approved and signing me to write it
- Megg Morin, for taking over developmental duties and approving changes to the outline after Jane left to spend more time with her family
- Joya Anthony, for handling the administration, schedule, and finances
- Dwight Spivey, for performing the technical review and providing helpful suggestions and encouragement
- Vasundhara Sawhney, for coordinating the project
- Bart Reed, for editing the text with care and a light touch
- Glyph International, for laying out the pages
- Elise Oranges, for proofreading the book
- James Minkin, for creating the index

Introduction

Your company or organization has a network built on Windows Server.

But you need to add Macs to the network.

Join the club. These days, pretty much every company or organization needs some Macs—anything from a handful to several departments' worth.

And Mac OS X 10.6 (Snow Leopard) can be a great corporate citizen on Windows—provided you know how to make it work.

Is This Book for Me?

Yes.

If you need to add Macs to a Windows network, this book is for you.

Read on for the details of what this book covers—or turn to the index to see if it contains the specific topics you're interested in.

What Will I Learn in This Book?

Here's what you will learn from this book:

- Chapter 1, "Planning Your Mac Rollout," walks you through deciding which members of the staff in your company or organization need Macs rather than Windows PCs, which kinds of Mac you'll buy for each of them, and how you'll manage the Macs on the network.

- Chapter 2, "Connecting the Macs to the Network and to Active Directory," explains how to create user and computer accounts in Active Directory for the Macs, how to connect the Macs physically to the network, and how to bind the Macs to Active Directory to make them members of the network at a basic level.

- Chapter 3, "Binding a Mac OS X Server to Manage Macs via a 'Magic Triangle,'" shows you how to bind a Mac running the Server version of Mac OS X to an Active Directory network so that you can use it to manage the Macs. You bind the Mac OS X server to the network, and then bind the Mac clients both to the Mac server and to Active Directory. The result is a magic triangle that enables you to manage the Macs through Mac OS X Server, even though the Macs are bound to Active Directory.

- Chapter 4, "Extending Active Directory to Handle Mac Clients Natively," takes you step-by-step through extending your Windows Server network's Active Directory schema so that it contains the attributes and classes it needs to store information about its Mac clients. Extending Active Directory is a complicated and tricky process—but when you get it right, it's not only richly rewarding but also can save you huge amounts of time and effort.

- Chapter 5, "Giving Your Macs Safe Access to the Internet," covers connecting your network's Macs to the Internet, using proxy servers to sanitize the raw content on offer there, and applying antivirus software to protect the Macs from any malware they encounter.

- Chapter 6, "Connecting Macs to Microsoft Exchange," shows you how to connect your Macs to Exchange Server so that Mac users can send e-mail using Mail, schedule appointments and to-do items with iCal, and look up contact information with Address Book.

- Chapter 7, "Providing Home Folders and File Services to Macs," takes you through your options for providing Macs with home folders and access to shared folders on the network. You'll learn to decide among giving the user a home folder on the Mac, creating a network home folder that acts like a local home folder, and setting up a mobile account for the user.

- Chapter 8, "Setting Up Printing on Macs," explains how to connect your network's Macs to printers on Windows print queues. Along the way, you'll learn about the peculiarities of Mac printing and how to cope with them.

- Chapter 9, "Installing and Updating Software," instructs you in the several essential methods of installing software on Macs. You could install all the applications the hard way—by sitting down at the Mac and slotting DVDs until the moon turns to blue cheese—but you'll probably want to save your time, fingernails, and hair by using the smarter, automated ways. And you'll certainly want to use Mac OS X's Software Update feature to download and install updates automatically.

■ Chapter 10, "Run Windows Programs on Macs," takes you through your options for running Windows programs on your network's Macs: using Remote Desktop Connection to run programs hosted by a Windows server, installing a virtual-machine application that can run Windows and Windows programs alongside the Mac applications, and using Boot Camp to run Windows directly on the Mac's hardware. After deciding which approach will suit you best, you'll learn how to set it up.

■ Chapter 11, "Providing Remote Access for and to Macs," shows you how to connect Macs to your Windows-based virtual private network (VPN) so that they can access your network securely by tunneling through the Internet from their existing Internet connections. You'll also learn how to make Macs inside your network accessible to Macs outside the network via the Internet.

■ Chapter 12, "Backing Up and Restoring Macs," explains how to use Mac OS X's built-in Time Machine application to back up files from Macs and restore them from backup after disaster strikes. The chapter also suggests other backup software you may want to investigate.

■ Chapter 13, "Recovering from Disasters on Macs," starts by explaining how to teach your network's Mac users to deal with application hangs, freezes, and system lockups. It then shows you how to repair permission errors and disk errors, use Safe mode to force a disk check and repair, "fsck" a hard disk to banish problems, and reinstall Mac OS X when all else fails.

■ Chapter 14, "Adding Macs to Small Windows Networks," takes a step back from the big picture of networks that run Windows Server. This chapter shows you how to add Macs to small Windows networks, such as those you may need to configure in branch offices or home offices.

■ The index—okay, you don't need me to tell you what that contains.

Conventions Used in This Book

To make its meaning clear and concise, this book uses a number of conventions, four of which are worth mentioning here:

■ The pipe character or vertical bar denotes choosing an item from the menu bar. For example, "choose Server | Connect" means that you should click the Server menu on the menu bar, and then click the Connect item on the menu that opens.

■ Note, Tip, and Caution paragraphs highlight information that's worth extra attention.

■ Sidebars provide extra information on important topics.

■ The ⌘ symbol represents the Mac Command key.

CHAPTER 1 | Planning Your Mac Rollout

S o you've decided to add some Macs to your Windows Server network.

Great move!

This chapter gets the ball rolling by running through the decisions you'll need to make before you place the order for the Macs:

- Which members of staff need Macs rather than Windows PCs.
- Which kind of Mac each eligible person gets.
- Which version of Mac OS X to run on the Macs (a much easier choice than with Windows).
- How you will manage the Macs on the network.

Choosing Who Gets a Mac

If you're running a Windows network, chances are that the majority of the computers on it will be Windows PCs. That means each person who gets a Mac will have a special need for it—otherwise, you'd just set them up with a PC like everyone else.

Normally, this means you're dealing with one (or both) of two groups of people:

- **Power users**   Computing areas such as desktop publishing, web design, graphics and illustration, and audio and video editing have long been Mac strongholds. If your company or organization has users who work in these areas, they may well be better off with Macs than with PCs—especially if most of their experience has been with Macs.
- **Executives**   If half your VPs decide they want Macs rather than PCs because they consider themselves the creative types that Apple's ads suggest prefer Macs to PCs, you may find you need to go along and provide the Macs. Given this group, it's most likely you'll provide high-end laptops.

Your company or organization may have other groups of people who need Macs for other reasons. For example, you may have customer-support techs who support Mac users and so need Macs themselves, software developers who develop for Mac OS X, web testers who need run-of-the-mill Macs to check that websites look okay on all important browsers, and so on.

Either way, draw up a list of the people who qualify for Macs—and note who's naughty and who's nice. Then follow through the next section to decide which type of Mac each should get.

Choosing Suitable Macs for Your Staff

Compared with the plethora of models that most PC manufacturers produce, Apple keeps its selection of Macs pared down to a minimum, maintaining admirably clear definitions between its different models. This means that choosing a Mac is a relatively straightforward process.

As usual, the first choice is between desktops and laptops. At this writing, laptops are now outselling desktops in the overall market—but because most companies and organizations are still buying more desktops than laptops, let's start with the desktop Macs.

Choosing Macs for Desktop Users

Apple sells three main families of desktop Macs: the Mac Pro, the iMac, and the Mac mini.

Mac Pro

The Mac Pro is the most powerful desktop Mac and the most expensive. The price includes the CPU (central processing unit—the main box of the computer, as it were) and a wired keyboard and mouse but no monitor. This gives you full flexibility in choosing your own monitor or monitors, but you pay for the privilege.

At this writing, the Mac Pro comes with either one or two quad-core processors and can contain up to 32GB of RAM and 4TB of storage. Out of the box, the Mac Pro can drive either one or two monitors (each up to 30 inches, such as Apple's 30-inch Cinema Display), but you can up the number to four by adding another graphics card.

This ferocious hardware means that the Mac Pro is great for demanding tasks such as graphic design, page layout, or editing music and video. For regular users, a Mac Pro is overkill.

Should You Buy Customized Macs or Buy Ready-Made Macs and Upgrade Them Yourself?

The Apple Store (http://store.apple.com) and most Apple-approved Mac retailers offer custom-built Macs as well as standard configurations, so you can tweak the Macs as needed. For example, you can increase the memory, bump up the hard drive by the odd terabyte, or add an extra monitor.

Normally, it's most convenient to buy your Macs configured the way you need them, so that you don't need to worry about upgrading them. But if you need to upgrade the memory on a Mac, take a minute to compare the price of third-party memory with the prices that Apple or Mac retailers charge, as the latter tend to be high. For example, at this writing, you can save the thick end of $2,000 by buying 32GB of RAM for a Mac Pro from a third-party retailer rather than the Apple Store.

NOTE　Unlike Apple's other Macs, the Mac Pro is designed to be easy to open and upgrade. This is good news if you need to add extra hard disks to provide additional storage or add RAM to improve the crunching power of the Mac Pro's virtual molars.

iMac

The iMac is an all-in-one desktop computer with the CPU built into the back of the LCD monitor. This makes for a sleek-looking unit with less cabling than computers that have the CPU in a separate box. It also means that you don't have to worry about finding a convenient place for the CPU in a cubicle or office: If you've got space for the monitor, keyboard, and mouse, you're all set.

 CAUTION　The iMac's integrated design means that most upgrades and maintenance involve major surgery. The RAM slots are easily accessible, but nothing else is.

The iMac comes as a complete package, including a wireless keyboard and the wireless Magic Mouse; you can substitute a regular, wired keyboard and wired mouse if you prefer.

At this writing, you can choose between a 21.5-inch screen and a 27-inch screen; the 21.5-inch screen is more than enough for general use, whereas the 27-inch screen gives high enough resolution (2560 × 1440 pixels) for advanced work with graphics, layout, or video. Both sizes come with dual-core processors, but you can also get the 27-inch model with a quad-core processor for extra grunt. Both models come with 4GB RAM standard, but you can increase it up to as much as 16GB to handle more demanding applications. Hard drives go up to 2TB; upgrading is a serious operation, so make sure you buy the size you need.

 NOTE　As well as its built-in monitor, the iMac can drive one external monitor (up to Apple's 30-inch Cinema Display), so you can easily set it up in a two-monitor configuration—great for knowledge workers who need to be able to see the contents of multiple windows at the same time.

Mac mini

The Mac mini is the smallest of the Mac models and comes as a single box containing only the CPU—you need to add the monitor, keyboard, mouse, speakers, and any other peripherals the user will require.

With a dual-core processor, 2GB or 4GB of RAM, and a 500GB hard drive, the Mac mini is plenty powerful enough for most work-related tasks. Compared to the iMac, though, the Mac mini offers less bang for the buck unless you already have monitors (and perhaps keyboards and mouses) that you want to continue using.

 NOTE　If you don't have monitors to reuse, the only reason to buy the Mac mini over the iMac is if you need to be able to place the CPU in a small space. Normally, this is more of a concern for servers than for desktop computers, because desktops tend not to be much use without at least a monitor, keyboard, and mouse attached.

Choosing Macs for Mobile Users

For those of your company or organization's mobile executives and knowledge workers who need Macs, you'll probably want to get MacBooks, MacBook Airs, or MacBook Pros. The choice here tends to be trickier than with desktops, as you'll see in a moment.

NOTE   Each MacBook (MacBook Pro, MacBook, and MacBook Air) uses a built-in battery that's not field-replaceable (battery replacement is a technician's job) but that gives better battery life than most replaceable batteries and should last for nearly twice as many charge cycles (around 1,000 instead of 500). The MacBook Pro and MacBook batteries give up to 7 hours of usable life; the MacBook Air gives more like 5 hours.

We'll start with the MacBook Pros.

MacBook Pro

The MacBook Pro is Apple's top-of-the-line series of laptops, providing a good balance between power and portability. Each MacBook Pro includes a DVD burner, so it's fully equipped for most tasks.

The MacBook Pro comes in three sizes, each of which can take up to 8GB of RAM and either a regular (spinning) hard drive or a solid-state device (SSD).

NOTE   SSDs give faster performance than regular hard drives, but they are still much more expensive, and their capacities are lower.

Using a Laptop Mac as a Desktop Mac

Apple doesn't sell docking stations for any of its laptops, but it's easy enough to use any of them as a desktop by connecting a keyboard, mouse, and monitor.

The easiest way to connect a keyboard and mouse is usually to connect the keyboard to the laptop via a USB cable, and to connect the mouse to the keyboard via USB (which allows you to keep it connected). Alternatively, you can connect a wireless keyboard (such as the Apple Wireless Keyboard) and a wireless mouse (such as the Apple Magic Mouse) using Bluetooth.

Each Mac laptop includes a Mini DisplayPort port that can drive a full-size monitor (up to Apple's 30-inch Cinema Display). After connecting the external display, you can either use the laptop's built-in display as an extra display or close the laptop's lid and use only the external display. When you close the lid, the laptop goes to sleep, but you can wake it by pressing a key on an external keyboard or clicking a button on an external mouse.

Third-party vendors do sell docking stations for some Mac laptops. For an example, see the OlympicControls Corp./BookEndz website (www .BookEndzDocks.com).

These are the MacBook Pro sizes:

■ **13-inch screen**   With 1280×800 pixel resolution, the baby of the litter offers great portability in a fully-spec'd laptop.

NOTE   The low-end MacBook Pros—the 13-inch MacBook Pro and the base model of the 15-inch MacBook Pro—use shared graphics, borrowing RAM for use as video memory. This means their graphics performance is acceptable rather than exciting. The high-end MacBook Pros—the two other 15-inch MacBook Pro models and all the 17-inch MacBook Pros—include a second graphics processor for improved performance.

■ **15-inch screen**   With 1440×900 pixel resolution, the mid-size MacBook Pro lets you see two decent-sized windows side by side.

■ **17-inch screen**   The 1900×1200 screen is large enough to see serious amounts of data at once, and the additional graphics processor delivers serious performance. To accommodate the screen, this MacBook Pro is necessarily larger, but it still weighs less than 7 pounds.

MacBook

The MacBook is Apple's lowest-priced laptop, although it's still substantially more expensive than many directly comparable PCs. Still, you're getting Mac OS X and the applications it includes—and with any luck, your company or organization is paying for it rather than you.

The MacBook has a dual-core processor, 2GB of RAM (upgradeable to 4GB), a DVD burner, and a medium-sized hard drive (the exact capacity depends on how much you care to pay). The MacBook isn't a screamer, but it's a solid laptop computer that works well for any user who doesn't need the power of a MacBook Pro or the ethereal lightness of a MacBook Air (discussed next).

NOTE   Visually, the main difference between the MacBook and the MacBook Pro line is that the MacBook's body is made of polycarbonate, whereas the MacBook Pro's body is made of aluminum.

MacBook Air

The MacBook Air is Apple's thin-and-light laptop—the one that omits a DVD burner in the interests of staying svelte. Weighing in at 3 pounds on the nose, the MacBook Air has a dual-core processor, 2GB of RAM, and a modest-sized hard drive or SSD.

NOTE   To keep down its size and weight, the MacBook Air omits an optical drive. You can add an external optical drive via USB, or use Mac OS X's Remote Disc feature to share another Mac's optical drive, but either solution is much more awkward than using a built-in optical drive.

The MacBook Air puts portability over performance, which tends to suffer both because the CPU has less grunt than that in the MacBook Pro models and because the RAM is limited to 2GB. This means the MacBook Air is great for traveling executives who need to work on reports, spreadsheets, or presentations, but it's not suitable for heavy-duty tasks.

NOTE   Apart from a Mini DisplayPort for connecting an external monitor, the MacBook Air has only two ports: an audio-out port and a single USB port. The MacBook Air comes with a USB-to-Ethernet network adapter that provides a pass-through USB port, so you can connect to a wired network and still connect a USB device. To connect multiple USB devices, you'll need to use a hub, which adds to the MacBook Air's traveling weight.

Choosing Which Version of Mac OS X to Use

At this point, if you were choosing Windows PCs, you'd need to choose which version of Windows to get: Windows 7 Ultimate for power users who need encryption, Windows 7 Professional for regular business types, or perhaps Windows 7 Enterprise if your corporation has managed to impose its delusions of grandeur on the regulatory authorities.

With Mac OS X, there's no such decision. Mac OS X comes in just two flavors, the client edition and the Server edition. You don't need me to tell you that the Server edition is for servers, and that you'll want to use the client edition on your non-server Macs. The client edition includes every client feature, from the iChat instant-messaging client to the DVD player, so users don't need to worry about missing out. In fact, the situation is rather the reverse: You may find that the Macs come with applications and features that you don't want to be available to the users. To fix this problem, you can turn off applications and features you don't want users to use, as discussed later in this book.

Running Mac OS X on Macs with Non-Intel Processors

Mac OS X version 10.6 (Snow Leopard) runs only on Macs that have Intel processors. That's most of the Macs that are still viable at this writing—but if your organization still uses Macs built around PowerPC processors, you won't be able to get them past Mac OS X version 10.5 (Leopard).

At this writing, there's no reason to buy Macs with PowerPC processors beyond historical curiosity, but if you already have them, the later PowerPC models will be viable for several years more.

Apart from including the PowerPC code, Leopard works largely in the same way as Snow Leopard, so if you have PowerPC Macs, you will be able to follow the instructions in this book with only minor variations.

Deciding How to Manage the Macs on the Network

Now that you've chosen your Macs, it's time to decide how you will manage them on the network. You have three main choices here:

- Use Active Directory authentication and network home folders only
- Manage the Macs through Active Directory
- Manage the Macs through Mac OS X Server

Let's look at each of these in turn.

NOTE Chapter 2 discusses how to connect the Macs to the network and bind them to Active Directory. Chapter 4 explains how to extend the Active Directory schema and manage the Macs through Active Directory. Chapter 3 walks you through adding a Mac OS X server to your Windows network and managing the Macs through it.

Use Active Directory Authentication and Network Home Folders Only

The lowest level of integrating the Macs in the Active Directory network is to use Active Directory to authenticate the Macs. It's the easiest arrangement to set up, and it's also the least expensive. At logon, each Mac user authenticates via Active Directory, so you can make sure nobody unauthorized is logging on.

You can also provide network home folders to the Mac users, which is good for desktop Macs. (For laptop Macs, you'll probably want to store the home folders on the Macs themselves so that they're available even when the Mac isn't connected to the network.)

Figure 1-1 illustrates using Active Directory authentication and network home folders only.

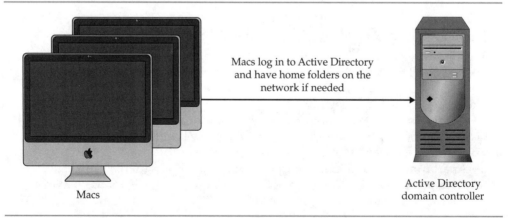

Macs log in to Active Directory
and have home folders on the
network if needed

Macs

Active Directory
domain controller

Figure 1-1. The simplest way to add the Macs to your network is to bind them to Active Directory but not manage them from it.

Manage the Macs Through Active Directory

You manage the Windows PCs on your network through Active Directory, so you'll probably want to do the same with the Macs. This requires some effort and some expense, but in many cases it's the best long-term solution for integrating the Macs into the Windows network. Figure 1-2 illustrates this arrangement.

To manage the Macs through Active Directory, you need to add 36 attributes and 10 classes to your Active Directory schema, extending it with the vital slots for holding the information needed to manage the Macs. Once these are in place, you can use Mac OS X Server tools such as Workgroup Manager to manage your Mac clients through Active Directory. These tools use Apple's client-management architecture called Managed Client for Mac OS X (abbreviated as MCX) or Managed Preferences.

Manage the Macs Through Mac OS X Server

Instead of extending the Active Directory schema to contain the information needed for the Mac OS X management tools, you can bind a Mac OS X Server to Active Directory and use it to manage the Macs. This arrangement, illustrated in Figure 1-3, is sometimes called a *magic triangle.*

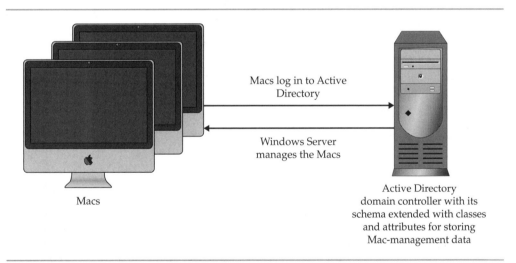

Macs log in to Active Directory

Windows Server manages the Macs

Macs

Active Directory domain controller with its schema extended with classes and attributes for storing Mac-management data

Figure 1-2.   By extending Active Directory with Mac-related attributes and classes, you can manage the Macs through Active Directory.

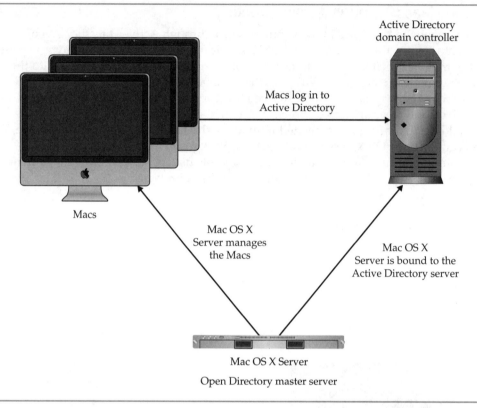

Figure 1-3.   By binding a Mac OS X Server to Active Directory, you can manage the Macs through Open Directory.

The Mac OS X Server enables you to manage the Macs much as you would if they were bound to a pure-Mac network rather than Active Directory, which is handy. However, this method also has a couple of drawbacks:

- First, of course, you need a Mac capable of running Mac OS X Server, plus a copy of Mac OS X Server to run on it. (See the sidebar on the next page for a couple of suggestions.)

- Second, you need to know how to set up Mac OS X Server and use the Mac OS X management tools.

Choosing a Server Mac and Getting Mac OS X Server

If you have a spare Mac, you can install Mac OS X Server on it, either by upgrading an existing installation of the client version of Mac OS X or by performing a clean install. Usually the clean install is the better way to go. If you need to be able to restore the Mac to the client version of Mac OS X afterward, repartition the hard drive and then install Mac OS X Server on the new partition.

Mac OS X Server will run on pretty much any Mac that has an Intel processor and 2GB of RAM, so you can test it on most any spare Mac you have. You can also install and run Mac OS X Server on a VMWare Fusion virtual machine, which is great for testing.

At this writing, the best-value new Mac server is the Mac mini that comes with Mac OS X Server preinstalled. If you have a spare Mac and you're in the U.S., you can get an evaluation copy of Mac OS X Server for free. Go to the Server page on the Apple website (www.apple.com/server/), look for Snow Leopard Server Evaluation, and follow the link.

CHAPTER 2 | Connecting the Macs to the Network and Active Directory

Once you've bought and gotten your Macs, you'll be ready to set them up and connect them to the network and to Active Directory. This chapter shows you how to do so. This book uses Windows Server 2008 R2 for its examples; if you have an earlier version of Windows Server, you may need to make minor alterations.

Normally, your first move will be to create user accounts in Active Directory for the users who will use the Macs, so we'll start there. You may also want to create Computer objects for the Macs in Active Directory before binding them—but, as you'll see, you can create them during the binding process instead.

With the accounts in place, you can connect the Macs physically to the network, either with Ethernet cables or wirelessly. We'll look at each of these in turn.

When you've connected a Mac, you can then bind it to Active Directory and verify the binding.

 NOTE   Chapter 3 explains how to set up a Mac OS X server, bind it to Active Directory, and use it to manage Macs on the network. Chapter 4 covers extending Active Directory so that you can manage Macs directly through it.

Creating User Accounts for the Mac Users

Start by creating user accounts on the Windows server for the Mac users. If you've already created the user accounts, you're set. For example, if you're transitioning existing Windows users to Macs, you can use the user accounts they already have.

To create the accounts, use Active Directory Users And Computers as usual. For example, expand the directory tree, right-click the Users object, and then choose New | User from the shortcut menu, as shown in Figure 2-1.

Fill in the details in the New Object – User dialog box (see Figure 2-2). Click the Next button, enter the user's initial password, and choose the password options—for example, whether the user must change the password the first time they log on and whether the password expires. Click the Next button again, check the details on the final screen, and then click the Finish button.

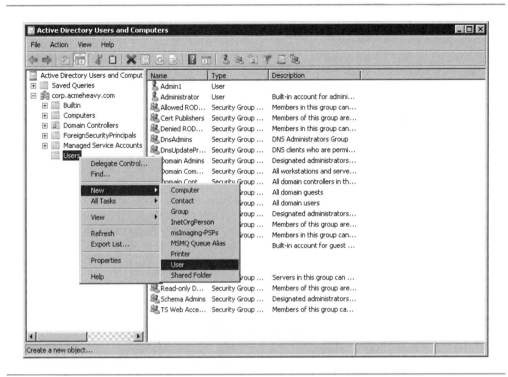

Figure 2-1.   Create user accounts for the Mac users in Active Directory Users And Computers as normal.

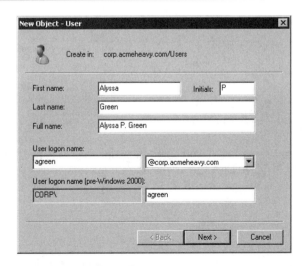

Figure 2-2.   Enter the details for the new user in the New Object – User dialog box.

Creating Computer Accounts for the Macs

At this point, you can also create Computer objects for the Macs you're going to add. Each Mac needs a unique Computer object on the network, just as Windows PCs do; you have the choice of either creating the Computer objects ahead of time in Active Directory or creating them during the binding process.

Whether you will do better to create the objects first probably depends on your network, your role in it, and whether you're adding a handful of Macs, a bucketful, or a boatload. If you need to implement a strict naming scheme, you may find it easier to create the Computer objects ahead of time and then go binding with a list in your hand. If the Macs are few and your naming scheme allows some flexibility, creating the objects during binding should work fine.

If you decide to create the Computer objects first, use Active Directory Users And Computers as normal. Expand the directory tree, right-click the Computers object, and then choose New | Computer. In the New Object – Computer dialog box (see Figure 2-3), type the name, choose the user or group, and then click the OK button.

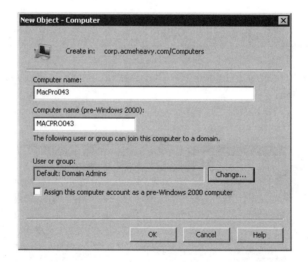

Figure 2-3.   If necessary, create a Computer object for each Mac by using the New Object – Computer dialog box in Active Directory Users And Computers.

Making the Physical Connection to the Network

Now that the network is ready to meet the Mac, it's time to introduce the Mac to the network. You'll first need to make the physical connection to the network, and then you can deal with all the protocol muck.

As you well know, there are two main ways of making the physical connection to the network:

- **Ethernet**   Use an Ethernet cable to connect the Mac to a wired network.
- **Wireless**   Use the Mac's built-in AirPort wireless network card.

We'll look at each of these ways in turn.

 NOTE   Apart from Ethernet and wireless networking, Mac OS X also supports several other types of networking. Wired network connections via FireWire cables are useful for small networks—a few computers in the same room—running at high speed; the cables are expensive, but you can assure yourself that you're worth it. Wireless network connections via Bluetooth enable you to set up small networks—again, a handful of computers within spitting distance of each other—running at low speed. Virtual private networks (which we'll examine in Chapter 11) enable you to connect securely to a remote network.

Connecting a Mac via Ethernet

When you plug an Ethernet cable into the Ethernet port of a running Mac, Mac OS X has a quick sniff to see what's happening on the wire. Out of the box, Mac OS X comes set up to look for a Dynamic Host Configuration Protocol (DHCP) server on the network, so normally the Mac automatically finds your DHCP server (assuming you have one), requests an address, and applies it.

If your network doesn't use a DHCP server, or if you connect a Mac that turns out to be configured not to use DHCP, you can configure the network address manually like this:

1. Open System Preferences. For example, click the System Preferences icon in the Dock or choose Apple | System Preferences.

2. In the Internet & Wireless area of the System Preferences window, click the Network icon to display the Network pane.

3. In the list of connections on the left, click Ethernet (it may already be selected) to display the options for it. Figure 2-4 shows the Network pane of System Preferences with the Ethernet connection selected.

 NOTE   If you need to make the Mac use DHCP, open the Configure IPv4 pop-up menu and choose Using DHCP. You also have the option of choosing Using DHCP With Manual Address, which enables you to specify the IP address manually but pick up other settings (such as the router and DNS servers) from the DHCP server. Using a manual address is useful for computers that you need to make reachable by their IP address (for example, servers).

Figure 2-4. When connecting a Mac to your network, you may need to change the Mac's Ethernet port from using DHCP to using a manual configuration.

4. Open the Configure IPv4 pop-up menu and choose Manually.

5. Type the details of the Ethernet connection in the text boxes:

   ■ **IP Address**   Type the IP address—for example, **10.0.0.99** or **192.168.1.25**.

   ■ **Subnet Mask**   Type the subnet mask—for example, **255.255.255.0**.

   ■ **Router**   Type the IP address of the router or gateway through which this Mac will connect to the Internet.

   ■ **DNS Server**   Type the IP address of your network's DNS server.

   ■ **Search Domains**   If your network requires one or more search domains, type it (or them) here—for example, **acmeheavy.com**. If you have two or more search domains, separate them with commas.

6. Click the Apply button to apply the settings you've chosen.

7. Quit System Preferences (for example, press ⌘-Q).

With the network settings in place, the Mac should be ready to connect to the network and to Active Directory.

Connecting a Mac to a Wireless Network

Every Mac includes a built-in wireless network adapter Apple calls AirPort—except for the Mac Pro, on which AirPort is a build option that you must select (and pay even more for) when choosing the Mac. So pretty much any Mac comes ready for connecting to a wireless network.

NOTE   Most AirPort adapters in Macs capable of running Snow Leopard can connect to networks running 802.11n as well as the slower 802.11g, 802.11a, and 802.11b (Wi-Fi) standards. The 802.11n standard will give you the best connections as long as your access points are fully compatible with the AirPort cards.

To set up the connection to the wireless network, follow these steps:

1. Open System Preferences. For example, click the System Preferences icon in the Dock or choose Apple | System Preferences.

2. In the Internet & Wireless area of the System Preferences window, click the Network icon to display the Network pane.

3. In the list of connections on the left, click AirPort to display the AirPort options. Figure 2-5 shows the Network pane of System Preferences with the AirPort connection selected.

4. If the Status readout at the top says Off, click the Turn AirPort On button to turn the AirPort on. The Status readout changes to On.

5. Open the Network Name pop-up menu and choose the wireless network to which you want to connect. If the network name doesn't appear in the pop-up menu, click the Join Other Network item to display the dialog box shown next.

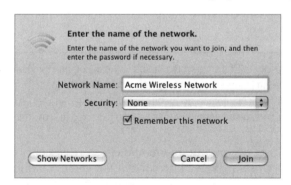

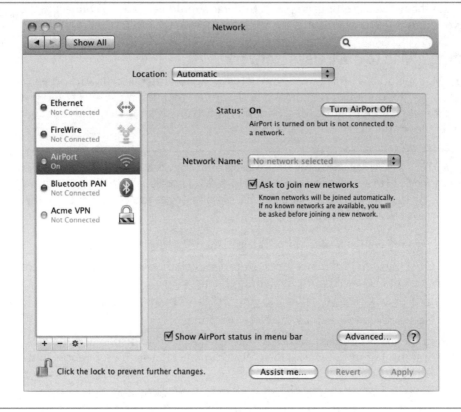

Figure 2-5. Click AirPort in the Network pane of System Preferences to display the options for configuring a Mac's AirPort to connect to your wireless network.

a. Type the network's name (its SSID or service set identifier) in the Network Name text box.

NOTE You can click the Show Networks button in the dialog box for joining another network, but usually doing so doesn't help—the resulting dialog box normally contains the same list of wireless networks as the Network Name pop-up menu. To join a closed network (one that doesn't broadcast its SSID and therefore doesn't appear in the list), you will need to type in the name manually.

b. Open the Security pop-up menu and choose the security type—for example, WPA Enterprise or WPA2 Enterprise. (For some unfathomable reason, Mac OS X selects the None item in the Security pop-up menu at first.) The dialog box then expands to show a Password text box and any other controls needed for authenticating the Mac. The next illustration shows an example.

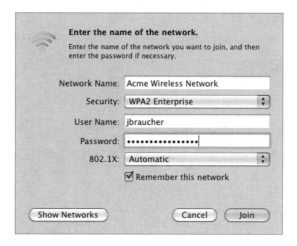

c. Type the password and provide any other means of authentication required—for example, the username.

d. Select the Remember This Network check box if you want Mac OS X to remember the network, as will normally be the case.

e. Click the Join button to join the Mac to the network.

6. Once Mac OS X has connected to the network, the Status readout near the top of the Network pane displays Connected and shows the name of the wireless network and the IP address assigned to the Mac. Figure 2-6 shows an example.

7. Select the Show AirPort Status In Menu Bar check box if you want the Mac to display an AirPort status indicator in the menu bar. This indicator shows the relative strength of the wireless network connection and provides menu commands for turning the AirPort off, switching networks, or opening Network Preferences, so it's handy for anyone who will need to manage their AirPort or be able to check its status at a glance. Desktop Macs in a stable wireless network may not need the AirPort status indicator.

8. Click the Apply button to apply the network settings.

9. Close System Preferences (for example, press ⌘-Q).

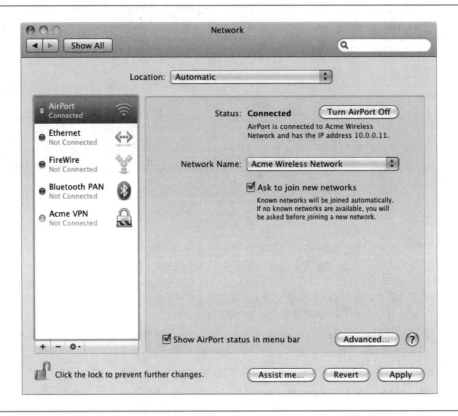

Figure 2-6.   The Status readout shows Connected when the AirPort has established the connection. You can see the network name and the Mac's IP address.

Adding Your Macs' MAC Addresses to a Wireless White List

If you have protected your wireless network by specifying a white list of MAC addresses that are permitted to connect to the network (and thus blocking any other MAC addresses), you will need to add the MAC address of each Mac's AirPort to the white list before the Mac can connect to the network.

To find out the MAC address for an AirPort, follow these steps:

1. Choose Apple | About This Mac to open the About This Mac dialog box.

2. Click the More Info button to launch System Profiler.

3. Click the Network item in the Contents pane to display the list of network interfaces. (You don't need to expand the Network list if it's collapsed—just click the Network item. But it's fine to expand the Network list if you want.)

4. Click the AirPort item in the list box to display its details in the lower pane.

5. Select the MAC address in the lower pane, as shown here, and then copy it to the Clipboard. For example, press ⌘-C; or either CTRL-click or right-click, and then choose Copy from the shortcut menu.

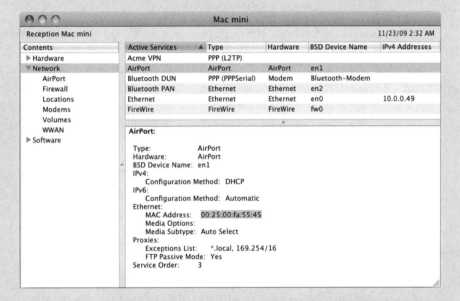

6. While you're in System Profiler, you may want to check which wireless technologies the AirPort supports. To do so, expand the Network item in the left pane, click the AirPort item, and then look at the Supported PHY Modes readout (PHY is the abbreviation for the physical layer of the Open Systems Interconnection—OSI—networking model). You'll see something like **802.11 a/b/g/n**, indicating that the AirPort can handle 802.11a, 802.11b, 802.11g, and 802.11n.

7. Quit System Profiler (for example, press ⌘-Q).

8. Click the Close button to close the About This Mac dialog box.

Binding a Mac to Active Directory

Now that the Mac knows the network is there, you can bind the Mac to Active Directory.

NOTE Normally you will want to bind your Mac clients to Active Directory so that they can consistently connect to directory services and shared folders. But in some cases you may choose to bind a Mac OS X server to Active Directory and then bind the Mac clients to the Mac OS X server via Open Directory.

Performing the Binding

To bind a Mac to Active Directory, follow these steps:

1. Open System Preferences. For example, click the System Preferences icon in the Dock or choose Apple | System Preferences.

NOTE If you're connecting a Mac running Leopard (Mac OS X 10.5) to Active Directory, you need to fire up Directory Utility directly from the Applications/Utilities folder rather than from the Accounts pane. (To launch Directory Utility, you can also press ⌘-SPACEBAR and type **dire** into the Spotlight field, then click the result.)

2. In the System area, click the Accounts icon to display the Accounts pane.
3. Click the Login Options button to display the Login Options pane (see Figure 2-7).
4. Next to Network Account Server, click the Join button to display the dialog box shown in Figure 2-8.

NOTE At this point, you can simply enter the server name in the Server box—either pick it from the pop-up menu or type it in if it doesn't appear in the pop-up menu—and then click the OK button. If all is well, the binding will work. But what you'll normally want to do is open Directory Utility and choose options for the binding, as detailed in the following steps.

5. Click the Open Directory Utility button to open Directory Utility.
6. Click the Services button on the toolbar to display the Services pane if it is not already displayed.
7. If the padlock icon in the lower-left corner of the Directory Utility window is snapped firmly shut, click it and then type your password in the dialog box that opens. (Just to be clear—this is your password for the Mac you're setting up, not for the Windows network.)

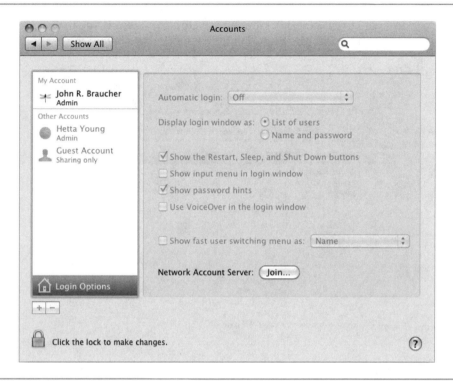

Figure 2-7.   To start binding a Mac to Active Directory, open the Login Options pane in Accounts preferences and click the Join button.

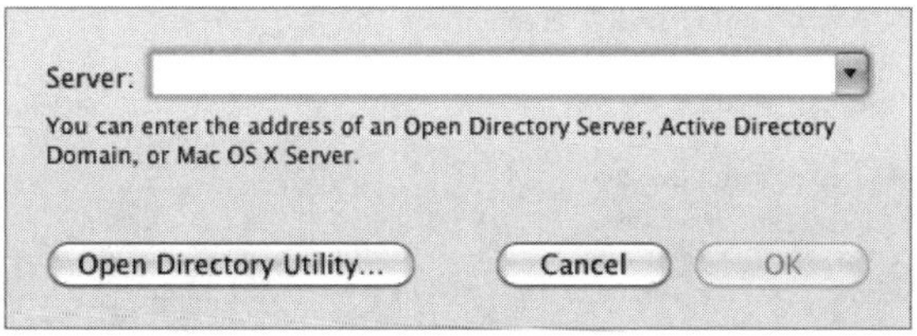

Server: [   ] ▾

You can enter the address of an Open Directory Server, Active Directory Domain, or Mac OS X Server.

(Open Directory Utility...)   (Cancel)   (OK)

Figure 2-8.   From this dialog box, you can either bind quickly by using the Server pop-up menu or click the Open Directory Utility button to open Directory Utility.

8. Once you've unlocked the controls in the Services pane of the Directory Utility window, as shown here, click the Active Directory item in the list box and then click the Edit button (the button with the pencil icon) below the list box.

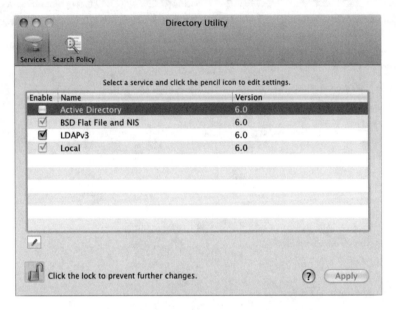

9. The Active Directory dialog box then opens, as shown next. As you can see, the Active Directory Forest text box is set to "– Automatic –," so leave it for Mac OS X to fill in automatically when you've chosen the domain.

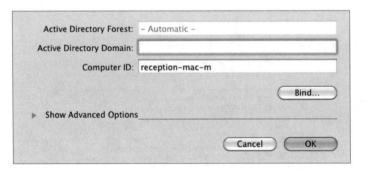

10. In the Active Directory Domain text box, type the domain to which you're binding the Mac—for example, **corp.acmeheavy.com**.

NOTE When binding a Mac to Active Directory, you can either provide the name of a Computer object that you've already created in Active Directory or provide a new name. If you provide a new name, the binding process creates a Computer object with that name for you. Normally, the name should be 19 characters or fewer for compatibility. The name must be unique in the directory.

11. In the Computer ID text box, type the name you want the Mac to have on the network. See the previous Note for details.

TIP At this point, you can decide whether to bind the Mac using default settings for what Apple terms "advanced options," or whether to set the options manually. If you choose to set them manually, see the next section for details, and then return to this list and go to step 12. If you want to go with default settings, go straight to step 12 without passing Go or collecting $200.

12. Click the Bind button, and then authenticate yourself in the dialog box that appears. (Again, this is your username and password for this Mac, not for the network—that's next.)

13. After you authenticate yourself, Mac OS X displays the Network Administrator Required dialog box (shown here).

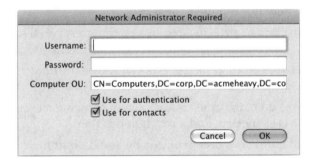

14. Type your administrator name in the Username text box and your administrator password in the Password text box.

15. Verify that the Computer OU text box shows the correct organizational unit for the computer. If not, fix the OU so that it is right.

NOTE The Computer OU text box shows the name split up into its components: the common name (CN) items and the domain content (DC) items. For example, you'll see an entry such as **CN=Computers,DC=corp,DC=acmeheavy,DC=com** rather than a single item such as **Computers .corp.acmeheavy.com**.

16. Select the Use For Authentication check box to use this credential for authentication for accessing the network.

17. Select the Use For Contacts check box to use this credential for contacts as well.

18. Click the OK button. Mac OS X tries to contact the directory server and, if it finds it, dances through a five-step sequence for binding the Mac to the directory. Once Mac OS X has managed the binding, the Bind button changes to an Unbind button, as you can see here.

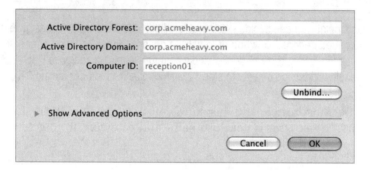

19. Click the OK button to close the Active Directory dialog box, and then quit Directory Utility (for example, press ⌘-Q).

20. In the Login Options pane in Accounts preferences, you'll see three things have changed:

    ■ The Network Account Server readout shows the domain to which you've bound the Mac.

    ■ Before the domain name appears a light showing its status: a green light if the Mac is connected, and a red light if it's not.

    ■ The Join button has been replaced by an Edit button.

21. Quit System Preferences (for example, press ⌘-Q).

Choosing Advanced Options for Binding a Mac to Active Directory

Instead of going ahead with the default settings for advanced options for binding a Mac to Active Directory, you can choose settings yourself. To do so, follow through steps 1–11 in the list in the previous section and then click the Show Advanced Options disclosure triangle to reveal the extra section of the Active Directory dialog box.

As you can see in Figure 2-9, the extra section contains three tabs: User Experience (shown in the figure), Mappings, and Administrative. We'll look at each of these in turn.

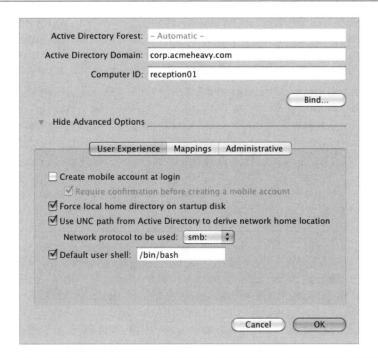

Figure 2-9. In the User Experience pane in the Advanced Options section of the Active Directory dialog box, you can choose whether to create a mobile account at logon and whether to derive the network home location using a UNC path from Active Directory.

Choosing User Experience Settings

In the User Experience pane in the Active Directory dialog box, you can choose settings for the following options:

■ **Create Mobile Account At Logon** Select this check box if you want to cache the account details on this Mac so that the user can log on when they're not connected to the network. Normally, you'll want to do this only for Mac laptops rather than Mac desktops (assuming you keep your desktops chained to the network). When you select this check box, Mac OS X selects the Force Local Home Directory On Startup Disk check box and makes it unavailable, so that you can't clear it.

NOTE You may want to select the Create Mobile Account At Logon check box for a Mac desktop if your domain controllers are balky or unreliable. Generally, though, making the domain controllers reliable is a better bet.

- **Require Confirmation Before Creating A Mobile Account**   If you selected the Create Mobile Account At Logon check box, you can select this check box if you want Mac OS X to prompt the user before it sets up the mobile account. Clear this check box if you want to force all the users of a particular Mac to use mobile accounts. (Again, you're normally looking at Mac laptops here.)

- **Force Local Home Directory On Startup Disk**   Select this check box to make Mac OS X store the user's home directory on the Mac's startup disk rather than on a network drive. Mac OS X puts the home directory in the /Users/ folder, as with local accounts.

- **Use UNC Path From Active Directory To Derive Network Location**   Select this check box if you want Mac OS X to pick up the Active Directory standard attribute for the home folder location. Then open the Network Protocol To Be Used pop-up menu and choose SMB.

NOTE   Apart from SMB (Server Message Block), the Network Protocol To Be Used pop-up menu offers AFP (Apple Filing Protocol) as a choice for accessing the network home folder. Don't try to use AFP with Windows Server 2008, because Microsoft removed AFP along with the other Services For Mac (SFM) components. Earlier versions of Windows Server do provide AFP.

- **Default User Shell**   To choose which UNIX shell is used in Terminal, SSH, and Telnet, select this check box and enter the path to the shell in the text box (for example, **/bin/bash** for the Bourne Again Shell, **/bin/csh** for the C Shell, **/bin/ksh** for the Korn Shell, **/bin/tcsh** for the Tenex C Shell, or **/bin/zsh** for the Z Shell).

Choosing Mappings Settings

Click the Mappings tab to display the Mappings pane (see Figure 2-10), and then choose settings to suit the user's needs:

- **Map UID To Attribute**   Select this check box if you want to map Mac OS X's unique user ID (UID) to an attribute in Active Directory. Type the Active Directory attribute name in the text box.

NOTE   The Map UID To Attribute text box suggests mapping the UID to the uniqueID attribute. You will need to add this attribute to Active Directory manually. If you have installed Services For UNIX on Active Directory, you can use the msSFU-30-Uid-Number attribute. Similarly, if you have included RFC 2307 in Active Directory, you can use the uidNumber attribute. You can also extend Active Directory with a custom attribute of your own.

- **Map User GID To Attribute**   Select this check box if you want to map the primary group ID (GID) in the user account to an attribute in Active Directory. Again, type the attribute name in the text box.

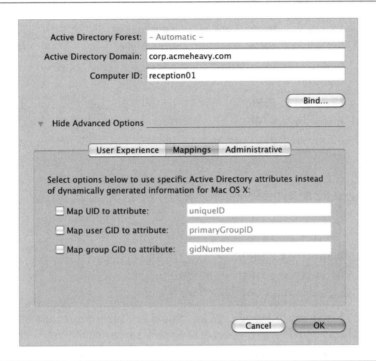

Figure 2-10.   In the Mappings pane, you can map Mac OS X's unique user ID and group IDs to Active Directory attributes.

- ■ **Map Group GID To Attribute**   Select this check box if you want to map the group ID (GID) in group accounts to an Active Directory attribute. Once more, type the attribute name in the text box.

CAUTION   Mapping the UID, user GID, and group GID to Active Directory attributes can be a great help in integrating your Mac users happily into Active Directory—but make sure you get the mappings right when you create the binding. If you change the mappings later, the user may not be able to access files they've created with the previous mappings in place.

So you can map the UID, the user GID, and the group GID—but which Active Directory attributes should you map them to? You can create your own custom attributes in Active Directory with names of your own choice, extending the schema, but you may find it easier to stick with the names Apple recommends, use the names built into Microsoft's Services For UNIX (which you can install on Active Directory), or follow the names used in RFC 2307 (which covers using LDAP as a network information service). Table 2-1 summarizes these names.

Item	Item Full Name	Recommended Name	Services For UNIX Name	RFC 2307 Name
UID	Unique user ID	uniqueID	msSFU-30-Uid-Number	uidNumber
User GID	User group ID	Primary GroupID	msSFU- 30-Gid-Number	gidNumber
Group GID	Group group ID	gidNumber	msSFU-30-Gid- Number	gidNumber

Table 2-1.   Suggested Active Directory Attribute Names for Mapping UIDs and GIDs

Choosing Administrative Settings

Click the Administrative tab to display the Administrative pane (see Figure 2-11), and then choose settings to suit the user's needs:

- **Prefer This Domain Server**   Select this check box to direct the Mac client to a particular Active Directory server. Type the server's DNS name in the text box.

- **Allow Administration By**   Select this check box if you want to specify who is permitted to administer the Mac. Mac OS X suggests a couple of suitable administrative groups in the list box. You can remove any of these groups by clicking it and then clicking the – button, or you can add a group by clicking the + button and then typing the group's name in the text box that appears.

- **Allow Authentication From Any Domain In The Forest**   Select this check box if you want to allow users to authenticate from any domain in the Active Directory forest. This setting is useful for users who work from different locations (for example, technicians). For users whom you prefer to chain to a particular domain, make sure this check box is cleared.

When you've finished choosing the advanced options in the Active Directory dialog box, click the Bind button to bind the Mac to Active Directory. When the binding is complete, click the OK button to close the Active Directory dialog box. You can then quit Directory Utility and System Preferences.

Changing the Mac's Search Policy for Active Directory

Apart from setting up bindings to Active Directory and other directories, Directory Utility also enables you to set the search policy for authentication and contacts. For each of these, you set up a list of domains in the order in which you want Mac OS X to search them to find the information it needs.

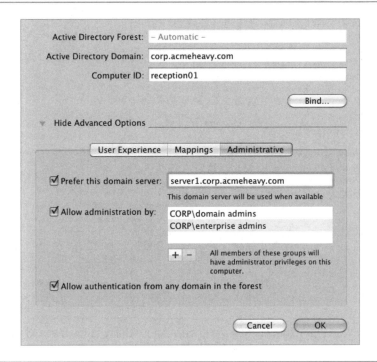

Figure 2-11. In the Administrative pane, you can set a preferred Active Directory server, choose who may administer the Mac, and decide whether to permit authentication from any domain in the forest.

To change the search policy, open the Search Policy pane of Directory Utility like this:

1. Open Directory Utility by clicking the Join button in the Login Options pane of Accounts preferences. If you've already set up the binding, the button you click is the Edit button rather than the Join button.

2. Click the Search Policy button on the toolbar of the Directory Utility window to display the Search Policy pane.

To set the authentication information that tells Mac OS X where in the directory to find the information to authenticate the Mac's users, click the Authentication tab and work in the Authentication pane (see Figure 2-12) like this:

1. In the Search pop-up menu, make sure that Custom Path is selected. This item gives the list of directory domains that include the Active Directory domains to which the Mac is bound.

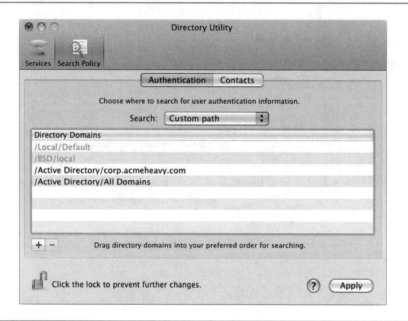

Figure 2-12.   Use the Authentication pane in Directory Utility to tell Mac OS X where to search for information on how to authenticate the user.

NOTE   The other choices in the Search pop-up menu are Local Directory and Automatic. Choosing either the Local Directory item or the Automatic item makes the Mac use the paths /Local/Default and /BSD/Local.

2.   To add a domain to the list, click the + button. In the dialog box that appears (as shown here), click the domain, and then click the Add button.

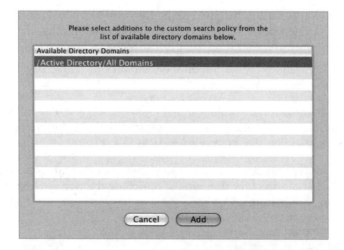

NOTE   If no domain appears in the Available Directory Domains list box, you've already added all available domains to the authentication list. If you selected the Allow Authentication From Any Domain In The Forest check box in the Administrative pane when binding the Mac or editing its binding, the /Active Directory/All Domains item already appears in the Directory Domains list box in the Authentication pane. Otherwise, you will find at least this item in the Available Directory Domains list box.

3. To remove a domain from the list, click it, click the – button, and then click the OK button in the Delete Directory Domain dialog box that appears (as shown here).

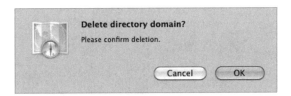

4. To change the order in which the Mac uses the domains, click a domain and drag it up or down the list. Put the first domain you want the Mac to use at the top of the list.

5. When you've finished making changes, click the Apply button.

To set the contact information that tells Mac OS X where in the directory to look for contacts, click the Contacts tab and work in the Contacts pane (see Figure 2-13). This pane works in a similar way to the Authentication pane:

1. In the Search pop-up menu, make sure that Custom Path is selected. Selecting the Custom Path item makes the Directory Domains list box show the directory domain to which the Mac is bound, but (unlike the Authentication pane) not the /Local/Default domain or the /BSD/Local domain. You can add these if needed.

2. To add a domain to the list, click the + button. In the dialog box that appears, click the domain and then click the Add button.

3. To remove a domain from the list, click it, click the – button, and then click the OK button in the Delete Directory Domain dialog box.

4. To change the order in which the Mac uses the domains, click a domain and drag it up or down the list. As before, the top domain is the one the Mac consults first.

5. When you've finished making changes, click the Apply button to apply them.

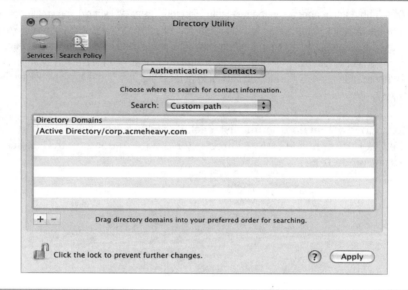

Figure 2-13. Use the Contacts pane in Directory Utility to tell Mac OS X where to search for contacts on the network.

Testing the Active Directory Binding with the id Command

To check that you've got the Mac firmly bound to Active Directory, use the id command in Terminal. This command returns not the part of the computer's mind governed by unrestrainable innate impulses but the identity of the item you ask about—in this case, a user.

1. Open Terminal. For example, click the Desktop, choose Go | Utilities, and then double-click the Terminal icon.

2. Type the **id** command followed by the name of a user you've added to Active Directory. If you're connected, you'll see a list of the user's items in the directory, as shown here.

```
Last login: Wed Nov 18 01:45:33 on ttys000
Reception-Mac-mini:~ jbraucher$ id jbraucher
uid=502(jbraucher) gid=20(staff) groups=20(staff),401(com.apple.access_screensharing
),204(_developer),100(_lpoperator),98(_lpadmin),81(_appserveradm),80(admin),79(_apps
erverusr),61(localaccounts),12(everyone),403(com.apple.sharepoint.group.2),402(com.a
pple.sharepoint.group.1)
Reception-Mac-mini:~ jbraucher$
```

3. Leave Terminal open so that you can read a user's record, as discussed next.

Testing the Active Directory Binding with the dscl Command

To get more information out of Active Directory, try using the dscl command to read a user's record—and to do a little exploring.

 NOTE dscl is the abbreviation for Directory Services Command Line.

Still in Terminal, type the **dscl** command at the prompt (here, **MacBook303:~**) and press RETURN. You'll see output as shown here (with the command in bold):

```
MacBook303:~ dscl
Entering interactive mode... (type "help" for commands)
 >
```

The > here indicates that dscl is running and ready to accept a command. Type the **ls** command, as shown in boldface here, to list the available folders:

```
MacBook303:~ dscl
Entering interactive mode... (type "help" for commands)
 > ls
Active Directory
BSD
Local

Contact
Search
>
```

As you can see, Active Directory is at the top of the list. You can now switch to it by using the **cd** command, as shown in boldface here.

 NOTE The cd command is the abbreviation for "change directory." You put "Active Directory" within quotes because the name contains a space, which makes the command choke without the quotes.

```
MacBook303:~ dscl
Entering interactive mode... (type "help" for commands)
 > ls
Active Directory
BSD
Local

Contact
Search
 > cd "Active Directory"
/Active Directory >
```

Now that you've changed to the Active Directory folder, type another **ls** command to list the contents of the folder, as shown in bold in the following (truncated) listing:

```
> cd "Active Directory"
/Active Directory > ls
All Domains
/Active Directory >
```

As you can see, the only folder in the Active Directory folder is the All Domains folder. So change to that folder next, as shown in bold here:

```
> cd "Active Directory"
/Active Directory > ls
All Domains
/Active Directory > cd "All Domains"
/Active Directory/All Domains >
```

Then use another **ls** command to list the contents, as shown in bold here:

```
> cd "Active Directory"
/Active Directory > ls
All Domains
/Active Directory > cd "All Domains"
/Active Directory/All Domains > ls
CertificateAuthorities
Computers
FileMakerServers
Groups
Mounts
People
Printers
Users
/Active Directory/All Domains >
```

Change to the Users folder and then list its contents. The two commands are shown in boldface here:

```
/Active Directory/All Domains > cd Users
/Active Directory/All Domains/Users > ls
admin1
administrator
agreen
guest
jbraucher
krbtgt
swills
/Active Directory/All Domains/Users >
```

Your list of users will be different from what's shown here (if it's not, I need to get you off of my network), but it will include the administrator, guest, and krbtgt accounts (see the note).

NOTE The krbtgt account in the Users folder is the Kerberos Ticket Granting Ticket account. This account is used by the Kerberos service for authentication. Don't try to log into this account, because you can't. Don't try to delete it either, because it's vital to making Kerberos authentication work.

Now use the **read** command to read the account details of one of the users who appears on your list. Here's an example showing the command and the first few lines of the screen that the command returns:

```
/Active Directory/All Domains/Users > read jbraucher
dsAttrTypeNative:accountExpires 9223372036854775807
dsAttrTypeNative:ADDomain: corp.acmeheavy.com
dsAttrTypeNative:badPasswordTime: 0
dsAttrTypeNative:badPwdCount: 0
dsAttrTypeNative:cn:
  John R. Braucher
```

On it goes, for several pages—but you should not be in doubt that you're getting the goods from Active Directory.

Now exit the dscl command by typing **quit** at the prompt and pressing RETURN. dscl bids you a friendly goodbye.

Quit Terminal by pressing ⌘-Q.

Troubleshooting the "Invalid Domain" Error Message when Binding to Active Directory

If you get the error message "Invalid domain: An invalid Domain and Forest combination was specified" (as shown next), which exhorts you to enter a fully qualified domain name, you've usually run into one of two problems.

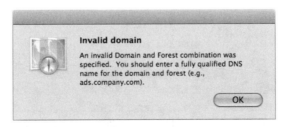

You can guess the first problem: You entered a partial domain name rather than a fully qualified domain name—for example, **acmeheavy.com** instead of **corp.acmeheavy .com**. And you can guess the solution to this problem: Add the missing qualifications and try again. Five times out of six, this will solve the problem.

If you *did* enter a fully qualified domain name, but you get the "Invalid domain" message anyway, you've probably run into the second problem: an issue with DNS. Usually the problem is that the Mac is using a DNS server other than your Active Directory DNS server. This typically means that the Mac is trying to connect to the domain server across the Internet rather than across the local network.

To see if this is the problem, follow these steps:

1. Open Network Utility. For example, click the desktop, choose Go | Utilities, and then double-click Network Utility.

2. Click the Lookup tab to display the Lookup pane.

3. Type the address of your network's domain server—for example, **server1.corp .acmeheavy.com**.

4. In the Select The Information To Lookup pop-up menu, choose Internet Address.

5. Click the Lookup button or press RETURN.

6. Look at the information in the main text box and see if the IP address for the server is on the Internet or on your local network. Figure 2-14 shows an example of an IP address on the Internet.

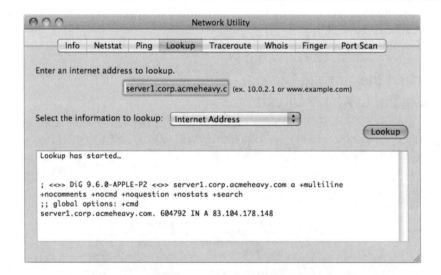

Figure 2-14. Use the Lookup pane in Network Utility to check whether a Mac is trying to connect to the domain server across the Internet instead of across the local network.

If you did indeed get an IP address on the Internet rather than one on your network, follow these steps to solve the problem. Leave Network Utility open for the moment, as you'll need it again.

1. Open System Preferences. For example, click the System Preferences icon in the Dock or choose Apple | System Preferences.

2. In the Internet & Wireless area, click the Network icon to display the Network pane (shown in Figure 2-15 with settings chosen).

3. If the padlock icon in the lower-left corner of the pane is locked, click it and then authenticate yourself in the dialog box that opens. Mac OS X opens the padlock.

4. In the list of network interfaces on the left, select the network interface you're using to connect to the network—for example, Ethernet.

Figure 2-15.   In the Network pane of System Preferences, change the DNS Server address to point to your network's DNS server.

NOTE   For a wireless connection, click AirPort in the list of network interfaces and then click the Advanced button to display the Advanced dialog box. Click the DNS tab and then work in the DNS Servers list box.

5. Select the contents of the DNS Server text box and then replace them with the IP address of your network's DNS server.

6. Click the Apply button to apply the change.

7. Quit System Preferences by pressing ⌘-Q.

Once you've sorted out the DNS, go back to Network Utility and click the Lookup button again to run the lookup once more. This time, lookup should return the address of the server on the local network rather than the Internet address.

Now pop back over to Directory Utility and try the binding again. With the DNS in place, it will work.

CHAPTER 3

Binding a Mac OS X Server to Manage Macs via a "Magic Triangle"

As you saw in the previous chapter, binding a Mac client to Active Directory and providing it with a home directory (either a mobile home directory or one on the network) is straightforward enough.

But odds are that you will want to manage your network's Mac clients, and simply binding them gets you only part of the way. To manage them effectively, either you will need to bind a Mac OS X server to Active Directory and then bind the Mac clients to both Active Directory and the Mac server's Open Directory (as described in this chapter) or you will need to extend Active Directory with the classes and attributes needed to manage the Macs through Active Directory (as described in the next chapter).

If your company or organization can afford an extra Mac for use as a server and a copy of Mac OS X Server to run on it, binding a Mac server can provide an easy way to manage the Macs. This arrangement is sometimes called a "magic triangle" because the management tools use the triangle depicted in Figure 3-1.

To set up the magic triangle, you need to do the following:

- Get the Mac you will use as the server.
- Install Mac OS X Server on your Mac (unless it came already installed) and configure it (even if it came installed).
- Update Mac OS X Server with the latest fixes.
- Bind the Mac server to Active Directory.
- Set your Mac clients to connect to both Open Directory and Active Directory.
- Set up Open Directory groups for managing your Mac users.

I'm assuming you've already gotten the Mac server (if not, flick back to the end of Chapter 1 for a couple of suggestions). So we'll start with installing Mac OS X Server on the Mac.

Installing Mac OS X Server on a Mac

If the Mac that will be your server doesn't already have Mac OS X installed on it, install it. These are the main steps:

1. Insert the Mac OS X Server DVD in the optical drive and then restart the Mac.
2. When you hear the startup sound, hold down c until you hear the Mac start reading the DVD.
3. When you see the Mac OS X Server screen, click your language and then click the arrow button.

NOTE If your server already has Mac OS X Server installed, skip ahead to the section "Performing the Initial Configuration," later in this chapter. If you've done that too, move on to the section "Updating Your Server with the Latest Fixes."

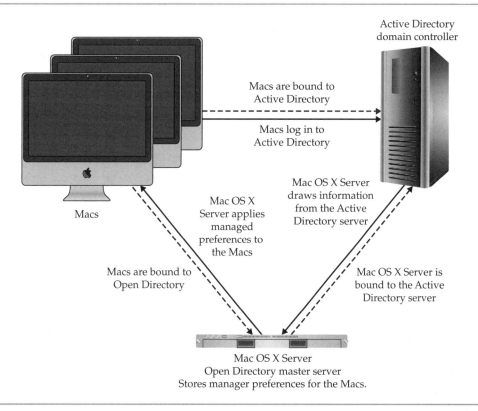

Active Directory
domain controller

Macs are bound to
Active Directory

Macs log in to
Active Directory

Mac OS X Server
draws information
from the Active
Directory server

Macs

Mac OS X
Server applies
managed
preferences to
the Macs

Macs are bound to
Open Directory

Mac OS X Server is
bound to the Active
Directory server

Mac OS X Server
Open Directory master server
Stores manager preferences for the Macs.

Figure 3-1.   In the "magic triangle" arrangement, you bind Mac clients to both Active Directory and Open Directory.

Choosing Which Disk to Install Mac OS X Server On

The next screen you see is titled Install Mac OS X Server. If your installation will simply take over the whole of the Mac's hard disk, or the whole of an existing volume, click the Continue button. But if you need to partition the Mac's hard disk before installing Mac OS X Server, choose Utilities | Disk Utility from the menu bar (see Figure 3-2). Then use Disk Utility to rearrange the partitions (see Figure 3-3). These are the main moves you'll need:

1. In the left column, click the hard disk you want to partition.
2. Click the Partition tab to display the Partition pane.

3. To delete a partition, follow these steps:

   a. Click the partition in the list of partitions.

   b. Click the Remove (–) button below the list box. Disk Utility displays a confirmation dialog box, as shown here.

c. Click the Remove button in the confirmation dialog box that Disk Utility displays.

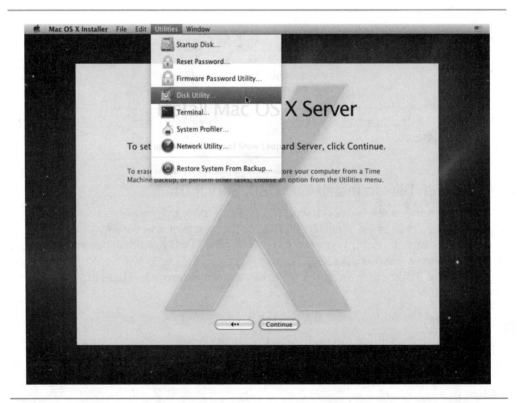

Figure 3-2. The Install Mac OS X Server screen has minimalist controls, but you can open the Utilities menu if you need to prepare the server's disk for the installation.

4. To create a partition from an existing partition, follow these steps:

   a. In the list of partitions, click the partition from which you want to take space to create a new partition.

NOTE   If the disk contains open space (for example, because you've deleted one or more partitions), just click the open space rather than carve out a new partition from an existing one. Go to step d in the sublist.

   b. Click the Add (+) button below the list of partitions. Disk Utility divides the partition into two, leaving the current partition with some free space and suggesting an amount of space for the new partition.

   c. Drag the horizontal divider bar between the partitions if you want to adjust the division of space.

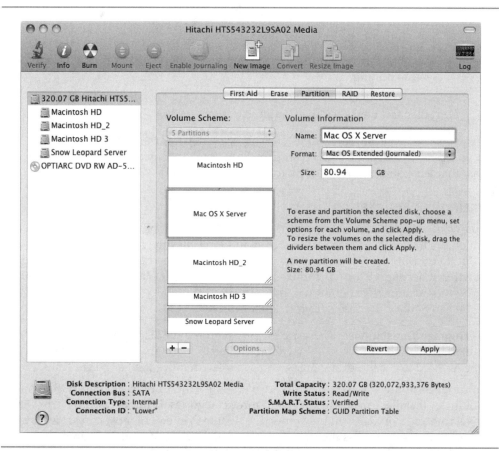

Figure 3-3.   Use Disk Utility if you need to rearrange the partitions on your server.

d. Click the new partition in the Volume Information area.

e. In the Name text box, type the name you want the new partition to have.

f. In the Format pop-up menu, choose the format for the new part. The default format, Mac OS Extended (Journaled), is usually the best choice.

g. Click the Apply button. Disk Utility confirms the actions it's going to take, as shown here.

h. Click the Partition button or the Remove button, depending on which move you're pulling.

5. When you've finished, choose Disk Utility | Quit Disk Utility to return to Installer and then click the Continue button.

The next screen is the software license agreement. Click the Agree button once you've waded through the small print. You then reach the Install Mac OS X Server screen that lets you select which disk to use (see Figure 3-4).

Customizing the Installation

If you want to install Mac OS X Server with its default options, just click the drive you want on the Install Mac OS X Server screen and then click the Install button.

But if you want to include the kitchen sink, or if you need to remove all items that you will not need, click the Customize button on the Install Mac OS X Server screen to display the Customize panel shown in Figure 3-5.

You can remove five items from the installation:

■ **Language Translations**   These are the files required for displaying the Mac OS X interface in other languages—for example, French, German, or Japanese. If you will never need to use these languages, you can safely remove the Language Translations.

■ **Printer Support**   These are printer drivers—and there are more than 2GB's worth of them. Installer breaks them up into three categories: Printers Used By This Mac, Nearby And Popular Printers, and All Available Printers. In most cases, Nearby And Popular Printers is the best choice, and is the default; you can add other printer drivers later if needed. To include all the printer drivers, select the All Available Printers check box.

Figure 3-4. Choose the disk on which you want to install Mac OS X Server.

- **X11** X11 is the window server used for running UNIX programs on Mac OS X. It takes up only about 160MB and is well worth having if you even think you'll need to run UNIX programs.

- **Rosetta** Rosetta is the Mac OS X application for running PowerPC-based applications on Intel-based Macs. If you've transitioned fully to applications with Intel code, you may not need Rosetta, but it takes up only a few megabytes, so usually it's a good idea.

- **QuickTime 7** If you need to run older multimedia files, you can include QuickTime 7.

NOTE If you make changes you need to undo, click the Restore Defaults button to restore the default settings.

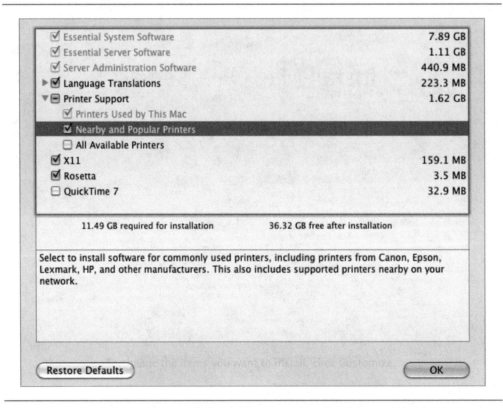

☑ Essential System Software	7.89 GB
☑ Essential Server Software	1.11 GB
☑ Server Administration Software	440.9 MB
▶ ☑ **Language Translations**	223.3 MB
▼ ⊟ **Printer Support**	1.62 GB
☑ Printers Used by This Mac	
☑ Nearby and Popular Printers	
☐ All Available Printers	
☑ X11	159.1 MB
☑ Rosetta	3.5 MB
☐ QuickTime 7	32.9 MB

11.49 GB required for installation   36.32 GB free after installation

Select to install software for commonly used printers, including printers from Canon, Epson, Lexmark, HP, and other manufacturers. This also includes supported printers nearby on your network.

Restore Defaults   OK

Figure 3-5. You can customize the Mac OS X Server installation by removing items you don't need, such as language translations.

When you've chosen which components to include, click the OK button to return to the Install Mac OS X Server screen.

Click the Install button to run the installation. Installer copies files, contemplates deep metaphysical questions, and then displays the Welcome screen.

NOTE If you're setting up a new Mac server that came with Mac OS X Server installed, you'll go directly to the Welcome screen.

Performing the Initial Configuration

From the Welcome screen (see Figure 3-6), you're ready to perform the initial configuration of your server.

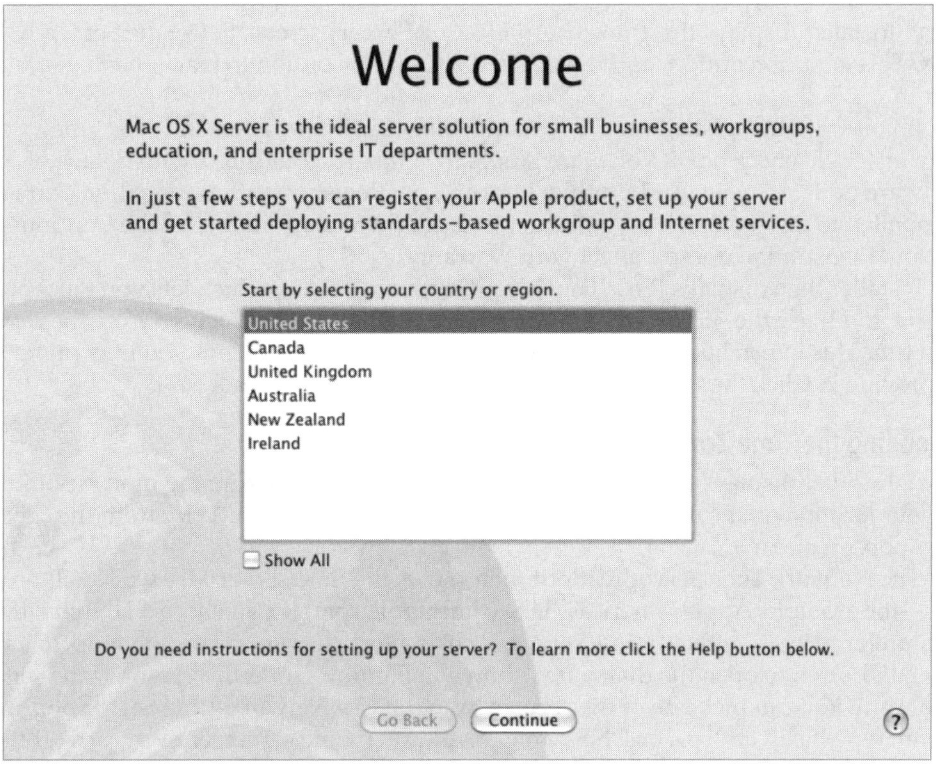

Welcome

Mac OS X Server is the ideal server solution for small businesses, workgroups, education, and enterprise IT departments.

In just a few steps you can register your Apple product, set up your server and get started deploying standards-based workgroup and Internet services.

Start by selecting your country or region.

United States
Canada
United Kingdom
Australia
New Zealand
Ireland

☐ Show All

Do you need instructions for setting up your server? To learn more click the Help button below.

(Go Back)   (Continue)   ⑦

Figure 3-6.   On the Welcome screen, pick your country or region, and then click the Continue button.

If your country or region appears on the short list, click it; otherwise, select the Show All check box and then click the country or region. Next, click the Continue button. Installer displays the Keyboard screen.

Choosing the Keyboard Layout

At first, the Keyboard list shows just a short list of keyboard layouts for the country or region you chose. If the keyboard layout you want appears, click it—for example, click U.S. for a standard U.S. keyboard layout. If you want a keyboard layout that doesn't appear, such as one of the Dvorak layouts, select the Show All check box to display the full list of keyboard layouts and then click the desired layout.

Entering the Serial Number

Click the Continue button. Installer displays the Serial Number screen. Enter the serial number and your registration information—type your name and organization name character- for- character, because the check is case sensitive—and then click the Continue button.

Choosing Whether to Transfer an Existing Server

Next, Installer displays the Transfer An Existing Server? screen. Select the Set Up A New Server option button, and then click the Continue button to reach the Registration screen.

If you want to register Mac OS X Server, fill in the information and select the Stay In Touch! check box if you want Apple to bombard your inbox with details of software updates, news, and product information. Registration is optional, so don't feel compelled to fill in the fields—you can just leave them blank and click the Continue button. Registration doesn't affect your warranty.

Installer then displays the A Few More Questions screen, which lets you tell Apple where you'll use the server, what type of clients you use, and which services the server will run. This information, too, is optional; it's useful for Apple, but you may prefer not to provide it. Click the Continue button when you're ready to move on.

Choosing the Time Zone

Next, Installer displays the Time Zone screen (see Figure 3-7). Aim the mouse pointer at your location on the map and click, and then choose the nearest city from the Closest City pop-up menu.

The Network Time Server readout then shows the time server Mac OS X will use—for example, Apple Americas/U.S. (time.apple.com) if you chose a U.S. city. If you prefer to use a different time server, such as a time server on your network, click the Edit button to open the dialog box shown in Figure 3-8 and then identify the server you want. You can pick one of the servers from the Use Network Time Server pop-up menu, type the IP address or DNS name of your own time server, or even turn off the use of network time by clearing the Use Network Time Server check box. Click the OK button when you've finished.

> **TIP**   To make your magic triangle work properly, you need to make sure that the Mac OS X server's clock is within five minutes of the clock on the Active Directory domain controller. Usually, the best way to ensure this is to use a network time server. If you have a time server on your network (for example, if your Windows Server is running the time service), use that; otherwise, point all the servers at the same time server on the Internet.

Click the Continue button when you're satisfied with your time server choices.

Setting Up the Administrator Account

On the next screen Installer displays, the Administrator Account screen (see Figure 3-9), you set up the account you will use to administer this server. Mac OS X stores this account on the server.

To set up the administrator account, follow these steps:

1. Type the full name for the account in the Name text box. For example, you may want to type your own name or a role name, such as Mac Administrator. You can change this name later if necessary.

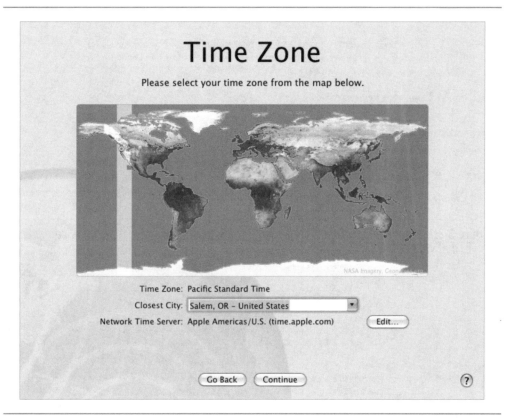

Time Zone

Please select your time zone from the map below.

Time Zone: Pacific Standard Time
Closest City: Salem, OR – United States
Network Time Server: Apple Americas/U.S. (time.apple.com)   Edit...

Go Back   Continue

Figure 3-7.   Click the map to indicate your general time zone, and then pick the nearest city from the Closest City pop-up menu.

2. Press TAB to move to the Short Name text box. Mac OS X automatically suggests a short name derived from the name you entered—for example, the same name but all in lowercase if the name is short enough.

NOTE   After you create the account, the short name is fixed, and you cannot change it. You can use uppercase and lowercase letters, numbers, underscores, hyphens, and periods, but no spaces or symbols. It's usually best to keep the name to eight characters or fewer, but you can use more if you want—the upper limit is 255 characters, but it's not sensible to use anywhere near that many.

3. Type a password in the Password text box and the Verify text box. For help creating a strong password, click the key icon to the right of the Password text box and use the Password Assistant to create a hard-to-crack password, as discussed in the nearby sidebar.

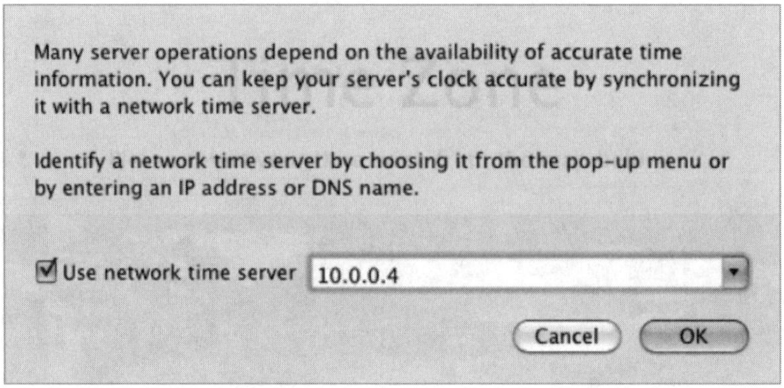

Many server operations depend on the availability of accurate time information. You can keep your server's clock accurate by synchronizing it with a network time server.

Identify a network time server by choosing it from the pop-up menu or by entering an IP address or DNS name.

☑ Use network time server 10.0.0.4 ▾

Cancel   OK

Figure 3-8.   Point Mac OS X Server at your network time server or at the same Internet time server that your Active Directory servers are using.

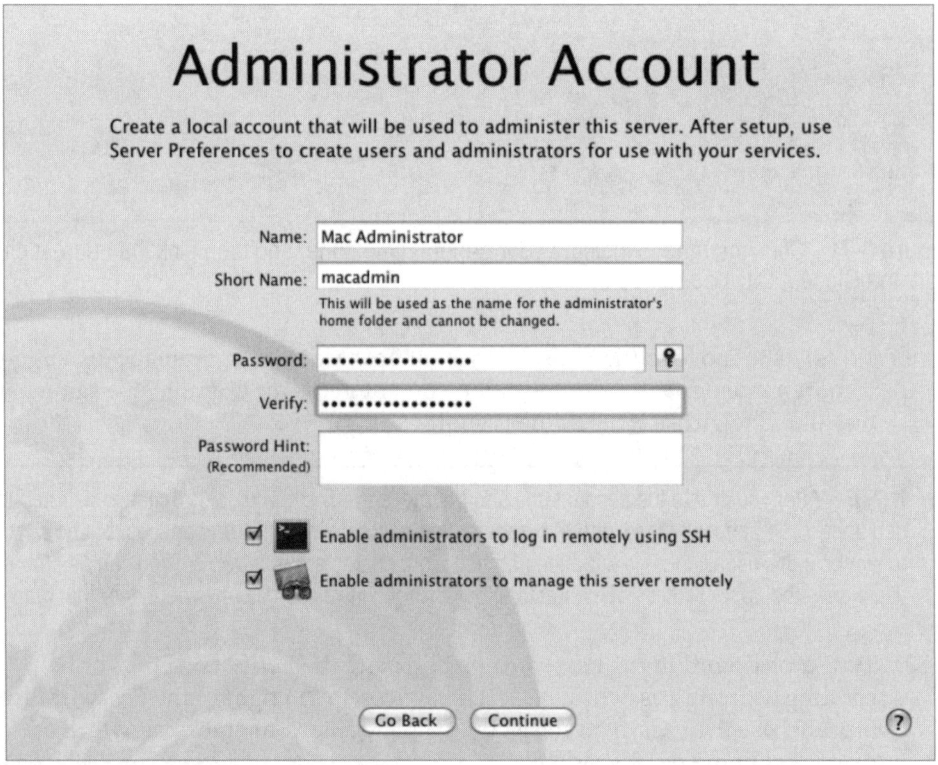

Administrator Account

Create a local account that will be used to administer this server. After setup, use Server Preferences to create users and administrators for use with your services.

Name: Mac Administrator

Short Name: macadmin
This will be used as the name for the administrator's home folder and cannot be changed.

Password: •••••••••••••••• 🔑

Verify: ••••••••••••••••

Password Hint:
(Recommended)

☑ Enable administrators to log in remotely using SSH

☑ Enable administrators to manage this server remotely

Go Back   Continue   ⑦

Figure 3-9.   On the Administrator Account screen, set up the local administrator account for the Mac OS X server.

4. Type a password hint in the Password Hint text box if you want to create a hint. Apple recommends creating a hint, because forgetting a password may prevent you from administering the Mac, but most security experts recommend against creating a hint. It's better simply to remember the password; if necessary, write it down, and keep it somewhere secure.

5. Select the Enable Administrators To Log In Remotely Using SSH check box if you will use the Secure Shell (SSH) protocol to connect to this Mac server from other servers. This capability is often useful.

6. Select the Enable Administrators To Manage This Server Remotely check box if you want to enable remote management. This lets you connect via Screen Sharing or Remote Desktop. This capability, too, is normally useful.

Click the Continue button when you've made your choices.

Choosing Network Settings for Your Server

Next, you'll see the Network screen, on which you can configure each of the server's network interfaces—for example, Ethernet, AirPort, and FireWire. In this section, we'll look at configuring Ethernet and AirPort because the chances are slim that you will use FireWire to connect your Mac server to your Windows network.

If you're using a wired network connection, click the Ethernet item in the list box on the left if it's not already selected. You then see the status and settings for the Ethernet interface. Figure 3-10 shows an example.

If your network has a DHCP server (as is likely), and the Mac has identified the server, you may not need to make any changes on this screen. Mac OS X selects the Using DHCP item in the Configure IPv4 pop-up menu by default, so the Mac automatically looks for a DHCP server on the network; if it finds a DHCP server, the Mac requests an address and applies it, together with the subnet mask, the router, the DNS server, and any search domains.

Giving the Mac Server a Fixed IP Address

DHCP is convenient, but you may well need to anchor the Mac server to a fixed IP address so that it's easy for your Macs and management tools to find. To do so, open the Configure IPv4 pop-up menu and choose Using DHCP With Manual Address; then type the IP address in the IP Address text box.

NOTE The Using DHCP With Manual Address choice in the Configure IPv4 pop-up menu lets you set the Mac's IP address but pick up the other configuration information from the DHCP server. If you want to set all the settings yourself, choose Manually and work as described in the section "Choosing Ethernet Settings Manually," a little later in this chapter.

Creating Strong Passwords with Password Assistant

For help creating a strong password, or to see how strong a password is, click the Password Assistant button—the button with the key icon—to the right of the Password text box to open Password Assistant (shown here with choices made).

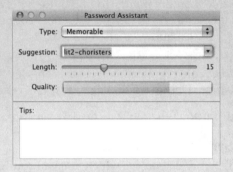

Open the Type pop-up menu at the top of the window and choose the type of password you want to create:

- **Manual**   You type the password yourself. Use this setting to check how strong your password is.

- **Memorable**   Password Assistant creates a password that's (relatively) easy to remember—for example, **curious!coffee** or **camel266squadron**. Memorable passwords are the easiest for general use, especially if you increase the Length slider setting to a suitable length.

- **Letters & Numbers**   Password Assistant creates a password that consists of uppercase and lowercase numbers but no symbols.

- **Numbers Only**   Password Assistant creates a password that consists only of numbers.

- **Random**   Password Assistant creates a password at random. These passwords tend to be very hard to memorize.

- **FIPS-181 Compliant**   Password Assistant creates a password that meets Federal Information Processing Standard 181 (FIPS-181), which covers automatic password generators. The FIPS-181 passwords that Password Assistant produces consist of only lowercase letters.

Drag the Length slider until it shows the number of characters you want the password to have. The Quality meter shows how strong the password is—red for an embarrassingly weak password, yellow for a fair or good password, and green for a good, strong password.

Open the Suggestion pop-up menu and then click the password you want, or click the More Suggestions item at the bottom to refresh the list of suggestions.

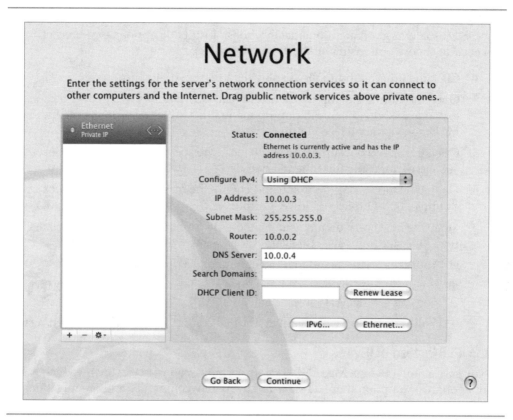

Figure 3-10. On the Network screen, you can configure each of your server's network interfaces. You'll probably want to start with Ethernet.

Changing the DNS Server

While on the Network screen, make certain the Mac has picked up the right DNS server. If it has the wrong server, you'll hit a rich vein of connectivity headaches.

If you need to change the DNS server, do so like this:

1. Open the Configure IPv4 pop-up menu and choose Manually. Mac OS X makes the DNS Server text box editable.

2. Open the Configure IPv4 pop-up menu again and choose Using DHCP. Mac OS X switches back to the DHCP values, but the DNS Server text box remains editable.

3. Type the address of your DNS server in the DNS Server text box. If you have multiple servers, separate them with commas—for example, **10.0.0.3, 10.0.0.12**.

Choosing Ethernet Settings Manually

Mac OS X usually is good at automatically choosing suitable options for Ethernet, but if you need to choose options manually, follow these steps:

1. Click the Ethernet button to display the Ethernet dialog box.

2. Open the Configure pop-up menu and choose Manually. The dialog box expands to show the Speed pop-up menu, the Duplex pop-up menu, and the MTU pop-up menu (see Figure 3-11).

3. Open the Speed pop-up menu and choose the speed. For example, choose 1000baseT for a Gigabit Ethernet network.

4. Open the Duplex pop-up menu and choose the means of duplexing—for example, Full-Duplex or Flow-Control.

5. Open the MTU pop-up menu and choose the size of the maximum transmission unit—the size (in bytes) of the largest data packet the interface can shift:

   ■ Your choices are Standard (1500), Jumbo (9000), and Custom.

   ■ If you choose Custom, the Ethernet dialog box displays a text box in which you can set the MTU size.

6. Click the OK button when you've finished configuring the Ethernet settings.

Using IPv6 Instead of IPv4

As you saw a moment ago, Mac OS X largely assumes you're using IPv4—which is still a fair-enough assumption these days, as relatively few companies and organizations

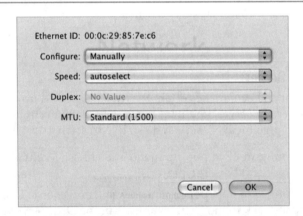

Figure 3-11. To configure the Ethernet adapter manually, choose Manually in the Configure pop-up menu and then provide the speed, duplex, and MTU settings you need.

have yet felt enough impetus to move to IPv6. But if your company or organization is one of the few, you can configure IPv6 like this:

1. Open the Configure IPv4 pop-up menu and choose Off to turn off the server's use of IPv4.

2. Click the IPv6 button to display the IPv6 dialog box (shown in Figure 3-12 with settings chosen). Normally, the IPv6 dialog box opens with the Automatically item chosen in the Configure IPv6 pop-up menu, and no other options in sight.

3. Open the Configure IPv6 pop-up menu and choose Manually. The dialog box expands to show a Router text box, an Address text box, and a Prefix Length text box.

4. Enter the router address, IP address, and prefix length.

5. Click the OK button.

Setting Up an AirPort Interface

For best performance, you'll typically want to connect your Mac server to your Windows network via Ethernet—preferably Gigabit Ethernet. But if you're heavily into wireless or you're setting up a temporary or flexible network, you may need to connect it via its AirPort interface.

NOTE   You cannot connect the Mac server to a closed wireless network (one that is not broadcasting its SSID) during setup. To get around this, either open the wireless network while you're setting up the server or set up the Mac using Ethernet and then add the closed wireless network afterward.

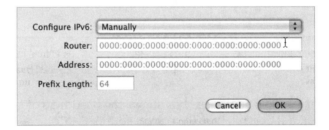

Figure 3-12.   For some networks, you may need to configure IPv6 manually by providing the router address, IP address, and prefix length.

Here's how to configure the AirPort interface:

1. In the list of network interfaces, click AirPort to display its configuration options.

2. Open the Network Name pop-up menu and choose the wireless network to which you want to connect.

3. When Mac OS X prompts you for the network password, type it and then click the OK button.

4. Open the Configure IPv4 pop-up menu, and then choose the way you want to select network settings. These are the three items you're most likely to need:

   - **Using DHCP** Select this item to have the Mac pick up the network settings from your existing DHCP server on the network. The IP address, subnet mask, router address, and DNS server addresses are all set for you; you just need to set the search domains if the Mac needs them.

   - **Using DHCP With Manual Address** Select this item when you need to set the IP address for the server manually but pick up the subnet mask, router address, and DNS server addresses from the DHCP server. Again, you can set the search domains and the DHCP client ID if your server needs them. This option lets you set a static IP address for your server rather than have it grab an address from the pool each time you start it or restart it.

   - **Manually** Select this item when you want to specify all the network settings manually.

NOTE The Configure IPv4 pop-up menu also offers the choices Using BootP, Off, and Create PPPoE Service. BootP is for Macs that boot from the network and is usually used for clients rather than servers. Off turns IPv4 off (so that you can use IPv6, as described earlier in this chapter). Create PPPoE Service lets you use Point-to-Point Protocol over Ethernet to establish a connection between two points in an Ethernet network; it is mostly used for DSL connections.

NOTE When entering multiple items in the same text box, such as entries in the DNS Server text box, separate them with commas—for example, **206.216.4.52, 206.216.4.43**.

5. Check that the DNS Server text box shows the IP address of your network's DNS server. If it doesn't, type the correct address.

NOTE If the DNS Server text box is not editable, open the Configure IPv4 pop-up menu and choose Manually. Then open the menu again and choose your previous setting—for example, Using DHCP.

6. If the network connection needs search domains, type them in the Search Domains text box.

Putting Your Network Connections in the Right Order

If you've set up two network connections—for example, Ethernet and AirPort—drag them up and down the list box on the left of the Network screen into the order in which you want the server to use them. Put the primary network service at the top of the list.

Giving Your Server a DNS Name and Computer Name

When you've finished configuring your server's network interfaces, click the Continue button to move along to the Network Names screen (see Figure 3-13).

If the Primary DNS Name text box shows a name that the Mac has picked up from the directory, check that it's the right one and change it if it's not. If the Mac hasn't found a name, type in the DNS name you want the Mac server to have—for example, **macserver.corp.acmeheavy.com**.

In the Computer Name text box, type the "friendly" name under which you want your server to appear on the network—the name users will see when they're browsing the network. For example, if this server is the network's only Mac server, you could call it **Mac Server** (there's nothing wrong with simplicity and clarity). You can use up to

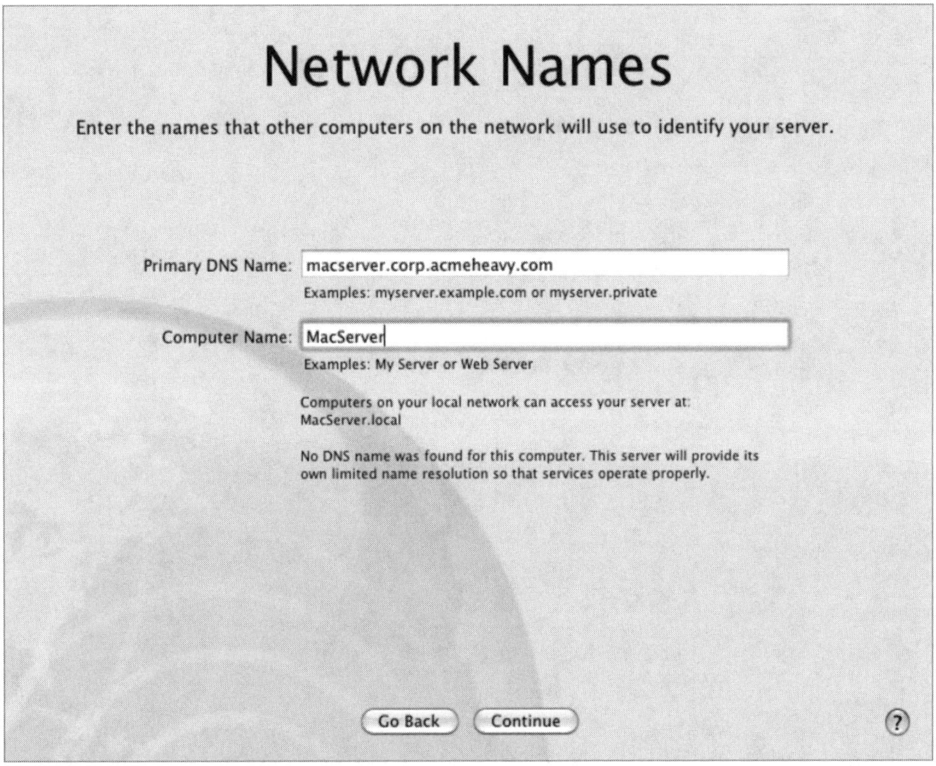

Network Names

Enter the names that other computers on the network will use to identify your server.

Primary DNS Name: `macserver.corp.acmeheavy.com`

Examples: myserver.example.com or myserver.private

Computer Name: `MacServer`

Examples: My Server or Web Server

Computers on your local network can access your server at: MacServer.local

No DNS name was found for this computer. This server will provide its own limited name resolution so that services operate properly.

Go Back   Continue

Figure 3-13. On the Network Names screen, give your server a DNS name and a computer name so that other computers on your network can access it.

63 characters for the name, including spaces or underscores, but a shorter name will be easier to read. Mac OS X suggests a name derived from the entry in the Primary DNS Name text box, but you can change it as needed.

When you've chosen the network names for your server, click the Continue button to move along.

Setting Up Users and Groups

The next screen you see is the Users And Groups screen (see Figure 3-14). What you want to do here is not create or import any users or groups yet. To do so, follow these steps:

1. Select the Configure Manually option button.

2. Click the Continue button. This brings you to a different Connect To A Directory Server screen, which is shown in Figure 3-15.

3. Make sure the Connect To A Directory Server check box is cleared, and then click the Continue button to move along.

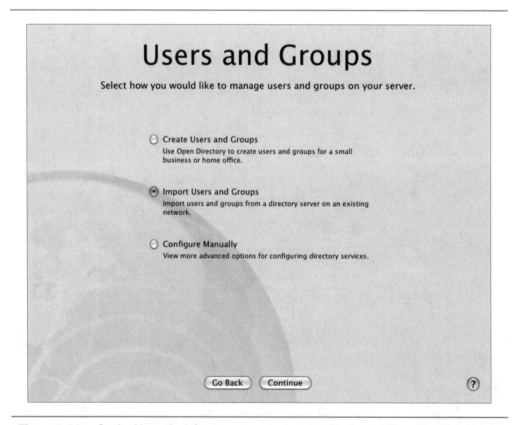

Figure 3-14. On the Users And Groups screen, select the Configure Manually option button to skip creating or importing users and groups for now.

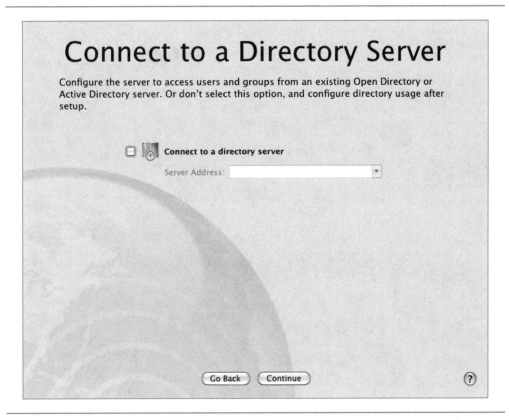

Figure 3-15.   From the Connect To A Directory Server screen, you can skip importing users and groups by leaving the Connect To A Directory Server check box cleared and then clicking the Continue button.

Setting Up Directory Services

After dealing with users and groups, you see the Directory Services screen shown in Figure 3-16. This screen gives you the option of making your Mac server an Open Directory master server. Now, you want your Mac server to be an Open Directory master server—but you don't want it to be one yet. First, you need to bind the Mac server to Active Directory. Then you can turn it into an Open Directory master.

So clear the Set Up An Open Directory Master check box, and then click the Continue button to move along to the last step of setup.

Reviewing Your Options for the Mac Server

Finally, Installer displays the Review screen (see Figure 3-17), which summarizes the main tools you use for configuring Mac OS X Server.

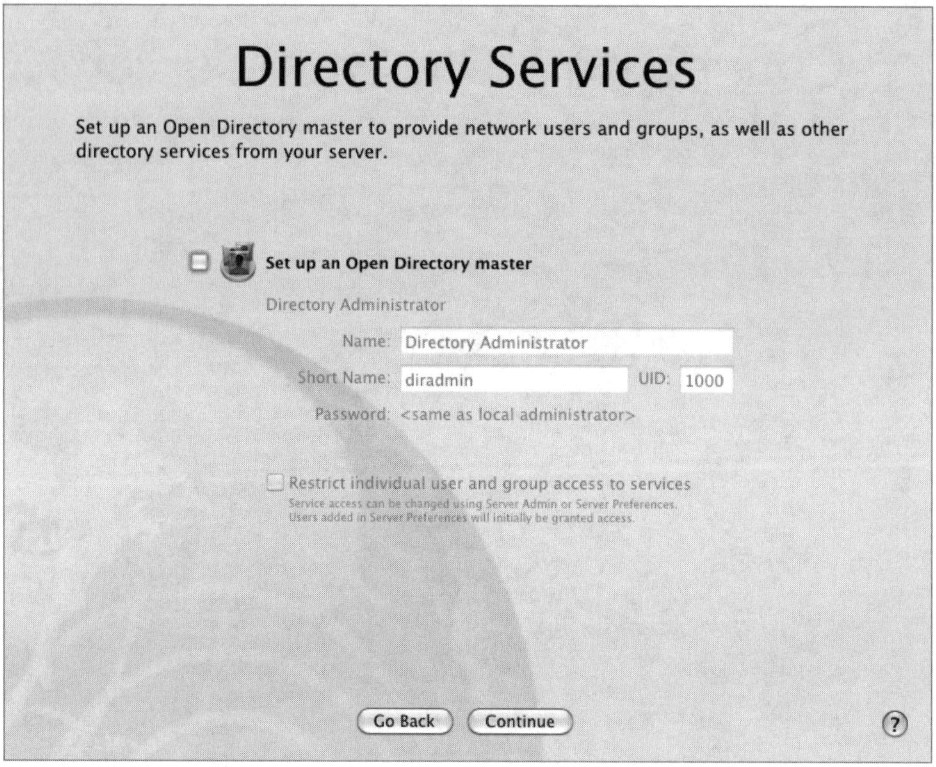

Directory Services

Set up an Open Directory master to provide network users and groups, as well as other directory services from your server.

☐ 📷 **Set up an Open Directory master**

Directory Administrator

Name: Directory Administrator

Short Name: diradmin   UID: 1000

Password: <same as local administrator>

☐ Restrict individual user and group access to services
Service access can be changed using Server Admin or Server Preferences.
Users added in Server Preferences will initially be granted access.

(Go Back)   (Continue)   ⑦

Figure 3-16. On the Directory Services screen, clear the Set Up An Open Directory Master check box.

If there's a problem, click the Go Back button and retrace your steps until you reach the screen on which you can fix it. Then make your way forward again using the Continue button.

NOTE   To see the details of the setup options you've chosen, click the Details button on the Review screen. Installer displays a screen with a breakdown of the options. From here, you can click the Save Setup Profile button to save your server's details as a profile that you can apply automatically to another server you set up. You can also click the Save Summary button to save a summary of the server's settings—for example, to put in your records.

Figure 3-17. Before you click the Set Up button on the Review screen, you may want to click the Details button to drill down to the settings.

If the settings look good to go, click the Set Up button. Installer then applies the settings to the server, displaying a Setting Up screen as it does so. When Installer displays the Go button, click it to launch your server.

When the server comes up, it automatically displays the Server Preferences application so that you can start configuring it.

You'll probably see the Mac OS X Server DVD on the desktop. If so, CTRL-click or right-click it, and then choose Eject from the shortcut menu to eject it.

Upgrading Mac OS X Client to Mac OS X Server

If your Mac already has the client version of Mac OS X installed on it, you can upgrade it to Mac OS X Server. Do this only if you're certain that you want to use the Mac as a server in the long term. If you may need to go back to the client version, you'll do better to create a new partition for Mac OS X Server and retain the existing Mac OS X client partition.

To upgrade, insert the Mac OS X Server DVD while the Mac is running. When the Finder opens the Mac OS X Server Install Disc window, double-click the Install Mac OS X Server icon. On the Install Mac OS X Server screen that appears, click the Install button to start the installation.

Go through the Welcome To The Mac OS X Server Installer screen and the Software License screen until you reach the Standard Install screen, where you choose the hard disk volume on which to install Mac OS X Server.

The installation routine assumes you want to upgrade the installation of Mac OS X on the Mac's current startup volume to Mac OS X Server. If you want to upgrade a different volume, click the Change Install Location button to reach the Select A Destination screen, click the volume you want, and then click the Continue button to return to the Standard Install screen. The volume you choose must also have Mac OS X 10.6 installed on it—you can't use this screen to install Mac OS X Server on a volume that has a different OS installed or no OS at all.

Click the Install button on the Standard Install screen, authenticate yourself by providing your password when Installer prompts you for it, and then Installer gets to work. Because most of the files needed for Mac OS X are already there, the upgrade is much quicker than a full installation. Usually, it's finished within five minutes. Click the Close button on the Installation Was Completed Successfully screen, and then restart your Mac.

When your Mac restarts, it displays the Welcome screen, and you can start configuring Mac OS X Server. Turn back to the section titled "Performing the Initial Configuration" and work through its steps to set up your server.

Updating Your Server with the Latest Fixes

Pretty much the first thing you should do after installing Mac OS X Server is install any updates that Apple has released since your installation disc came out of the press. Apple is so eager for you to apply these updates that it makes Mac OS X Server run the Software Update utility automatically the first time you start the server.

So see if there's a Software Update window somewhere on your screen checking for updates or (if it has already found them) bouncing its Dock icon at you like a spaniel levitating at the prospect of a walk.

If Software Update isn't running, choose Apple | Software Update to launch it manually. Give it a minute or two to check for updates.

Figure 3-18. Click the Show Details button in the first Software Update dialog box.

Usually, there will be at least a few updates, and Software Update will display a dialog box like the one shown in Figure 3-18 telling you that software updates are available for your Mac but not spelling out what they are.

Click the Show Details button to learn the details of what the updates are and how big they are (see Figure 3-19), and then clear the check box for any update you don't want to install.

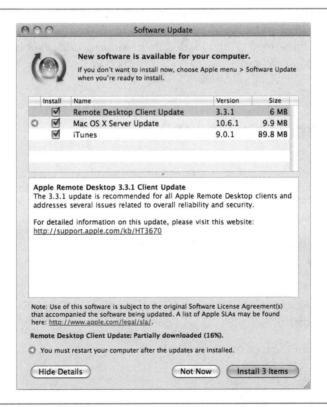

Figure 3-19. When you see the list of updates, clear the check box for any update you don't want to install.

Figure 3-20. You may need to restart the server to finish installing the updates.

TIP The reversed Play symbol that appears alongside the Mac OS X Server Update in Figure 3-19 means you'll need to restart the server after installing the update. While you're configuring the server, that's no problem—but you may want to watch out for it in future when the server has clients connected to it.

Click the Install button, accept any license agreements that Mac OS X displays, and then authenticate yourself by typing your password. Software Update downloads the updates (unless it has already downloaded them for you) and installs them.

If Software Update prompts you to restart the server (see Figure 3-20), click the Restart button.

Binding the Mac Server to the Network

Next, you need to sort out the configuration of your Mac server and bind it into the magic triangle. There are six steps you need to perform here:

1. Turn on the Open Directory service on your Mac server.

2. Turn your Mac server into a standalone directory server.

3. Bind your Mac server to Active Directory.

4. Turn your Mac server into an Open Directory master server.

5. Turn off Kerberos on your new Open Directory master server.

6. Join your Mac's Open Directory services with your Active Directory server's Kerberos realm.

Let's take it from the top.

Turning On the Open Directory Service

Start by turning on the Open Directory service on your Mac server. Follow these steps:

1. Click the Server Admin icon on the Dock to open Server Admin (see Figure 3-21). What you see at first is the overview pane, which briefly details the Mac's hardware, software, services, and status.

2. Expand the server's entry in the Servers pane on the left by clicking the gray disclosure triangle or (usually easier) double-clicking the server's name. You'll see a list of the services the server is running. (This is the same list as you see in the Services area of the overview pane, but it also gives you access to services.)

Figure 3-21.   Server Admin opens showing the overview of the server. From here, you can see which services are running and what the service status is.

3. If the Open Directory service doesn't appear in the list of services, add it like this:

   a. Click the Settings button in the toolbar to display the Settings pane.

   b. Click the Services tab in the tab bar to display the Services pane (see Figure 3-22).

   c. In the Select The Services To Configure On This Server list box, select the Open Directory check box.

   d. Click the Save button to save the change. Server Admin adds the Open Directory service to the list of services under the server in the left pane but doesn't show a green light next to it because the service isn't configured yet.

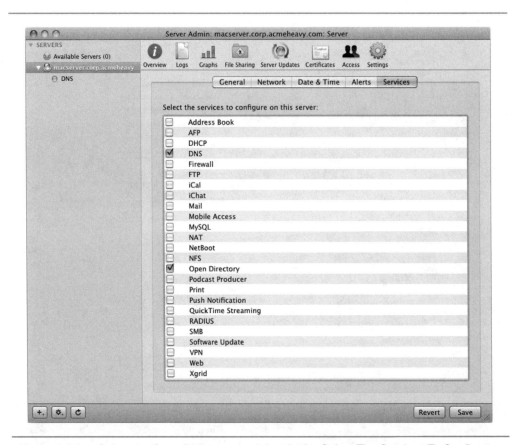

Figure 3-22.   Select the Open Directory check box in the Select The Services To Configure On This Server list in the Services pane, and then click the Save button.

Turning Your Mac Server into a Standalone Directory Server

Now make sure that your Mac server is running a standalone directory service—one in which it is using only its local directory domain, not another directory domain on the network. To do this, follow these steps in Server Manager:

1. In the left pane, click the Open Directory service under the server to display the configuration screens for Open Directory.

2. Look at the readouts in the Overview pane. If the top readout says "Open Directory is: Standalone directory," you're all set; skip the rest of this list.

3. If not, click the Settings tab to display the Settings pane, and then make sure the General pane (see Figure 3-23) is displayed (click the General tab if it isn't).

4. Click the Change button to launch the Open Directory Assistant. The Assistant displays the Change Directory Role screen (see Figure 3-24).

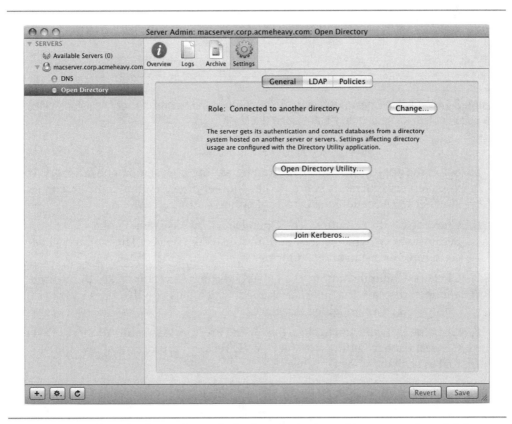

Figure 3-23.   From the General pane in Settings for the Open Directory service, click the Change button to change the Mac server's role to a standalone directory service.

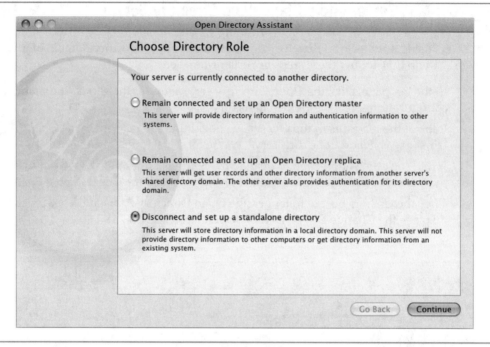

Figure 3-24.   On the Change Directory Role screen of the Open Directory Assistant, select the option button for setting up a standalone directory.

5. Select the appropriate option button for setting up a standalone directory. If your server is currently connected to another directory, this is the Disconnect And Set Up A Standalone Directory option button.

6. Click the Continue button. The Open Directory Assistant displays the Confirm Settings screen, which briefly summarizes your choice: "This server will be configured as a standalone directory."

7. Click the Continue button. The Open Directory Assistant makes the change and then displays the Summary screen, which tells you that the server has been configured as a standalone directory.

8. Click the Done button to close the Open Directory Assistant. You'll see that the General pane in Settings for the Open Directory service now shows the server's role to be Standalone Directory.

Leave Server Admin open for the moment—you'll need it again shortly.

Binding the Mac OS X Server to Active Directory

Now it's time to use Directory Utility to bind your Mac OS X server to Active Directory by following the steps in the section "Performing the Binding" in Chapter 2. To get started, open System Preferences, click the Accounts icon in the System area, click the Login Options item in the left pane, and then click the Join button next to the Network Account Server readout.

NOTE In the User Experience pane in Advanced Options within Services in Directory Utility for Active Directory, you almost certainly won't want to create a mobile account on the server, so clear the Create Mobile Account At Login check box. Similarly, clear the Force Local Home Directory On Startup Disk check box to make sure Mac OS X doesn't create a local home directory—the network one should be fine.

If you're using the name of an existing Computer object in Active Directory rather than creating a new object during the binding, Mac OS X displays the Join Existing Account? dialog box, shown here:

Normally, you'll want to click the OK button here. But if this message means you've gotten the wrong computer account, click the Cancel button, go back, and fix the name.

Next, because you're binding a server to Active Directory rather than binding a client, you'll see the Join Kerberos Realm dialog box, shown here:

There's no choice except to click the OK button, so do that. But don't follow the instructions in the dialog box just yet—we'll do that in a moment. Before that, we need to turn the Mac server into an Open Directory master and disable Kerberos on it.

Click the OK button to close the Active Directory dialog box, and then quit Directory Utility and System Preferences.

Identifying and Resolving DNS Problems when Binding

If your Mac server cannot bind to Active Directory, the problem may lie in DNS. To see if there is a DNS problem, open Terminal and check that your Mac server and your Active Directory server agree on hostnames and IP addresses.

Click the Terminal icon in the Dock to open a Terminal window, then type the **hostname** command and press RETURN. You'll get back something like this, where **macserver:~** is the prompt and the command you type is in boldface:

```
macserver:~ hostname
macserver.corp.acmeheavy.com
```

Now use the host command to return the IP address for the hostname you just got:

```
macserver:~ host macserver.corp.acmeheavy.com
macserver.corp.acmeheavy.com has address 10.0.0.3
```

Next, use the host command again to make sure the IP address is associated with the hostname in DNS:

```
macserver:~ host 10.0.0.3
3.0.0.10.in-addr.arpa domain name pointer macserver.corp.acmeheavy.com
```

This is all fine: You can put in the hostname and get the IP address, or put in the IP address and get the hostname.

Now, again from Terminal, do the same thing with your Active Directory server. First, use the host command to return the IP address:

```
macserver:~ host server1.corp.acmeheavy.com
server1.corp.acmeheavy.com has address 10.0.0.4
```

That's fine. So try to return the hostname from the IP address:

```
macserver:~ host 10.0.0.4
4.0.0.10.in-addr.arpa domain name pointer acmeheavy.com
```

As you can see, what I've got here is a pointer to the domain name as a whole, not to the server on it. You'll need to fix a DNS problem such as this in order to get binding to work. In this case, the problem is a messed-up pointer in the reverse-lookup zone in DNS on the Active Directory server, and the solution is to create a pointer that points to the right machine.

When you've sorted out the DNS on Windows Server, go back to Terminal and try returning the hostname from the IP address again:

```
macserver:~ host 10.0.0.4
4.0.0.10.in-addr.arpa domain name pointer server1.corp.acmeheavy.com
```

Now that DNS knows where to find the server, we're back in business and can get binding again.

Turning Your Mac Server into an Open Directory Master Server

Next, turn your Mac server from a standalone directory server to an Open Directory master server. Follow these steps:

1. Go back to Server Admin and click the Open Directory service under the server in the left pane to display the configuration screens for Open Directory. (If Server Admin is already displaying the Open Directory service, you're fine.)

2. Click the Settings button to display the Settings pane, and then click the General tab to display the General pane under it. You'll see that the Role readout now says "Connected to another directory" because you've bound the server to Active Directory.

3. Click the Change button to launch the Open Directory Assistant. The Assistant displays the Change Directory Role screen, which you met earlier in the chapter.

4. This time, select the Remain Connected And Set Up An Open Directory Master option button.

5. Click the Continue button to reach the Directory Administrator screen.

NOTE If the Open Directory Assistant displays the Single Sign-On Unavailable screen, close the Open Directory Assistant and check that the DNS service is running.

6. On the Directory Administrator screen (see Figure 3-25), set up the details of the directory administrator account:

   ■ In the Name text box, either accept the default name for the directory administrator (Directory Administrator) or type a name you've chosen.

   ■ In the Short Name text box, either accept the default short name for the directory administrator (diradmin) or type your preferred name.

   ■ In the UID text box, either accept the default user ID number for the directory administrator (1000) or type a number of your choice.

   ■ Type a strong password in the Password text box and the Verify text box.

7. Click the Next button to move along to the Domain screen (see Figure 3-26).

8. Check out the Open Directory Assistant's suggestion in the LDAP Search Base text box, and correct it if necessary.

9. Click the Continue button. The Open Directory Assistant displays the Confirm Settings screen, which summarizes your choices.

10. Check through the details, and then click the Continue button if everything's right. (If not, click the Go Back button and fix the problem.) The Open Directory Assistant creates the Open Directory master and then displays the Summary screen to tell you it has done so.

11. Click the Done button to close the Open Directory Assistant.

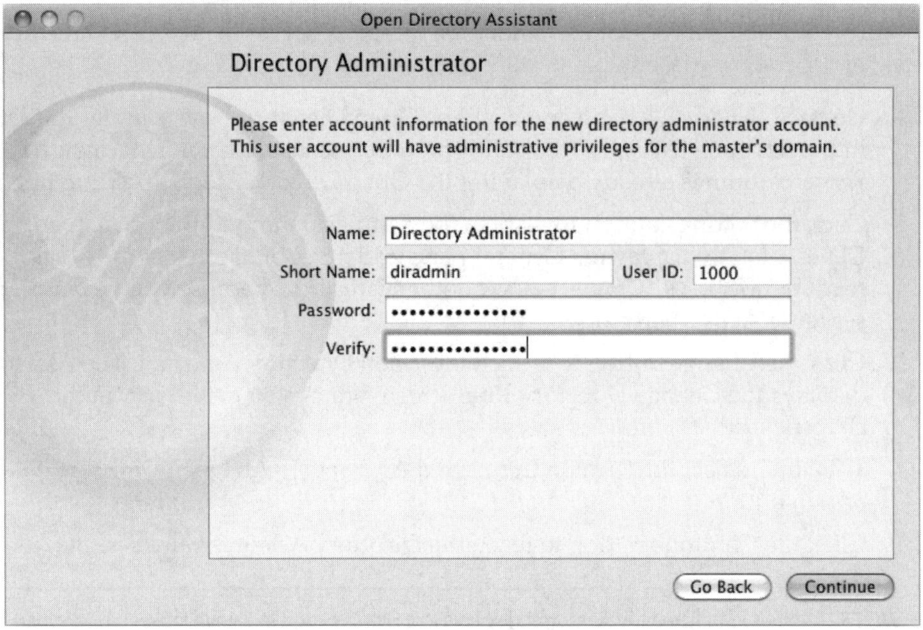

Figure 3-25.   Set the directory administrator account details for the Open Directory on the Directory Administrator screen.

Disabling Kerberos on Your Open Directory Master

Now that you have set up your Open Directory master server, disable Kerberos on it. You need to do this to prevent conflicts occurring between the Open Directory master server's Kerberos realm and the Active Directory Kerberos realm.

Follow these steps:

1. Open Terminal (for example, click the Terminal icon in the Dock).

2. Type the **sso_util** command with the **remove –k** flag, as shown next, providing your Open Directory administrator name and password and the name of your Open Directory Master's Kerberos realm:

    ```
    sudo sso_util remove -k -a username -p password -r realm_name
    ```

3. Type your account password when Mac OS X demands to know what right you have to use the sudo command.

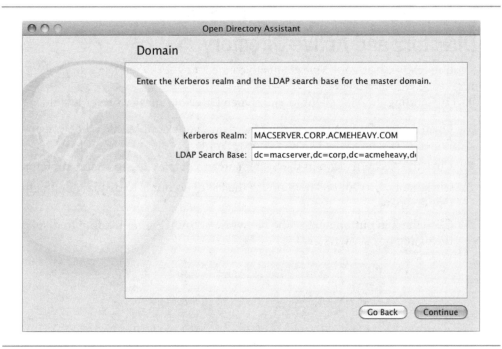

Figure 3-26. On the Domain screen of the Open Directory Assistant, check the Kerberos Realm and the LDAP search base to use for the master domain. Change them if necessary.

 NOTE To see your Kerberos realm, look at the Kerberos Realm readout in the Overview pane for the Open Directory service in Server Admin.

Leave Terminal open for now because you'll need it in the next section.

Joining the Mac Server to the Active Directory Kerberos Realm

After disabling Kerberos on the Open Directory master server, use the `dsconfigad` command to join the Mac server to the Active Directory Kerberos realm.

Still in Terminal, type the following command and then press RETURN:

```
sudo dsconfigad -enableSSO
```

You'll get the laconic message "Settings changed successfully."

Now check that you've safely bound the server to Active Directory by returning the entries in your keytab. Still in Terminal, type this command and press RETURN:

```
sudo klist -ke
```

If all is well, you'll get back a tidal wave of information about the Mac OS X Server services and the Kerberos realms.

Setting Your Mac Clients to Connect to Open Directory and Active Directory

Now you're ready to set your Mac clients to connect to your Open Directory server and to your Active Directory server.

Start by binding the Mac client to your Open Directory master server like this:

1. Open System Preferences on the Mac client. For example, click the System Preferences icon in the Dock or choose Apple | System Preferences.

2. Click the Accounts icon in the System area to display the Accounts preferences.

3. Click the Login Options item under the list of accounts to display the Login Options pane.

4. Click the Join button next to the Network Account Server readout to display the dialog box shown here.

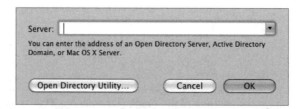

5. Open the Server pop-up menu and see if your Open Directory master server appears on it. If not, type either the name (for example, **macserver.corp .acmeheavy.com**) or the IP address (for example, **10.0.0.3**) of the server in the text box.

6. Click the OK button, and then authenticate yourself when Mac OS X prompts you to do so. Mac OS X then tries to connect to the server, and if it is able to do so, it displays its name or IP address next to the Network Account Server readout in the Login Options pane in Accounts preferences.

With the Mac bound to the Open Directory server, you can now bind it to the Active Directory server as well. Follow these steps:

1. From the Login Options pane in Accounts preferences, click the Edit button to display the dialog box for connecting to a directory service.

2. Click the Open Directory Utility button to open Directory Utility.

3. Click the padlock icon, type your password in the authentication dialog box, and then click the OK button. Directory Utility removes the locking from the options in the Services pane.

4. Click the Active Directory item in the list of services, and then click the Edit button (the pencil button) to display the Active Directory dialog box.

5. In the Active Directory Domain text box, type the Active Directory domain to which you're connecting the Mac.

6. If you need to choose advanced options, click the Show Advanced Options disclosure triangle and then choose advanced options as discussed in the previous chapter.

7. When you've chosen the options and you're ready to bind the Mac to Active Directory, click the Bind button and then provide your username and password in the Network Administrator Required dialog box that opens. Select the Use For Authentication check box to use the credentials for authentication, and select the Use For Contacts check box to use the credentials for contacts too. Then click the OK button to perform the bind.

After binding the Mac to Active Directory, Directory Utility will show the two servers to which the Mac is bound. When you quit Directory Utility (just press ⌘-Q as usual), you'll see that the Network Account Server readout in the Logout Options pane in System Preferences shows Multiple to indicate that multiple bindings are in place.

Setting Up Open Directory Groups for Managing Your Macs

With the magic-triangle arrangement, you manage your Macs through Open Directory rather than through Active Directory. To manage the Macs easily, you'll need to create groups in Open Directory and add the users to them.

In most cases, the most straightforward approach is to create groups in Open Directory for your Mac users and then add users or groups from Active Directory to these Open Directory groups. When you create an Open Directory group like this, the group contains references to the users and groups you've added; the user records and group records remain within Active Directory, where you can manipulate them using Windows Server's tools as usual. But to the Open Directory group, you can add the Mac-specific policies that the Macs need.

Creating an Open Directory Group

To create an Open Directory group and add records to it from Active Directory, follow these steps:

1. Open Workgroup Manager. For example, click the Workgroup Manager icon in the Dock. Workgroup Manager displays the Workgroup Manager Connect dialog box (shown here).

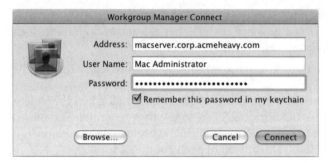

 NOTE   You can run Workgroup Manager on either your Mac server or on a Mac client on which you've installed the Server Administration Tools.

2. Type the server's name in the Address box.

3. Type your administrator username in the User Name text box and the corresponding password in the Password text box.

4. Select the Remember This Password In My Keychain check box if you want to store the password in your Mac OS X keychain so that you won't have to type it in again in future.

5. Click the Connect button to connect to the server. You'll see the full Workgroup Manager window. As you can see in Figure 3-27, the Workgroup Manager window has these main features:

    ■ **Toolbar**   The toolbar across the top of the window contains buttons for launching Server Admin, switching between viewing accounts and viewing preferences, creating a new item (such as a new user), and other important operations.

    ■ **Authentication bar**   Below the toolbar is the authentication bar, which shows which directory you're viewing and whether you're authenticated. The globe icon at the left end opens the Change Directory pop-up menu, which you use to navigate to other directories. The lock icon at the right end shows whether the directory is locked or is open for editing.

Change Directory
pop-up menu   Toolbar   Authentication
bar   Lock icon

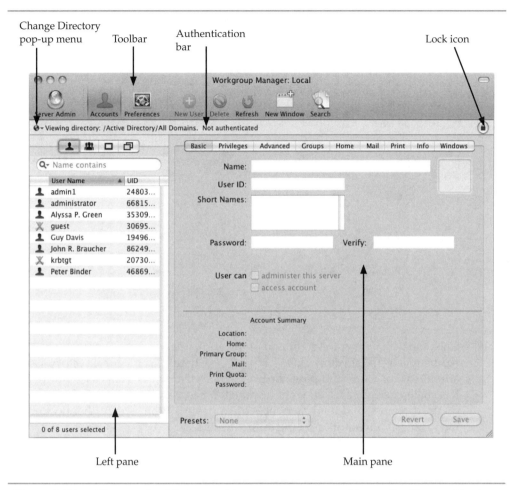

Figure 3-27. After opening Workgroup Manager, you may need to use the Change Directory pop-up menu to change the directory displayed.

Left pane   Main pane

- **Left pane** The tab bar at the top of the left pane lets you switch among users, groups, computers, and computer groups. Once you've displayed the right type of object, click an object in the list to work with it.

- **Main pane** The main pane shows the details of the object you're working with. You can switch from one pane of details to another by clicking the appropriate tab on the tab bar across the top of the pane.

6. Look at the Authentication bar and see which directory you're viewing. If it's the /LDAPv3/127.0.0.1 directory, you're all set. However, chances are you'll be at the /Active Directory/All Domains directory. In this case, open the Change Directory pop-up menu and choose /LDAPv3/127.0.0.1. If this item doesn't

appear on the menu, click the Other item, use the Select A Directory dialog box (shown here) to choose the directory, and then click the OK button.

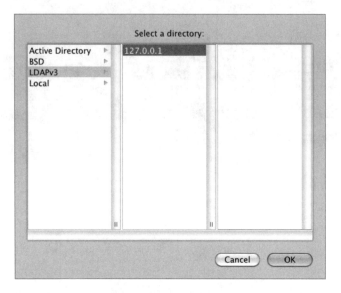

7. Click the lock icon at the right end of the authentication bar to open the Authenticate To Directory dialog box (shown here). Type your directory administrator name and password, select the Remember This Password In My Keychain check box if you want to store the password to speed up future raids on the directory, and then click the Authenticate button. The Authentication bar then shows your status as being authenticated.

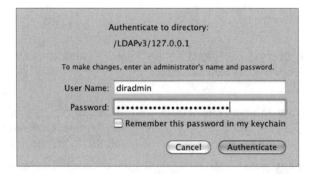

8. Click the Groups tab at the top of the left pane to display the list of groups.

9. Click the New Group button on the toolbar to create a new group. Workgroup Manager gives the new group a default name such as Untitled 1.

10. Type the name for the group in the Name text box—for example, **Mac Users**. Workgroup Manager automatically suggests a short name derived from this name but without capitals or spaces (for example, **macusers**). Figure 3-28 shows the Basic pane in the Groups pane displayed and some information entered.

11. Edit the short name in the Short Name text box if necessary.

12. Change the group ID number in the Group ID text box if need be. Normally, it's fine to go with Workgroup Manager's suggested number.

13. Optionally, type a comment about the group in the Comment text box.

14. Click the Save button to save the changes you've made so far. Workgroup Manager applies the group name in the left pane.

15. Click the Members tab to display the Members pane.

16. Click the Add (+) button in the upper-right corner of the Members pane to open the drawer of users and groups. Figure 3-29 shows the Members pane with the drawer open.

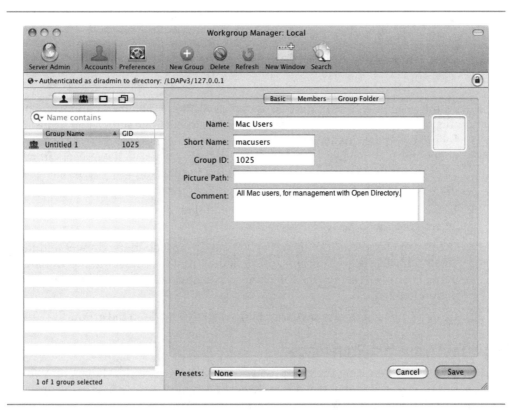

Figure 3-28.   Creating a new group in Workgroup Manager.

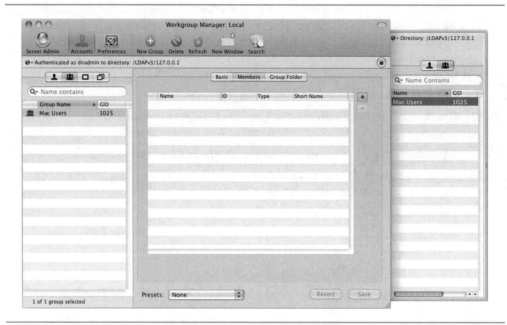

Figure 3-29.   Switch to the Members pane, and then open the drawer of users and groups.

17. At this point, the drawer may be as bare as Mother Hubbard's cupboard—but this is because you're looking at the directory of the Mac server you've just set up. Open the Change Directory pop-up menu at the top of the drawer and choose the /Active Directory/All Domains item from it. A list of users from Active Directory appears in the drawer (or a list of groups, if you're viewing the Groups tab in the drawer).

18. In the drawer, select the users you want and then drag them across to the Members pane.

19. If you need to add groups as well, click the Groups tab in the drawer and then click and haul the appropriate groups across from the drawer to the Members pane. Figure 3-30 shows the Members pane with a small handful of users and a group added.

20. Click the Save button to save the changes you've made to the group.

Adding a Test Managed Preference

You've now finished creating the group, so you can exit Workgroup Manager if you choose. But what you'll probably want to do is apply a managed setting to the group for a quick test to make sure your policies are working.

Figure 3-30. Add users and groups from the drawer to the Members pane.

Yes? Okay, good. Then follow these steps:

1. With the group you just created still selected in the left pane of Workgroup Manager, click the Preferences button to switch to the Preferences pane. Figure 3-31 shows the Overview pane you should see first (if not, click the Overview tab to display it).

2. We'll make this change dramatic, so click the Finder icon to display the preferences for managing the Finder. There are three panes of Finder preferences, and Workgroup Manager should select the Preferences pane (the first of the three) by default. If not, click the Preferences tab to display this pane.

3. At first, the Never option button in the Manage bar at the top will be selected, so all the remaining controls will be grayed out. To start managing preferences, click the Always option button. All the controls become available, as shown in Figure 3-32.

4. Select the Use Simple Finder option button at the top of the pane. Simple Finder is a stripped-down version of Finder that's normally kept for less experienced and less confident users. You probably won't want to inflict Simple Finder on any competent Mac user in your company or organization— but it's good for a test.

5. Click the Apply Now button to apply the change you've made.

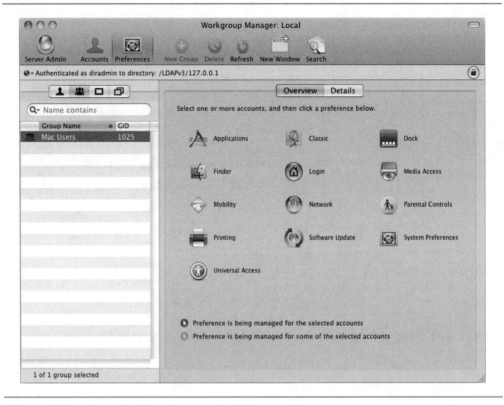

Figure 3-31.   From the Overview pane in Workgroup Manager, you can set managed preferences for the selected user, group, computer, or computer group.

NOTE   We'll dig into the details of what you can do with Workgroup Manager in the following chapters.

Testing the Managed Preference for the Group

Leave Workgroup Manager to continue instructing the Mac server on metaphysical questions and the nonexistence of Schrödinger's cat, and go to one of the client Macs you've bound to Active Directory and Open Directory.

Log in using one of the accounts you added to the group, and verify that you get the Simple Finder, with only the Finder, File, and Help menus rather than the full set of menus.

If you get the Simple Finder, you're signing in correctly to Open Directory and receiving the managed preference. So far, so good. Log out.

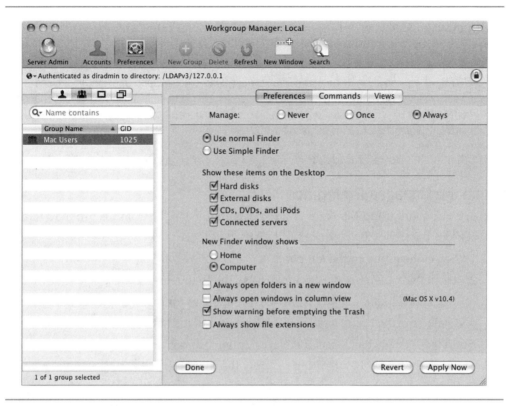

Figure 3-32.   In the Preferences pane of Finder preferences, select the Use Simple Finder option button to provide an easily identifiable managed preference.

NOTE   If you don't get the Simple Finder when you log in, first check that the Mac is bound to Open Directory. Then go to Workgroup Manager and make sure that the account you're using is part of the group for which you set the managed preference.

Now make sure that an administrator gets the option of skipping the managed preference. Log in using an administrator account (for example, a domain administrator account, but see the next Note). If all is well, Mac OS X displays a dialog box that lets you choose to skip Workgroup Management.

NOTE   To check which accounts Mac OS X is treating as administrator accounts, open Directory Utility and authenticate yourself. In the Services pane, click the Active Directory item and then click the Edit button to open the Active Directory dialog box. Click the Show Advanced Options button, and then click the Administrative tab to display the Administrative pane. Make sure the Allow Administration By check box is selected, and then examine the groups in the list box.

For your third check, try to log in as an Active Directory user whom you have not added to your Open Directory group. If everything's working right, the Mac will refuse to log you in, because you're not part of Open Directory.

 NOTE   If you can log in as an Active Directory user who is not in Open Directory, your Open Directory server isn't correctly bound into Active Directory. You need to unbind the server, change it from an Open Directory master to a standalone server, and then once more go through the steps for binding it, promoting it to a master, and so on.

If all is well, you can remove the managed preference, as described next.

Removing the Managed Preference

Go back into Workgroup Manager and remove Simple Finder from the group to which you applied it. The easiest way to do this is as follows:

1.   Select the group in the left pane.

2.   Click the Preferences button to display the Preferences panes.

3.   Click the Finder icon to display the preferences for managing the Finder.

4.   Make sure the Preferences pane is displayed (if it's not, click the Preferences tab).

5.   In the Manage bar, select the Never option button.

6.   Click the Apply Now button to apply the change.

7.   If you've finished messing with your Mac users, quit Workgroup Manager. Otherwise, dig into the other preferences that you actually want to set for the Mac users.

CHAPTER 4 | Extending Active Directory to Handle Mac Clients Natively

As you saw in the previous chapter, one way of managing the Mac clients you've bound to Active Directory is to bind a Mac OS X server into your network and use it to manage the Macs. Like the other computers on the network, the Macs get their authentication from Active Directory; but unlike the other computers, the Macs get their policy from Open Directory running on the Mac server.

This arrangement can work well, and it saves you from having to modify Active Directory in order to manage your Mac clients. But if you don't want to use this kind of "magic triangle" or dual-directory setup, and prefer to manage the Macs through Active Directory without involving Open Directory, you need to take a different approach.

This different approach is to extend the Active Directory schema so that it contains the attributes and classes that the Apple tools require. The schema extensions enable you to store the Mac-related information in Active Directory, connect Workgroup Manager directly to Active Directory, and use Workgroup Manager to apply policy to the Macs.

This chapter shows you how to extend Active Directory. We'll start by going over what's involved, then assemble the equipment you need, and then perform the deed. After that, we'll test that the setup is working.

Understanding the Essentials of Extending the Active Directory Schema

This section discusses the essentials of extending the Active Directory schema to accommodate your network's Macs, starting with the essential question—why extend it?

Understanding the Limitations of a Straightforward Bind

In Chapter 2, you saw the most straightforward way to connect a Mac to your Windows network: to perform a straightforward bind of the Mac to Active Directory. When you bind a Mac to Active Directory like this, you get a basic level of policy:

- First, each user (let's assume it's you) gets a home directory. When you log in, the Mac mounts the home directory and puts a reference to it in the Dock. You can then synchronize the data between the network home directory and your local home directory on the Mac.

- Second, you can use Address Book or Mail to access the contacts in Active Directory—for example, to send e-mail to your colleagues.

- Third, you can connect to printers that are available in Active Directory and print on them.

This is a start, but it doesn't get you far. To apply further policy to the Mac, you need to trundle around to it and set the preferences you want. In most networks, you'll want to manage policy centrally and consistently without touring the workstations—so you need to take the next step.

Why Do You Need to Extend the Schema?

As you know, Active Directory is governed by a *schema*, a set of formal rules that state which objects the directory can contain, what attributes they can have, and where you can create them. For example, you normally create a User object for each user, with attributes such as the user's name, office, e-mail address, and so on. The schema dictates that you must give each User object a unique name, that you can add information to other attributes (anything from the user's address to assigning them a personal virtual desktop), and that you can create the User object only in an organizational unit (OU) or a container.

That's great for Windows-based users, for whose needs Active Directory is designed to cater fully straight out of the box. But Mac users require extra information for which Active Directory doesn't have storage slots built in. So you need to add these storage slots to Active Directory—by extending the schema—in order to store the extra, Mac-related information in it. You can then use Managed Client For Mac OS X (MCX for short) to manage the Mac clients through Active Directory. MCX stores policy in XML documents inside attributes in Active Directory and applies policy at the user level, at the group level, or at the computer level.

NOTE   Not only do you need to extend the storage, but Mac policy is applied in different ways. Windows stores its group policy objects (GPOs) in the SysVol object, from which Active Directory references them and applies them at three levels: site level, domain level, and organizational unit level. By contrast, Mac OS X lets you apply policy at four different levels: user level, group level, computer level, and computer list level.

Storing Mac OS X Data in Active Directory

To store the Mac OS X data in Active Directory, you need to extend the Active Directory schema with 10 classes (formally, objectClasses) and 36 attributes. To make sure you don't step on any other data, each of these classes and attributes is unique within the directory. For clarity, the name of each class begins with "apple-", so you can easily distinguish it from native Active Directory objects; similarly, the name of each attribute (with one exception) begins with "apple-" as well.

NOTE   Extending the schema works with Windows Server 2003 R2 and later versions. This is because of the UNIX attributes these versions of Windows Server have.

Understanding How the Process of Extending the Schema Works

The first step in extending the schema is to compare Open Directory with Active Directory. For this, you need to have access to the Open Directory schema that Mac OS X Server uses.

Comparing the two directories gives you a list of the attributes and classes you need to add to the Active Directory schema in order to store the policy information for managing the Macs.

You then create an LDAP Data Interchange Format (LDIF) file that contains the differences, and then edit the LDIF file, changing some of the class and attribute names, altering some of the attribute values, and adding some extra information that's needed to make things work smoothly.

Once you've done that, you can apply the LDIF file to the Active Directory domain controller. The domain controller then replicates the schema changes throughout the Active Directory forest.

You can then bind a client to Active Directory and make sure that the schema extensions are working.

Getting Ready to Extend the Schema

To extend the schema, you'll need a Windows server, a Mac client, and a Mac server. The following sections have the details. You may also need a Windows client as well.

NOTE You can use a virtual-machine application such as VMWare Fusion, Parallels Workstation, or VirtualBox for the Windows server and (if you need it) the Windows PC. If you use VMWare Fusion, you can run the Mac server on a virtual machine as well. The Mac client has to be a real Mac.

Windows Server

The Windows server must be running Windows Server 2003 R2 or higher; Windows Server 2008 R2 is preferable unless your company or organization is tied to an earlier version. The examples in this chapter use Windows Server 2008 R2.

You need to make this server an Active Directory domain controller and load your current schema on it, so that you can extend your actual schema.

CAUTION Although it's undoubtedly possible to use your actual domain controller right off the bat, you'll almost certainly want to set up a test domain controller first to get things working without risking laying your career on the altar of unemployment.

You also need to add the Active Directory Lightweight Directory Services (AD LDS) role to your Windows server if you haven't added it already. You need to install this role in order to have the AD DS/LDS Schema Analyzer tools installed on your server; you don't actually have to create and run an instance of AD LDS, even though Windows assumes that you will do so.

NOTE   If you're running the ADAM tools on Windows XP, you don't need to add the Active Directory Lightweight Directory Services role to your Windows server.

To add the Active Directory Lightweight Directory Services role, follow these steps:

1. Pick a time when a restart wouldn't be grossly inconvenient. There's a 50-50 chance you'll need to reboot your server after installing AD LDS.

2. Open Server Manager. For example, click the Server Manager button on the Taskbar or choose Start | All Programs | Administrative Tools | Server Manager.

NOTE   If you haven't already pinned Server Manager to the Taskbar or Start menu, now might be the time to do one, the other, or both.

3. Right-click Roles in the left pane and choose Add Roles to launch the Add Roles Wizard. If the wizard hits you with the Before You Begin screen, select the Skip This Page By Default check box (unless you want to see the screen again) and then click the Next button to reach the Select Server Roles screen (see Figure 4-1).

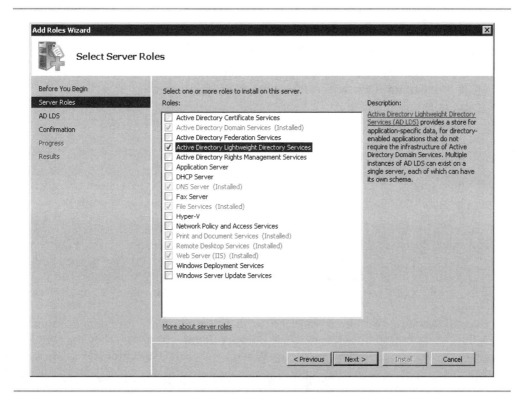

Figure 4-1.   Select the Active Directory Lightweight Directory Services check box on the Select Server Roles screen of the Add Roles Wizard.

4. In the Roles list box, select the Active Directory Lightweight Directory Services role.

5. Click the Next button, and then work your way through the setup. There aren't any more decisions to make, just information screens to read.

6. If Windows prompts you to restart it, do so as soon as is convenient. (I know—a restart is *never* convenient. But do it anyway.)

Mac Server

For your Mac server, start the installation of Mac OS X Server as described in the previous chapter and follow through the early stages.

On the Users And Groups screen, skip the process of importing users and groups. Use the same move as in the previous chapter:

1. Select the Configure Manually option button and click the Continue button to reach the Connect To A Directory Server screen.

2. Make sure the Connect To A Directory Server check box is cleared, and click the Continue button.

This brings you to the Directory Services screen (see Figure 4-2). This time, you do want an Open Directory master server from the start, so proceed like this:

1. Select the Set Up An Open Directory Master check box.

2. In the Name text box, either accept the default name for the directory administrator (Directory Administrator) or type a name you've chosen.

3. In the Short Name text box, either accept the default short name for the directory administrator (diradmin) or type your preferred name.

4. In the UID text box, either accept the default user ID number for the directory administrator (1000) or type a number of your choice.

5. Select the Restrict Individual And Group Access To Services check box if you want to limit users' access to services on the server. You can change these settings later.

Now click the Continue button to move along to the Services screen (see Figure 4-3), which lets you decide which standard services you want to run on your server: File Sharing, Address Book, Calendar, Instant Messaging, Mail, or Web. Because you want this server only for its body—I'm sorry, for its schema—you can safely clear all these check boxes.

Click the Continue button to reach the Review screen, review your configuration (click the Details button if you want to see the gory details), and then click the Set Up button to apply your choices to the server. When you see the Go button, click it to start your server.

Figure 4-2.   On the Directory Services screen of Mac OS X Server setup, select the Set Up An Open Directory Master check box.

Mac Client

The last of the three machines you'll need is a Mac client—just a regular Mac with Mac OS X installed on it. Update Mac OS X to the latest version before you start—there's no point in stumbling around over problems that Apple has solved in updates.

You shouldn't need to install Mac OS X on the Mac unless you've just done something horrible to it, but you do need to install the Server Admin Tools package, which you can download for free from the Downloads section of Apple's website (http://support.apple.com/downloads/; search for "Server Admin Tools" and grab the latest version). You'll use Workgroup Manager (which is part of Server Admin Tools) to apply policy to the Mac, and you'll then use the client to make sure the policy is working on the Mac. (If you discern an element of sadomasochism here, don't worry—computers don't go in for that kind of thing.)

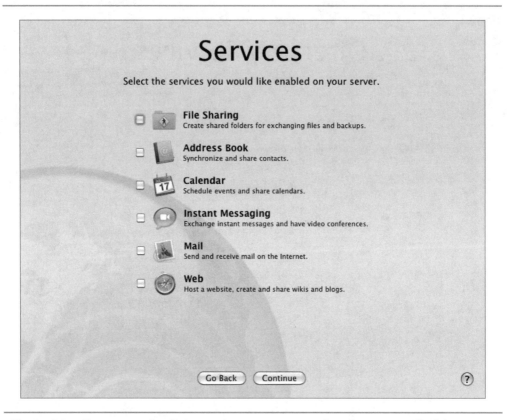

Figure 4-3.   Because you're setting up the server to create its schema, turn off all the services that the Services screen offers.

After you download the Server Admin Tools package, install the tools. If Safari doesn't automatically mount the disk image for you, double-click the disk image file to mount the disk image and display its contents in a Finder window.

Double-click the ServerAdministrationSoftware.pkg file to launch Installer, and then follow through the installation process. There's no option for installing only Workgroup Manager—you have to install the whole set of Server Administration Software. No matter, though—you'll probably find it handy to have the other tools on your Mac because they will enable you to administer your Mac server remotely. You can choose to install the tools on a different volume, but that's the only choice.

When Installer finishes, open the Utilities folder on the Server Administration Tools disk image and then drag the PackageMaker application to a folder on your Mac. The /Applications/Server/ folder is usually the best place. You may need PackageMaker to create packages for distributing applications (see Chapter 9 for details).

Next, eject the disk image (for example, drag it to the Trash) and store the disk image file somewhere handy.

Windows PC

If you don't want to install Active Directory Lightweight Directory Services on your Windows server, you can take another approach—but one that requires another PC, either physical or virtual.

The Windows PC must be running Windows XP Professional with Service Pack 2 or Service Pack 3. Install the Microsoft .NET 2.0 Framework, and then download the Active Directory Application Mode (ADAM) tools from the Windows Server 2003 Active Directory Application Mode website (www.microsoft.com/windowsserver2003/adam/default.mspx). You can then run the ADSchemaAnalyzer.exe program on Windows XP and use it to analyze the difference between the Open Directory schema and the Active Directory schema.

Getting the Schema Extensions You Need

Now you're ready to get the schema extensions you need for extending Active Directory. As you'll remember, you first need to grab the schema from Open Directory and then compare it with Active Directory to find out the differences. You then save those to an LDIF file and edit the file to make some minor adjustments to it.

Follow these steps:

1. Choose Start | Run to open the Run dialog box.

2. Type in **C:\Windows\ADAM\ADSchemaAnalyzer.exe**, or navigate to it by clicking the Browse button and using the Browse dialog box. (If you type in the path, lowercase is fine. I've used uppercase to make the name easier to read.)

3. Click the OK button. Windows launches AD DS/LDS Schema Analyzer, which at first displays a supremely uninformative window (shown here at a suitably small size).

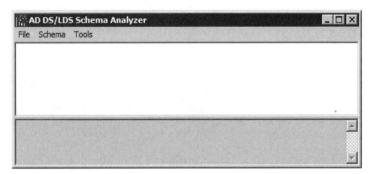

4. Choose File | Load Target Schema to open the Load Target Schema dialog box (shown here).

5. In the Server text box, type the IP address or host address of your Mac OS X Open Directory master server.

6. In the Bind Type area, select the Simple option button to connect to the Open Directory master server without authentication.

7. Click the OK button. The Load Target Schema dialog box closes, and the schema appears in the AD Schema Analyzer window. At first, you'll see just a collapsed folder of Classes, a collapsed folder of Attributes, and a Property Sets folder, as shown here.

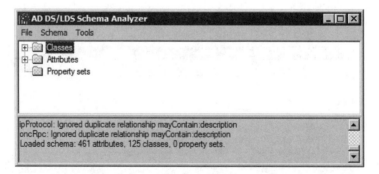

8. Expand the Classes category by double-clicking the Classes category heading or clicking the + sign to its left. You'll see a list of the classes, as in Figure 4-4. You can see many of the Mac-related classes, whose names start with "apple-" (for example, apple-computer).

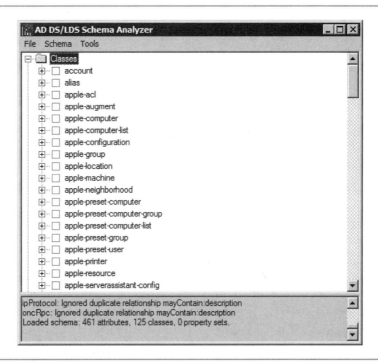

Figure 4-4.   If you expand the Classes folder in the AD DS/LDS Schema Analyzer, you can see some of the Mac-related classes, such as apple-machine and apple-preset-user.

9. Now choose File | Load Base Schema to display the Load Base Schema dialog box (shown here).

10. In the Server text box, type the IP address or hostname of your Active Directory domain controller.

11. Type your administrator username for the Active Directory domain controller in the Username text box, and type the corresponding password in the Password text box.

12. In the Bind Type area, select the Secure option button instead of the Simple option button. The Active Directory domain controller requires you to authenticate before it will surrender the precious details of the schema. When you select the Secure option button, AD DS/LDS Schema Analyzer makes the Domain text box available.

13. In the Domain text box, type the domain for the domain controller.

14. Click the OK button. AD DS/LDS Schema Analyzer closes the Load Base Schema dialog box, hauls in the base schema, and analyzes the target schema against it.

15. Choose Schema | Hide Present Elements to hide the elements that are present in both the base schema and the target schema. Doing this enables you to see only the elements that are different in the target schema—the elements that we are interested in here.

16. Now expand the Classes folder so that you can select the classes you need.

CAUTION   Select the attributes only within the Classes list—don't expand the Attributes folder and select the attributes there.

17. Select the classes and attributes listed in Table 4-1. Take your time—you need to get this right. Here's how to proceed:

   ■ Expand the class you want to affect, so that you can see the attributes under it.

   ■ Click in the box next to the class, placing a heavy black plus (+) sign in the box and a grayed-out heavy plus sign in each attribute's box.

   ■ Click the box for each item you want to remove, so that the check box displays a black X. Figure 4-5 shows the apple-group class with its boxes containing the appropriate plus signs and Xs.

NOTE   There are 36 different attributes, but many of them appear for multiple different objects—so there's a lot of repetition in the list.

18. Once you've checked your list, and maybe gone over it twice to make sure, choose File | Create LDIF File (or press CTRL-L if you like keyboard shortcuts). AD DS/LDS Schema Analyzer displays the Select LDIF File dialog box (see Figure 4-6), which may well be the most oddly named dialog box you've come across in a week of Sundays.

Class	Attributes
apple-computer	subclassOf: top rdnAttId: cn mayContain: apple-category mayContain: apple-computer-list-groups mayContain: apple-keyword mayContain: apple-mcxflags mayContain: apple-mcxsettings mayContain: apple-networkview mayContain: apple-service-url mayContain: apple-xmlplist mayContain: macAddress mayContain: ttl
apple-computer-list	subclassOf: top rdnAttId: cn mayContain: apple-computer-list-groups mayContain: apple-computers mayContain: apple-keyword mayContain: apple-mcxflags mayContain: apple-mcxsettings
apple-configuration	subclassOf: top rdnAttId: cn mayContain: apple-data-stamp mayContain: apple-keyword mayContain: apple-xmlplist mayContain: ttl
apple-group	subclassOf: top rdnAttId: cn mayContain: apple-group-homeowner mayContain: apple-group-homeurl mayContain: apple-keyword mayContain: apple-mcxflags mayContain: apple-mcxsettings mayContain: apple-user-picture mayContain: ttl
apple-location	subclassOf: top rdnAttId: cn mayContain: apple-dns-domain mayContain: apple-dns-nameserver

Table 4-1. Classes and Attributes for Extending the Active Directory Schema to Handle Mac OS X Clients

Class	Attributes
apple-neighborhood	subclassOf: top rdnAttId: cn mayContain: apple-category mayContain: apple-computeralias mayContain: apple-keyword mayContain: apple-neighborhoodalias mayContain: apple-nodepathxml mayContain: apple-xmlplist mayContain: ttl
apple-serverassistant-config	subclassOf: top rdnAttId: cn mayContain: apple-xmlplist
apple-service	subclassOf: top rdnAttId: cn mayContain: apple-dnsname mayContain: apple-keyword mayContain: apple-service-location mayContain: apple-service-port mayContain: apple-service-url mayContain: ipHostAddress mustContain: apple-service-type
apple-user	subclassOf: top rdnAttId: cn mayContain: apple-imhandle mayContain: apple-keyword mayContain: apple-mcxflags mayContain: apple-mcxsettings mayContain: apple-user-authenticationhint mayContain: apple-user-class mayContain: apple-user-homequota mayContain: apple-userhomesoftquota mayContain: apple-user-mailattribute mayContain: apple-user-picture mayContain: apple-user-printattribute mayContain: apple-webloguri
mount	subclassOf: top rdnAttId: cn mayContain: mountDirectory mayContain: mountDumpFrequency mayContain: mountOption mayContain: mountPassNo mayContain: mountType

Table 4-1.   Classes and Attributes for Extending the Active Directory Schema to Handle Mac OS X Clients (*continued*)

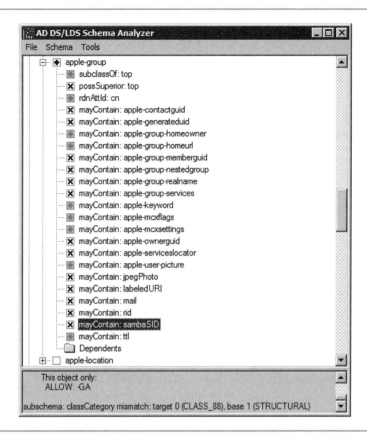

Figure 4-5.   Select each whole class, and then knock out the attributes you don't need to keep.

19. Choose the destination as usual (I'm using the Desktop\Temp folder here), type a filename that you won't forget, and then click the Save button. AD DS/LDS Schema Analyzer saves the LDIF file containing the classes and attributes.

20. Take a squint at the pane at the bottom of the AD DS/LDS Schema Analyzer window and make sure that "LDIF file created" reads "36 attributes, 10 classes, 0 property sets, 0 updated present elements."

   ■ If so, chances are you got the right items (although you could have gotten some of the wrong classes and attributes if you've been creative). Proceed as described next.

   ■ If not, you'll need to go back and work out which classes or attributes you missed or included when you shouldn't have. When you've fixed the problem, export the LDIF file again, and make sure it comes out right this time.

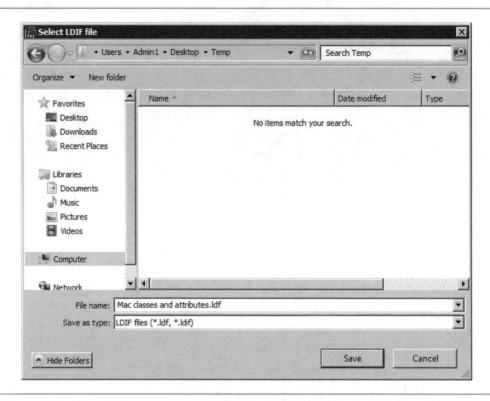

Figure 4-6.   Despite its name, you use the Select LDIF File dialog box like a regular Save As dialog box.

Editing the LDIF File to Make It Right

Next, you need to edit the LDIF file you've exported to make it exactly right for applying to Active Directory. You must make a bunch of small changes to the file so that it contains precisely the information needed.

Here's how to edit the LDIF file:

1. Launch your favorite document editor—for example, Microsoft Word or WordPad. This example uses WordPad, because it'll be installed on your server unless you've forcibly removed it. (Relax—WordPad isn't my favorite document editor. I don't expect it's yours either.)

2. In the document editor, open the LDIF file you exported from AD DS/LDS Schema Analyzer.

NOTE For most document editors, you'll need to choose All Documents in the Files Of Type drop-down list to enable the editor to open the LDIF file. The file is plain text, so any old editor can open it, but Windows doesn't normally have a file association for the LDIF file, so you can't open it by double-clicking it.

3. At the top of the file (see Figure 4-7), you'll find instructions for importing the file using the ldifde command, as we'll do when the file is finished. Below that is the long list of attributes, followed by a shorter list of classes.

NOTE A pound sign (#) at the beginning of a line indicates a comment line that the ldifde command will ignore.

4. Scroll down to the classes list, or search for **# Class** (a pound sign, a space, and "Class") to jump to the first class.

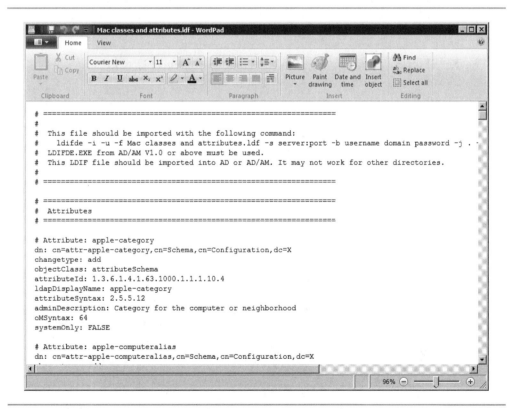

Figure 4-7. Open up the LDIF file in a text editor such as WordPad so that you can make the edits needed to its contents.

5. Find the apple-computer class (it should be the first class) and change the
objectClassCategory value to 3, as shown in boldface in the following partial
listing:

```
# Class: apple-computer
dn: cn=cls-apple-computer,cn=Schema,cn=Configuration,dc=X
changetype: add
objectClass: classSchema
governsID: 1.3.6.1.4.1.63.1000.1.1.2.10
ldapDisplayName: apple-computer
adminDescription: computer
objectClassCategory: 3
systemOnly: FALSE
...
```

NOTE   Changing the objectClassCategory of the apple-computer class, the apple-group class,
and the apple-user class makes these classes feed additional information into Active Directory
rather than creating new objects.

6. Scroll down to the apple-group class and change its objectClassCategory to 3
as well.

7. Scroll down to the apple-user class and change its objectClassCategory to 3
as well.

8. Now go to the end of the LDIF file and type in the following lines to extend the
Active Directory Computer class with the apple-computer auxiliary class:

```
# Extend the Active Directory Computer class
# with the apple-computer auxiliary class
dn: CN=User,CN=Schema,CN=Configuration,DC=X
changetype: modify
add: auxiliaryClass
auxiliaryClass: apple-computer
-
```

9. Copy that section, paste it in twice, and then edit it to match the listing
shown next (the new sections appear in boldface). The edits extend the Active
Directory Group class with the apple-group auxiliary class and the Active
Directory User class with the apple-user auxiliary class:

```
# Extend the Active Directory Computer class
# with the apple-computer auxiliary class
dn: CN=User,CN=Schema,CN=Configuration,DC=X
changetype: modify
add: auxiliaryClass
```

```
auxiliaryClass: apple-computer
-


# Extend the Active Directory Group class
# with the apple-group auxiliary class
dn: CN=User,CN=Schema,CN=Configuration,DC=X
changetype: modify
add: auxiliaryClass
auxiliaryClass: apple-group
-


# Extend the Active Directory User class
# with the apple-user auxiliary class
dn: CN=User,CN=Schema,CN=Configuration,DC=X
changetype: modify
add: auxiliaryClass
auxiliaryClass: apple-user
-
```

 NOTE   At the end of each extension is a line that consists of a single hyphen. After that, you must include a blank line before the next extension—otherwise, the schema extension will crash and burn when you try to import it.

10. Save the changes you've made to the file.

11. Now go through the file and change each instance where AD DS/LDS Schema Analyzer has automatically added the attr- prefix to attributes unnecessarily. The easiest way to do this is to search for **dn: cn=attr-**, replace it with **dn: cn=**, and hit the Replace All button.

12. In the same way, replace all instances of **dn: cn=cls–** with **dn: cn=** to remove the unneeded "cls–" from the beginning of class names where AD DS/LDS Schema Analyzer has added it.

13. Now add the apple- prefix to the Mac-specific classes and attributes that lack it. Most of the classes and attributes already have the apple- prefix, but you need to add it to a handful of items:

   ■ Change **dn: cn=mountDirectory** to **dn: cn=apple-mountDirectory**.

   ■ Change **dn: cn=mountDumpFrequency** to **dn: cn=apple-mountDumpFrequency**.

   ■ Change **dn: cn=mountOption** to **dn: cn=apple-mountOption**.

   ■ Change **dn: cn=mountPassNo** to **dn: cn=apple-mountPassNo**.

   ■ Change **dn: cn=mountType** to **dn: cn=apple-mountType**.

   ■ Change **dn: cn=mount** to **dn: cn=apple-mount**.

14. Save the changes you've made to the file.

15. Now add the possSuperiors attribute to the apple-computer-list class, specifying organizationalUnit as one possible parent object and container as another:

```
apple-computer-list
possSuperiors: organizationalUnit
possSuperiors: container
```

16. Copy the two possSuperiors lines, and then paste them in for each of these six other classes:

- apple-configuration
- apple-location
- apple-neighborhood
- apple-serverassistant-config
- apple-service
- apple-mount

NOTE   If any of these classes has a possSuperiors attribute already, remove it.

17. Save the changes you've made to the file.

Double-Checking the LDIF File

Now scan quickly through the file to make sure everything's in place:

- **Thirty-six attributes**   Check that there are 36 attributes in the Attributes section.
- **Ten classes**   Check that there are 10 classes in the Classes section.
- **attributeID**   Make sure the attributeID for each attribute starts with 1.3.6.1.4.1.63.1000.1.1.1, so that they're all in the Apple namespace.
- **governsID**   Make sure the governsID for each class starts with 1.3.6.1.4.1.63.1000.1.1.2. Again, this is to make sure that the classes are all in the Apple namespace.
- **apple- prefixes**   Check that the dn: and ldapDisplayName for each attribute and class start with the apple- prefix. The one exception is ttl.
- **objectClassCategory**   Verify that the apple-computer class, the apple-group class, and the apple-user class have the objectClassCategory attribute set to 3.
- **possSuperiors**   Check that the apple-computer-list, apple-configuration, apple-location, apple-neighborhood, apple-serverassistant-config, apple-service, and apple-mount classes have possSuperiors of organizationalUnit and container.

If you've made any changes to the file, save it again. The file is now ready for applying to your domain controller.

Applying the Schema Extensions to Active Directory

After you create the LDIF file that contains the classes and attributes required to extend Active Directory, you can apply it to your domain controller.

 CAUTION   As mentioned earlier, first extend the schema in a test environment so that you can work out any problems before rolling out the extensions to your production environment.

To apply the schema extensions, you use the ldifde command. Follow these steps:

1. Log on to your Windows Server as a member of the Schema Admin group.

2. Open an administrator-level Command Prompt window. For example, choose Start | All Programs | Accessories, right-click Command Prompt, choose Run As Administrator from the shortcut menu, and then click the Continue button in the User Account Control window.

3. Change the directory to the folder in which you've saved the LDIF file of schema modifications. For example, if you're using the Temp folder on your Desktop, type the following command and press ENTER:

```
cd desktop\temp
```

4. The ldifde command takes several parameters, so we'll build it in stages, with each new part we add appearing in boldface. First, type the command itself:

```
ldifde
```

5. Then add the /j parameter to tell ldifde to log its results to a file. Type the path to the folder in which you want ldifde to store the log file, or type a period (.) to use the current folder, as we'll do here:

```
ldifde /j .
```

6. Add the /k parameter to tell the import to ignore Constraint Violation and Object Already Exists errors:

```
ldifde /j . /k
```

7. Add the /i parameter to tell ldifde that you want it to import a file, then add the /f parameter followed by the filename (if the name contains spaces, put it in double quotation marks):

```
ldifde /j . /k /i /f "Mac classes and attributes.ldf"
```

8. Add the /v parameter to use verbose logging rather than laconic logging, so that you get full details on any problems that occur:

```
ldifde /j . /k /i /f "Mac classes and attributes.ldf" /v
```

9. To substitute your network's real domain name in place of the placeholder data in the LDIF file, add the /c parameter and specify the placeholder and what to replace it with. This example (which you'd enter all on one line rather than broken onto two lines) replaces **DC=X** with **DC=CORP,DC=ACMEHEAVY,DC=COM**:

```
ldifde /j . /k /i /f "Mac classes and attributes.ldf" /v /c
"DC=X" "DC=CORP,DC=ACMEHEAVY,DC=COM"
```

10. Double-check the command, and then give the ENTER key a ceremonial tap to run the command. If all goes well, you'll see a readout such as this at the end of a long list of changes:

```
51 entries modified successfully.
The command has completed successfully.
```

NOTE   If the ldifde import fails with an "insufficient access rights" error, you're probably using an account that's not a member of the Schema Admins group. If necessary, change to an account that is a member of this group, or add your current account to it.

11. Close the Command Prompt window.

TIP   If the ldifde import fails with the message that your LDIF file contains an error on a particular line, open the file in a text editor that can show line numbers rather than in WordPad (which can't). Notepad is generally horrible, but it can show line numbers if you display the status bar (choose View | Status Bar).

Turning Workgroup Manager on to Active Directory

Now that you've extended Active Directory with the Mac-related classes and attributes, you can open Workgroup Manager and point it at Active Directory. You'll need to have installed the Server Administration tools on the Mac you're using, as described earlier in this chapter.

Follow these steps to bind the Mac to Active Directory and to connect Workgroup Manager:

1. Bind the Mac to Active Directory as described in Chapter 2.

2. Open Workgroup Manager—for example, if you've placed Workgroup Manager on the Dock, click its icon there. Failing that, launch it from the /Applications/ Server folder or by typing the dreaded word **work** into Spotlight.

3. When Workgroup Manager opens, it displays the Workgroup Manager Connect dialog box (shown here), which you use for connecting to Mac OS X servers.

4. Click the Cancel button to close the Workgroup Manager Connect dialog box.
5. Choose Server | View Directories to open a Workgroup Manager window showing the /Active Directory/All Domains directory, as shown in Figure 4-8.

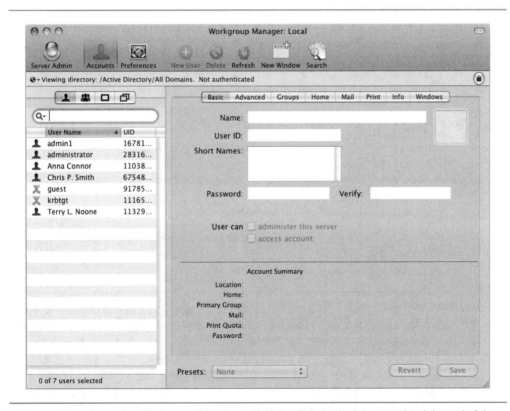

Figure 4-8. From the Workgroup Manager window, click the lock icon at the right end of the authentication bar to authenticate yourself to Active Directory.

6. To work with the contents of the directory, click the lock icon at the right end of the authentication bar—the bar that goes across the Workgroup Manager window just below the toolbar. Workgroup Manager displays the Authenticate To Directory dialog box (shown here).

Authenticate to directory:

/Active Directory/All Domains

To make changes, enter an administrator's name and password.

User Name:

Password:

☐ Remember this password in my keychain

Cancel   Authenticate

7. Type your Windows administrator's name in the User Name text box and the corresponding password in the Password text box.

8. Select the Remember This Password In My Keychain check box if you want Mac OS X to store your password so that you don't need to type it in again.

9. Click the Authenticate button. Workgroup Manager authenticates you to Active Directory, and the authentication bar shows your status as Authenticated.

You can now make changes to the directory, as described in the next section.

Applying Test Policy to Users and Groups

Now that you've connected Workgroup Manager to Active Directory, you can apply some test policy to your Mac users or groups so that you can test whether everything is working as it should be. This section contains a simple example that lets you check that all is well.

To apply some test policy, follow these steps:

1. In Workgroup Manager, having authenticated yourself as described in the previous section, click the Group tab at the top of the left pane to display the list of groups.

NOTE   If you haven't yet created a group such as Mac Users in Active Directory and added to it the users of Macs on your network, you may want to do so before continuing. Alternatively, apply the test policy to a single user—for example, yourself.

2. In the left pane of Workgroup Manager, select your group of Mac users so that you can apply test policy to them. Figure 4-9 shows the Mac Users group selected on the test network.

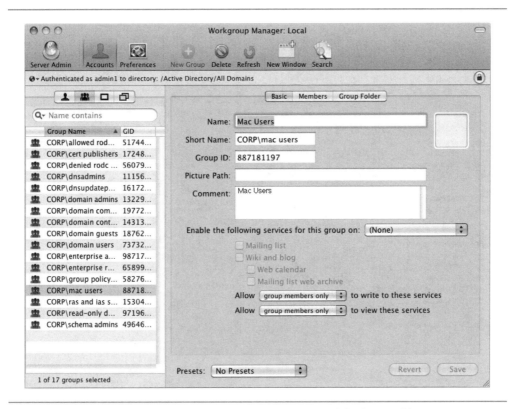

Figure 4-9.   Choose your Mac users group in the left pane of Workgroup Manager.

3. Click the Preferences button on the toolbar to display the Preferences pane (see Figure 4-10).

4. Click the Dock icon to display the Dock category.

5. Click the Dock Display tab to show the Dock Display pane (shown in Figure 4-11 with settings chosen).

6. In the Manage bar below the tab bar, select the Always option button. Selecting this option button makes your policy choices apply always, so that the user cannot change them.

7. In the Position On Screen area, select the Right option button to make Mac OS X position the Dock on the right of the screen for the members of your Mac users group.

8. Open the Minimize Using pop-up menu and choose Scale rather than Genie, to make windows minimize to the Dock using the Scale effect instead of the default Genie effect.

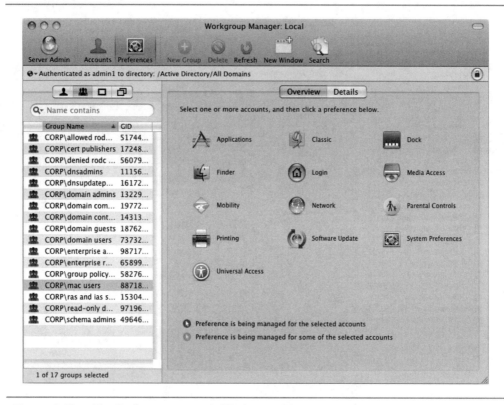

Figure 4-10. The Preferences pane in Workgroup Manager gives you access to the major categories of policy you can set on networked Macs.

9. Click the Apply Now button to apply the policy change.

10. Click the Done button to return to the main Preferences screen.

11. Leave Workgroup Manager open for the moment—you'll probably want to remove the Dock policy after testing that it works.

Checking That Your Test Policy Works

Now check that your test policy works. Follow these steps:

1. Bind the Mac to Active Directory as described in Chapter 2.

NOTE   If the Mac you're using was already bound to Active Directory before you extended the schema, you must refresh the directory settings. You can do this either by running the **sudo killall DirectoryService** command in a Terminal window or by restarting Mac OS X.

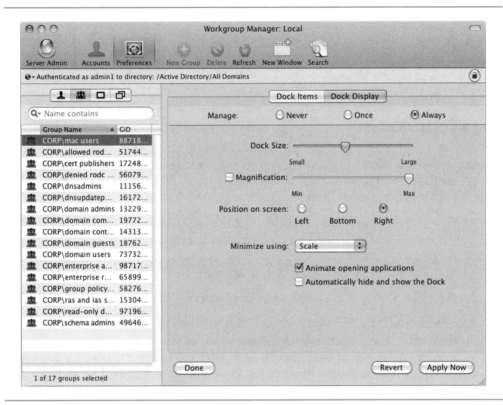

Figure 4-11. The Dock Display pane in Workgroup Manager preferences enables you to choose how the Dock appears for a managed user.

2. Log in using one of the accounts in the Mac users group for which you just changed the Dock policy. If your Mac is using Fast User Switching, it's fine to use that.

3. Verify that the Dock appears on the right.

4. Launch an application from the Dock—any application is fine. Finder is usually the quickest to lob a window onto the screen.

5. Minimize the application window, and check that it zooms down with the straightforward Scale effect rather than the Genie whoosh.

6. CTRL-click or right-click the Dock divider bar and choose Dock Preferences from the pop-up menu to open the Dock preferences pane in System Preferences.

7. Confirm that the Size, Magnification, Position On Screen, and Minimize Windows Using controls are grayed out and unavailable.

8. Quit System Preferences. For example, choose System Preferences | Quit System Preferences.

9. Log out from the account.

Now return to your account, go back into Workgroup Manager, and remove the test policy—unless you actually want to restrict what the Mac users can do with the Dock.

Creating a Computer List

In theory, you can create a computer list from Workgroup Manager in an Active Directory schema you've extended, but the process is complex and tends to fail with errors about lack of permissions or lack of storage. If you want to try it and see if things have improved since this writing, here's what to do:

1. Open Workgroup Manager, connect to Active Directory, and authenticate yourself as an Active Directory administrator, as usual.

2. Choose Workgroup Manager | Preferences (or press ⌘-,) to open the Workgroup Manager Preferences dialog box (see Figure 4-12).

3. Select the Show "All Records" Tab And Inspector check box.

4. Click the OK button to close the Workgroup Manager Preferences dialog box.

5. Back in the main Workgroup Manager window, you'll see that the left pane now has a fifth tab at the right end of its tab bar. This fifth tab, which bears a bull's-eye icon, is the All Records tab; click it to display the All Records pane (see Figure 4-13).

6. Open the pop-up menu at the top of the All Records pane and choose ComputerLists from it.

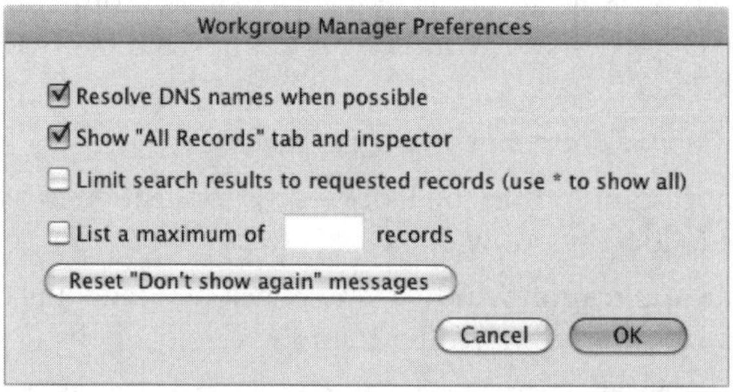

Figure 4-12. In the Workgroup Manager Preferences dialog box, select the Show "All Records" Tab And Inspector check box to enable yourself to view computer lists.

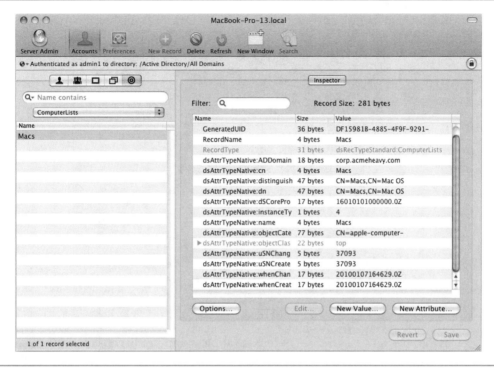

Figure 4-13. Choose ComputerLists in the pop-up menu in the All Records pane to try to create a computer list in Workgroup Manager.

7. Click the New Record button to create a new computer list.

8. Fill in the name and other details of the computer list.

Another possibility is to open Terminal and fire up the dscl (Directory Services Command Line) utility. Specify your Active Directory, and give the **–create** command with the **/ComputerLists** parameter and the name of the list you want to create. For example, the following command creates a computer list named "Macs" in the Active Directory for our long-suffering corp.acmeheavy.com:

```
dscl -u admin1 "/Active Directory/corp.acmeheavy.com" -create
   /ComputerLists "Macs"
```

All too often, though, this also fails with permission errors. So usually the best bet is to use ADSI Edit on your Windows server like this:

1. Choose Start | Administrative Tools | ADSI Edit to open ADSI Edit.

2. Double-click the Default naming context to expand it if it's currently collapsed.

3. Double-click the domain's folder to expand it if it's collapsed.

4. Right-click the CN=Mac OS X container, and then choose New | Object from the shortcut menu to display the first Create Object dialog box (shown here).

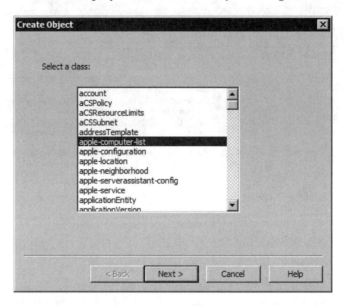

5. In the Select A Class list box, select the apple-computer-list object and then click the Next button to display the second Create Object dialog box (shown here).

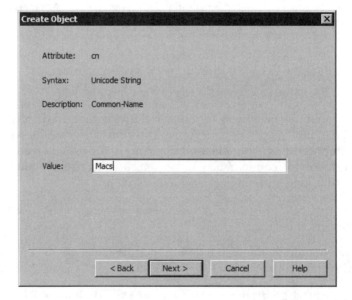

6. In the Value text box, type the name you want to give the list. In this example, I've gone for the laconic "Macs," but you may prefer to use more letters.

7. Click the Next button to display the third Create Object dialog box. From here, you can click the More Attributes button if you want to set attributes via ADSI Edit, but you can safely go with the default values.

8. Click the Finish button to create the list.

Once you've done this, you can add members to the computer list in Workgroup Manager like this:

1. Open Workgroup Manager, connect to Active Directory, and authenticate yourself as an Active Directory administrator, as usual.

2. Click the Accounts button on the toolbar if it's not already firmly clicked.

3. Click the Computer Groups button on the tab bar in the left pane to display the Computer Groups pane (shown in Figure 4-14 with additions underway).

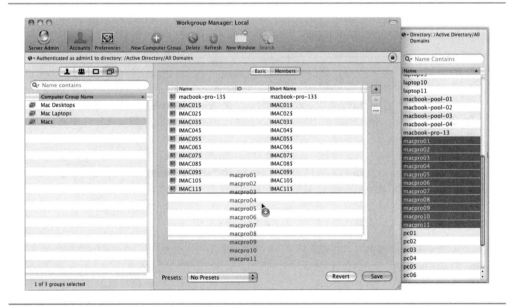

Figure 4-14. Use the Computer Groups pane to add your Macs to the computer list you've created.

4. In the list of computer groups, select the computer list you just created.

5. In the main part of the pane, click the Members tab to display the Members pane.

6. Click the Add (+) button at the upper-left corner of the list in the Members pane to display the drawer containing computers.

7. Drag the appropriate computer accounts to the Members pane.

8. Click the Save button to save your changes.

Indexing the macAddress Attribute to Speed Up Active Directory Searches

If your Active Directory domain controllers give you Warning events or Information events about inefficient searches, the problem may be that your Mac OS X clients are struggling to locate their computer accounts on Active Directory. To solve this problem, you can index the macAddress attribute in Active Directory.

NOTE Inefficient searches are more likely to occur on Mac clients running Mac OS X 10.5 (Leopard) rather than Mac OS X 10.6 (Snow Leopard).

To index the macAddress attribute, follow these steps:

1. Launch the Active Directory Schema snap-in.

NOTE If you haven't already added the Active Directory Schema snap-in to a console, open an Administrator-level Command Prompt and give the **regsvr32 schmmgmt.dll** command. Then use the **mmc** command to launch a Console window, choose File | Add/Remove Snap-in, and add the Active Directory Schema snap-in. Save the console (choose File | Save) if you don't want to repeat this rigmarole.

2. Double-click the Console Root folder in the left pane to display the Active Directory Schema object.

3. Double-click the Active Directory Schema folder in the left pane to display the Classes folder and the Attributes folder.

4. Click the Attributes folder to display its contents in the right pane (see Figure 4-15).

5. Double-click the macAddress attribute to open its Properties dialog box (see Figure 4-16).

6. Select the Index This Attribute check box.

7. Click the OK button to close the Properties dialog box.

8. Close the console window.

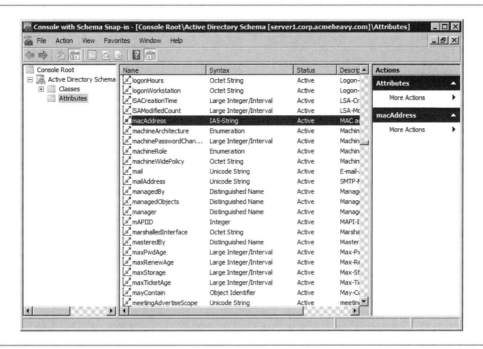

Figure 4-15. Use the Active Directory Schema snap-in to open the list of attributes.

Figure 4-16. Select the Index This Attribute check box in the Properties dialog box for the macAddress attribute.

CHAPTER 5 | Giving Your Macs Safe Access to the Internet

Unless you can lock your Mac users in a lead-lined room and keep them firmly cordoned off from the outside world, you'll almost certainly need to give your network's Macs access to the Internet, just as you provide it to your network's PCs.

You can give the Macs Internet access in exactly the same way as PCs. In fact, you may already have given the Macs access to the Internet simply by connecting them to your network—so your starting point may not be providing connectivity so much as limiting it. You can do this by directing the Macs to use your network's proxy server, which can both filter out content you want to block and cache data that many users will want to access.

Whether you use a proxy server or let the Macs run wild, you should protect your Macs against viruses and malware by running an effective antivirus application. This chapter briefly outlines the main possibilities here but leaves you to choose the best solution for your needs.

Establishing Basic Internet Connectivity

When you bind a Mac to the network as discussed in Chapter 2, you normally give the Mac access to the Internet through the network. The Mac picks up the routing information along with its IP address and subnet mask from the network's DNS server. The Mac can then learn where to find other IP addresses, including those on the Internet.

Checking for Internet Connectivity

The easiest way to check that the Mac has Internet connectivity is to open Safari and point it at a website if it doesn't open one automatically. If the website loads, you're in business; if not, try another site in case you've caught the first one napping.

Checking Which DNS Server the Mac Is Using

If the Mac is unable to access the Internet, check that it's using the right DNS server. In most cases, the easiest way to do this is to use the dig command, which shows you both the DNS server's IP address and its fully qualified name.

NOTE   You can also check the DNS server's IP address by looking in Network preferences. We'll do this in a moment.

1. On the Mac, open a Terminal window: Press ⌘-SPACEBAR to open the Spotlight field, type **term**, use the arrow keys to select the Terminal hit, and then press RETURN. (Or, if you prefer, open the Utilities folder and double-click the Terminal icon.)

NOTE The dig command is short for *domain information groper* and is useful for giving DNS servers an elbow in the ribs.

2. Type the **dig** command, using the **–t** parameter with the value **SRV** to specify that the type of record you're looking for is the server and specifying your domain name after the **_ldap._tcp.** term. The following example returns the domain controller for the domain corp.acmeheavy.com:

```
dig -t SRV _ldap._tcp.corp.acmeheavy.com
```

3. Press RETURN, and you'll see several sections of information. The Answer Section shows the server's name, and the Additional Section shows both the server's name and IP address.

4. Quit Terminal (for example, press ⌘-Q).

If the dig command unearths a server other than your domain controller, there are two main possibilities:

■ *Your DNS server is pointing in the wrong direction.* You can check this quickly by seeing whether your Windows PCs are confused as well. If the PCs are happy as pigs in slop, the DNS server is behaving itself.

■ *The Mac is using the wrong DNS server.* In this case, change the Mac's DNS server as described next.

To change the DNS server for the Mac, follow these steps:

1. Open System Preferences—for example, click the System Preferences icon on the Dock.

2. In the Internet & Wireless section, click the Network icon to open the Network pane.

3. In the left list box, select the network interface the Mac is using to connect to the network—for example, Ethernet. Usually, this interface is the one at the top of the list. The Network pane displays the settings for that interface. Figure 5-1 shows an example for an Ethernet interface. If you're using AirPort instead, you need to go into the Advanced dialog box to set the DNS server, as described in step 5.

4. Check the IP address in the DNS Server text box. If it's wrong, type in the right address.

 NOTE If the DNS Server item has a readout rather than a text box, open the Configure IPv4 pop-up menu and choose Using DHCP With Manual Address. The Network pane displays the DNS Server text box, in which you can change the IP address.

Figure 5-1. Use the Network pane in System Preferences to change the DNS server for an Ethernet connection.

5. If you need to change the DNS server address for an AirPort connection, change it like this:

   a. Click the AirPort item in the list of network interfaces.

   b. Click the Advanced button to display the Advanced dialog box.

   c. Click the DNS tab in the tab bar to display the DNS pane (see Figure 5-2).

   d. If the wrong address appears in the DNS Servers pane, click it and then click the Remove (–) button to administer a quick coup de grace.

   e. Click the Add (+) button below the DNS Servers pane. Mac OS X adds an entry and displays a text box for you to type in the address. Type it, and then press RETURN.

   f. Click the OK button to close the Advanced dialog box and return to the Network pane.

6. Click the Apply button to apply the change.

Now try the Internet connection again and verify that it works.

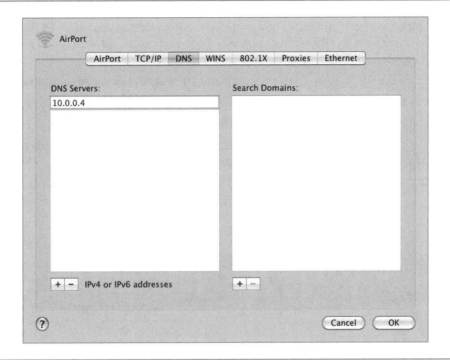

Figure 5-2.   Use the DNS pane in the Advanced dialog box to set up the DNS servers for an AirPort connection.

Restraining Mac Clients with Proxy Servers

If your company or organization chooses to limit the smorgasbord of depravity freely available on the Web to those few bland and tasteless morsels that haven't yet attracted censorship, you've probably got a proxy server of some kind running on the network. To get your network's Macs to use the proxy server rather than tasting unsanitized Internet content, you'll need to tell them where it is.

You can set up your Macs to use a proxy server either by using policy or by making the changes manually. As usual, using policy normally saves time and effort, but you may sometimes need to configure a machine manually, so we'll look at both ways here.

Using Policy to Set Macs to Use a Proxy Server

To set up your Macs to use a proxy server, follow these steps on the Mac (client or server) from which you're running Workgroup Manager:

1. Open Workgroup Manager. For example, click the Workgroup Manager icon in the Dock.

2. When the Workgroup Manager Connect dialog box appears, click the Cancel button to dismiss it.

3. Choose Server | View Directories or press ⌘-D to connect to Active Directory.

4. Click the lock icon at the right end of the authentication bar to open the Authenticate To Directory dialog box, type your administrator name and password, and then click the Authenticate button.

5. Click the user, group of users, computer, or computer list you want to affect.

6. Click the Preferences button on the toolbar to display the Preferences pane.

7. Click the Network icon to display the Network pane.

8. If the Proxies tab is not already selected, click it to display the Proxies pane (shown in Figure 5-3 with settings chosen).

9. In the Manage bar, select the Always option button to enable the controls.

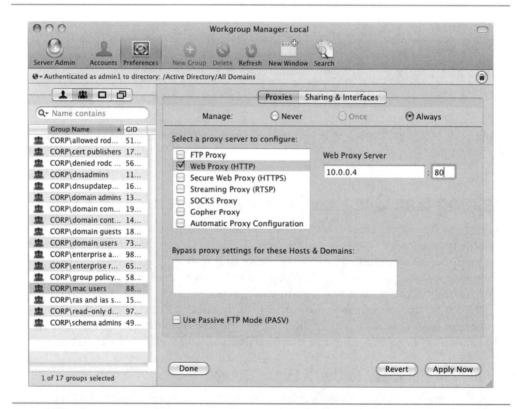

Figure 5-3.   Use the Proxies pane in Workgroup Manager to set up proxy servers for a user account, group, or computer.

10. In the Select A Proxy Server To Configure list box, click the proxy server you want to set up. Workgroup Manager displays text boxes to the right of the Select A Proxy Server To Configure list box so that you can enter the proxy server's details.

11. Enter the details of the proxy server in these text boxes. For example, for a web proxy server, type the server's address in the Web Proxy Server text box and type the port number in the second text box.

12. In the Select A Proxy Server To Configure list box, select the check box for the proxy server to activate it.

13. Repeat the previous three steps to configure the other proxy servers the account needs.

NOTE   If your proxying arrangement uses an automatic proxy configuration, select the Automatic Proxy Configuration check box and then enter the URL for the proxy auto-config (.pac) file in the URL text box that Workgroup Manager displays.

14. In the Bypass Proxy Settings For These Hosts & Domains text box, type the addresses of hosts and domains that the user or computer should connect to directly rather than going through the proxy.

    ■ You can enter a target server's name (such as server2.corp.acmeheavy.com), an IP address (such as 10.0.0.27), or a domain name (such as corp.acmeheavy .com).

TIP   When you add a domain name, the bypassing is only for that domain—not for any of its subdomains. To add an entire website and all its subdomains, put an asterisk before it—for example, ***.acmeheavy.com**.

    ■ To create an easy-to-read list, put each item on a new line. Alternatively, separate items with commas, semicolons, or spaces.

15. Select the Use Passive FTP Mode (PASV) check box if you want the user or computer to use passive FTP mode for FTP.

16. Click the Apply Now button to apply the changes.

17. Click the Done button to return to the Preferences pane.

Manually Setting a Mac to Use a Proxy Server

Here's how to manually set a Mac to use a proxy server:

1. Open System Preferences. For example, choose Apple | System Preferences.

2. In the Internet & Wireless section, click the Network icon to open the Network pane.

3. In the left list box, select the network interface the Mac is using to connect to the network—for example, Ethernet. Usually, this interface is the one at the top of the list. The Network pane displays the settings for that interface.

4. Click the Advanced button to display the Advanced dialog box.

5. Click the Proxies tab on the tab bar to display the Proxies pane (shown in Figure 5-4 with settings chosen).

6. In the Select A Protocol To Configure list box, click the protocol you want to proxy. The Proxies pane displays controls for configuring the protocol. For example, when you select the Web Proxy (HTTP) protocol, the Proxies pane displays the Web Proxy Server controls.

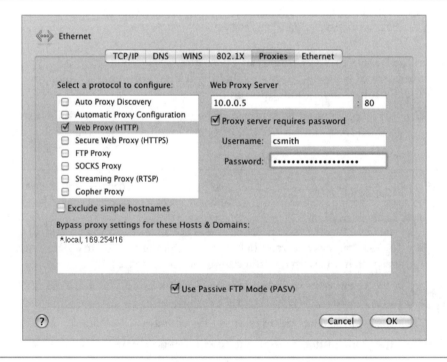

Figure 5-4.   You can set up proxies manually in the Proxies pane of the Advanced dialog box for a network interface.

7. Type the IP address of the proxy server in the left text box and the port in the right text box.

8. If the proxy server requires authentication, select the Proxy Server Requires Password check box. Type the username in the Username text box and the password in the Password text box.

9. Repeat steps 6 to 8 for each other protocol you want to proxy.

10. Select the Exclude Simple Hostnames check box if you want the Mac to contact computers on your network directly rather than going through the proxy server.

11. In the Bypass Proxy Settings For These Hosts & Domains text box, list any computers or any domains that you want the Mac to contact directly rather than using the proxy server.

   ■ You can enter a target server's name (such as server2.corp.acmeheavy .com), an IP address (such as 10.0.0.27), or a domain name (such as corp .acmeheavy.com).

   ■ To bypass a single domain but not its subdomains, use the name—for example, acmeheavy.com. To bypass a domain and all its subdomains, put an asterisk before the domain—for example, *.acmeheavy.com.

   ■ Mac OS X suggests the *.local domain and the 169.254/16 link-local address range for bypassing. (The link-local address range is the range that devices use to automatically assign IP addresses when there's no DHCP server.) It's usually fine to leave these two items in.

   ■ To create an easy-to-read list, put each item on a new line. Alternatively, separate items with commas, semicolons, or spaces.

12. Select the Use Passive FTP Mode (PASV) check box if you want the Mac to use passive FTP mode for FTP.

13. Click the OK button to close the Advanced dialog box.

14. Click the Apply Now button to apply the changes to the network interface.

15. Quit System Preferences by pressing ⌘-Q.

Checking That Proxying Is Working

After applying proxying, check that it is working as it should:

1. Log in to a client Mac using an account you haven't exempted from proxying. If you've set up proxying manually, you should already be logged in.

2. Open Safari and try to access a site you put on your blocked list. Make sure the server prevents you from accessing the website.

3. Try to access a site you haven't blocked, such as the McGraw-Hill Professional website (www.mhprofessional.com). Make sure the proxy server doesn't block the site.

Protecting Macs Against Viruses and Malware

In general, Macs suffer less from viruses and malware than Windows PCs, partly because the Mac OS X code base appears to be more secure than the Windows code base (although experts argue the details) but mainly because Windows is a much bigger and more profitable target for the brutes who create such software. Even so, Macs aren't immune to viruses and malware, and there are specific attacks that target Mac OS X and its applications—so you'll almost certainly want to protect your Macs against viruses and malware.

Given that the Mac market is smaller than the Windows market, it should be no surprise that fewer antivirus applications are available for the Mac than for Windows. But there's still a fair selection, such as the following:

- **Norton Antivirus for Mac**   Symantec (www.symantec.com/Norton/index .jsp) sells several different antivirus and security products for Mac OS X. The basic version, Norton AntiVirus For Mac ($49.95), provides protection against viruses, Trojans, spyware, and other widespread attacks. If that's not enough, you can go for Norton Internet Security For Mac ($79.99), which adds further protection such as antiphishing features and authentication of popular banking and shopping sites. To confuse the issue, Symantec also offers Dual-Protection versions of both Norton Antivirus ($69.99) and Norton Internet Security ($89.99) for Macs that run Windows as well as Mac OS X.

- **VirusBarrier**   Intego (www.intego.com) sells VirusBarrier ($49.99 for one or two Macs), which provides pretty solid protection against viruses, spyware, and so on. Intego's kitchen-sink offering is Internet Security Barrier ($79.99 for one or two Macs), which adds antispam, parental control, backup, and data-protection features. Clearly acquainted with Symantec's offerings, Intego also sells Dual-Protection versions of both VirusBarrier ($89.99; one or two Macs and one version of Windows) and Internet Security Barrier ($119.99; likewise) for Macs that run Windows as well. Figure 5-5 shows VirusBarrier at work.

Figure 5-5.   VirusBarrier is a full-featured antivirus application from Intego.

- **Sophos Anti-Virus**   Sophos (www.sophos.com) makes business-oriented security software including Sophos Anti-Virus (antivirus protection) and Sophos Computer Security (which adds a firewall and data protection). Pricing varies depending on how many years' coverage you buy at once but is generally in line with other commercial packages.

- **ClamXav**   ClamXav (http://clamxav.com) is a free virus checker for Mac OS X. ClamXav (see Figure 5-6) offers many fewer features than the full antivirus applications, but if your network's Mac users use the Internet sensibly (or are protected from its excesses by a proxy server), checking for viruses may be all you need.

NOTE   Whichever antivirus application you choose, you need to run it consistently and keep it updated to get maximum protection.

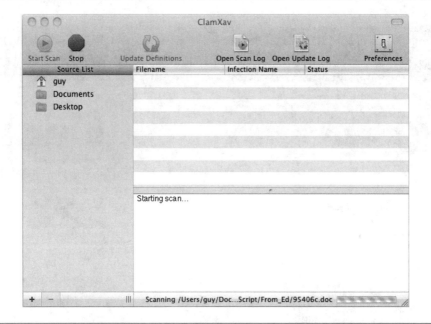

Figure 5-6.   ClamXav lets you scan for viruses using a straightforward interface.

CHAPTER 6

Connecting Macs to Microsoft Exchange

I f you're running Windows Server, chances are you're using Exchange Server for e-mail and organization—and that you'll want to connect your network's Macs to Exchange as well.

Mac OS X 10.6 makes connecting to Exchange Server a snap. This chapter shows you how to create mailboxes in Exchange for Mac users, connect Mail to Exchange, and configure settings in Mail, iCal, and Address Book for using Exchange.

Creating a Mailbox for a Mac User in Exchange

Your first step is to set up a Mac user to use Exchange. Once you've created the person's user account in Active Directory, create a mailbox for the user using the New Mailbox Wizard:

1. Run Exchange Management Console. Choose Start | Exchange Management Console if the Exchange Management Console appears directly on your Start menu. Otherwise, choose Start | All Programs | Microsoft Exchange Server | Exchange Management Console.

NOTE This chapter shows Exchange Server 2010, but the procedure is pretty much the same as Exchange Server 2007. These are the two versions of Exchange to which Mac OS X 10.6 is designed to connect seamlessly. For earlier versions of Exchange, you'll need to take extra steps that this book doesn't cover.

2. In the left pane, expand the Microsoft Exchange tree until you can see the Recipient Configuration node.

3. Expand the Recipient Configuration node so that you can see its contents.

4. Click the Mailbox item to display the current list of mailboxes.

5. In the Actions pane on the right, click the New Mailbox item. The New Mailbox Wizard starts up and then displays the Introduction screen (see Figure 6-1).

NOTE If you like using the context menus, you can right-click the Mailbox item in the left pane and choose New Mailbox from the context menu.

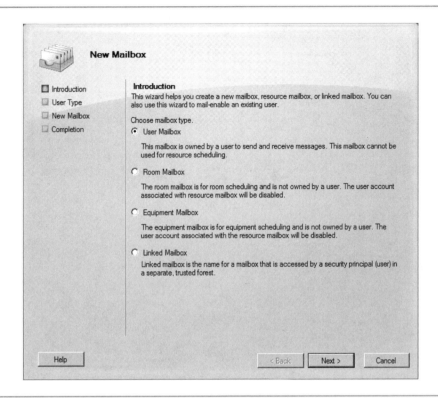

Figure 6-1.   On the Introduction screen of the New Mailbox Wizard, select the User Mailbox option button and then click the Next button.

6. In the Choose Mailbox Type list, select the User Mailbox option button (it may be selected already) and then click the Next button. The wizard displays the User Type screen (see Figure 6-2).

7. Select the Existing Users option button.

8. Click the Add button to open the Select Users dialog box. Select the user or users—search for them using the Search box if necessary—and then click the OK button to close the dialog box and add them to the User Type screen.

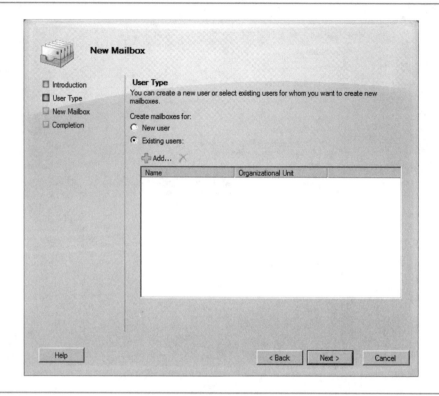

Figure 6-2. On the User Type screen of the New Mailbox Wizard, select the Existing Users option button, click the Add button, and then choose the user in the Select User dialog box.

NOTE You can create mailboxes for multiple users at once by adding each user to the list on the User Type screen. When you do this, you can't enter an alias for the mailbox user—you have to accept the default aliases that the New Mailbox Wizard generates.

9. Click the Next button. The wizard displays the Mailbox Settings screen (see Figure 6-3).

10. To create a custom alias for the user, type the alias in the Alias text box.

11. If you want to override the default location for the mailbox database, select the Specify The Mailbox Database Rather Than Using A Database Automatically Selected check box. Click the top Browse button, select the database location in the Select Mailbox Database dialog box, and then click the OK button.

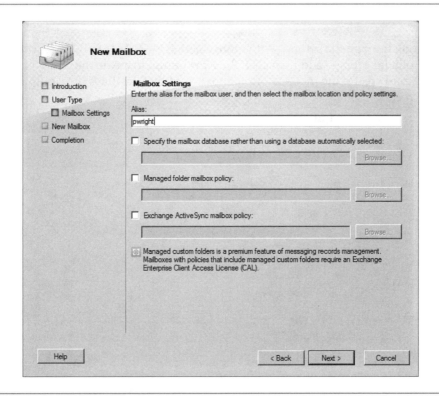

Figure 6-3.   On the Mailbox Settings screen of the New Mailbox Wizard, enter a custom alias and mailbox database if necessary. You can also choose managed folder mailbox policy and Exchange ActiveSync mailbox policy.

12. If you want to apply a managed folder mailbox policy to the mailbox, select the Managed Folder Mailbox Policy check box (but see the nearby Caution). Click the middle Browse button, select the policy in the Select Managed Folder Mailbox Policy dialog box, and then click the OK button.

CAUTION   You need to have an Exchange Enterprise Client Access License for managed custom folders.

13. If you want to apply Exchange ActiveSync mailbox policy to the mailbox, select the Exchange ActiveSync Mailbox Policy check box. Click the bottom Browse button, select the policy in the Select ActiveSync Mailbox Policy dialog box, and then click the OK button.

14. Click the Next button. The New Mailbox Wizard displays the New Mailbox screen (see Figure 6-4).

15. Look through the settings—if you're creating a single account here, checking won't take long—and then click the New button to create the mailbox. The wizard creates the mailbox or mailboxes and then displays the Completion screen.

16. Click the Finish button to close the wizard.

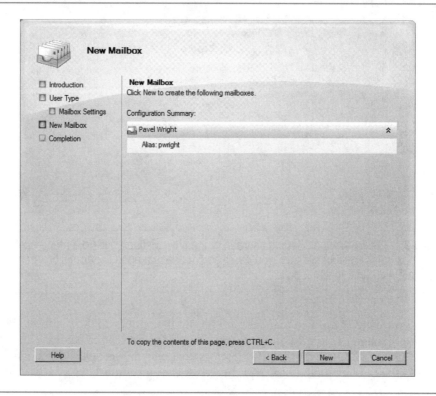

Figure 6-4.   On the New Mailbox screen of the New Mailbox Wizard, check the settings for the mailbox or mailboxes and then click the New button to proceed.

Connecting Mac OS X Mail to Exchange

When you've created the mailbox for a user, you can set up Mail for the user in moments. Follow these steps on the Mac the user normally uses:

1. Open Mail. For example, click the Mail icon on the Dock.

2. If Mail doesn't yet contain an e-mail account, Mail automatically displays the Welcome To Mail Assistant (see Figure 6-5), which walks you through the process of setting up an account. If Mail already contains one or more accounts, start creating a new account like this:

    a. Choose Mail | Preferences to open the Preferences window.

    b. Click the Accounts button on the toolbar to display the Accounts pane (see Figure 6-6).

    c. Click the Add (+) button at the bottom of the Accounts list to launch the Add Account Assistant. This assistant works in the same way as the Welcome To Mail Assistant—in fact, the two assistants are really two similar faces on the same assistant.

Figure 6-5.   The Welcome To Mail Assistant springs into action if Mail doesn't yet contain an e-mail account.

Figure 6-6. To start setting up an e-mail account in Mail, click the Add (+) button at the bottom of the Accounts list in the Accounts pane.

3. In the Full Name text box, approve or edit the Assistant's suggestion for the user's name.

4. In the Email Address text box, type the user's e-mail address for your Exchange server.

5. In the Password text box, type the user's password for your Exchange server.

6. Click the Continue button. Mail roots around on the network until it discovers the mail server, then gives the mail server a poke and sees how it responds to the credentials you've provided. If all is well, you see the Account Summary dialog box (see Figure 6-7).

Figure 6-7. In the Account Summary dialog box, choose whether to set up Address Book contacts and iCal calendars as well as the e-mail account.

7. Look through the details and make sure that the account type, full name, e-mail address, and server address are all correct.

8. In the Also Set Up area, select the Address Book Contacts check box if you want to set Address Book up to use the Active Directory address book. This is usually helpful.

9. Still in the Also Set Up area, select the iCal Calendars check box if you want to set iCal up to use the calendars on the Exchange server. This, too, is usually helpful.

10. Click the Create button. Mail creates the account and then displays the Inbox.

Making Mail Trust a Self-Signed Certificate

When you connect Mail to your Exchange server, Mail checks the server's digital certificate to make sure the server is legitimate.

Normally, your server will be running a digital certificate signed by a public certificate authority. In this case, Mail verifies that the certificate is current and that it's valid for e-mail, and then proceeds with setting up the e-mail account. But if you're testing a new configuration or planning a network migration, you may be using a self-signed certificate for the time being. In this case, Mail displays the Verify Certificate dialog box (shown here) to warn you that there may be a problem.

From here, you can simply click the Connect button to tell Mail to damn the torpedoes and get on with setting up the account. But what you may want to do is make Mail and Mac OS X trust the certificate so that Mail and other applications don't keep bugging you about it.

To do so, click the Show Certificate button to expand the Verify Certificate dialog box, as shown here. You can then select the Always Trust *Server* When Connecting To *Server Address* check box to put your seal of approval on the certificate.

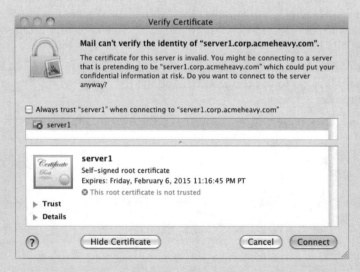

You don't need me to tell you that you shouldn't blindly trust anybody else's self-signed certificates—only certificates you've created yourself and have nurtured carefully since their inception. If you see the Verify Certificate dialog box in any other context, click the Show Certificate button and then dig into the Trust section and the Details section to see what's wrong with the server you're connecting to.

Choosing Mail Account Settings

After you've set up Mail as described in the previous section, the user can send and receive Mail using the Exchange server. But to enable the user to get the most out of Mail, you may need to adjust the settings that Mail automatically applies to the account.

To choose settings, open the account like this:

1. Choose Mail | Preferences or press the trusty old ⌘-, keyboard shortcut (⌘ and the COMMA key) to open the Preferences window.

2. Click the Accounts button on the toolbar to display the Accounts pane.

3. In the Accounts list box on the left, click the account you want to affect. (If Mail contains only the one account, it'll already be selected.)

You can then click the Account Information tab, the Mailbox Behaviors tab, or the Advanced tab on the tab bar, and then choose settings as described in the following sections.

Choosing Account Information Settings

You probably won't need to make many changes in the Account Information pane in Accounts preferences (see Figure 6-8) because most of its fields contain information that Mail fills in with suitable values when you connect Mail to the Exchange server.

The Account Information pane contains these fields:

- **Account Type**   This readout shows Exchange 2007 when Mail is connecting to Exchange Server 2007 or Exchange Server 2010.

- **Description**   In this text box, enter the account name as you want it to appear for the user in the Mail interface. The default setting is the e-mail address, but you (and the user) may prefer a descriptive name.

- **Email Address**   This text box shows the user's e-mail address. If Mail is working with Exchange Server, you shouldn't need to change this.

- **Full Name**   In this text box, enter the user's name the way it should appear on outgoing messages. The default setting picks up the user's name from Active Directory; you or the user may want to change it.

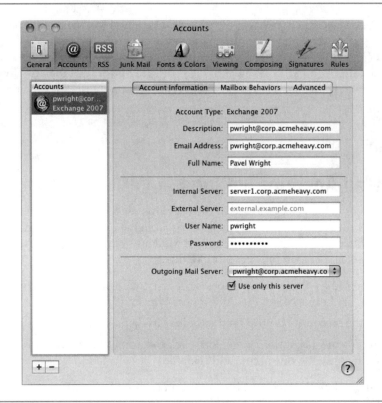

Figure 6-8.   The Account Information pane in Accounts preferences includes the e-mail address, the server names, and the username and password.

- **Internal Server**   This text box shows the Exchange server used within the network. Again, if Mail is working, you shouldn't need to change this.

- **External Server**   If you have set up an external server for Exchange, so that users can connect to Exchange across the Internet but without using a VPN connection, enter it in this text box. Otherwise, leave this text box empty. Mail doesn't configure the external server by default, because in most cases the user won't need it.

NOTE   Don't set up an external server for VPN users—the VPN brings them into the network, so they can access mail via the internal server. The external server is only for users who connect to Exchange across the Internet.

- **User Name**   This text box shows the user's account name for the mail server. Once more, if Mail is working, you shouldn't need to change this.

- ■ **Password**   This text box contains the user's password, blanked out by security-conscious dots.

- ■ **Outgoing Mail Server**   In this pop-up menu, make sure the Exchange entry is selected. The list shows the user's e-mail address first, followed by "(Exchange)," so you may need to open the pop-up menu to verify that it's the Exchange entry.

- ■ **Use Only This Server**   Select this check box if you want to limit Mail to using this outgoing mail server. Normally, this is a good idea.

Choosing Mailbox Behaviors Settings

The Mailbox Behaviors pane of Accounts preferences (see Figure 6-9) lets you choose how to handle drafts, notes, sent messages, junk mail, and trash. These are the settings you can choose:

- ■ **Store Draft Messages On The Server**   Select this check box if you want to store draft messages on the server rather than on the client. This setting is helpful for anyone who accesses their Exchange e-mail from multiple computers.

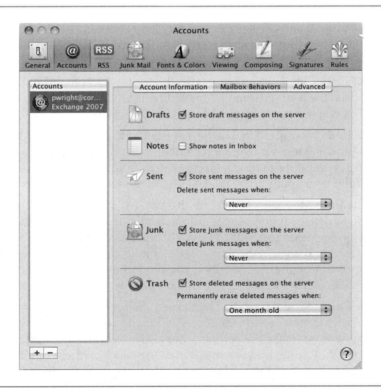

Figure 6-9.   In the Mailbox Behaviors pane of Accounts preferences, choose which items to store on the server and whether to display notes in the Inbox.

- **Show Notes In Inbox** For an IMAP or POP account, you can select this check box to make Mail display notes in the Inbox as well as in the Notes category. Some people apparently like to lump their notes in with their messages like this—there's no accounting for taste. But this setting doesn't apply to Exchange accounts.

- **Store Sent Messages On The Server** Select this check box if you want to store sent messages on the server rather than on the client. This setting is good for users who use multiple computers.

- **Delete Sent Messages When** In this pop-up menu, choose whether (and, if so, when) to delete sent messages automatically. These are your choices:

  - **Never** This is the standard setting, and usually the best. Mail keeps sent messages until the user deletes them manually.

  - **One Day Old** Mail automatically deletes messages one day after sending them. Usually it's better to keep messages for longer than this—for example, in case the user needs to be able to refer back to sent messages.

  - **One Week Old** Mail automatically deletes messages one week after sending them.

  - **One Month Old** Mail automatically deletes messages one month after sending them. Of the options for deleting messages automatically, this is the only option that strikes a balance between keeping mailbox size down and being able to track sent messages.

  - **Quitting Mail** Mail automatically deletes the contents of the Sent folder when the user quits mail. This setting is too trigger-happy for normal use, but you may need it under special circumstances.

- **Store Junk Messages On The Server** Select this check box if you want to store junk messages on the server rather than on the client. As before, this setting is useful for people who check mail from multiple computers; it's also helpful if your spam filters mistakenly categorize some messages as spam.

- **Delete Junk Messages When** In this pop-up menu, choose whether (and when) to delete junk messages automatically. The options are the same as for Delete Sent Messages When, but you'll typically want to treat junk mail more aggressively than sent messages. For example, deleting junk mail after a week is reasonable enough—but only if you remind users to check their junk mail folders regularly for messages that have been wrongly convicted.

- **Store Deleted Messages On The Server** Select this check box if you want to store deleted messages on the server rather than on the client. Again, you'd probably want to use this setting for users who check mail from multiple computers. You can also use the deleted messages on the server as a backup when the user accidentally deletes a vital message on the client.

- **Permanently Erase Deleted Messages When**   In this pop-up menu, choose whether (and when) to wipe deleted messages off the face of your mail server. The options are the same as for Delete Sent Messages When, but you'll probably want to use one of the auto-deletion settings. For example, erasing deleted messages after one day can work well, or when quitting Mail.

Choosing Advanced Settings

You can choose the following settings in the Advanced pane of Accounts preferences (see Figure 6-10):

- **Enable This Account**   Select this check box to make the account active, as you'll normally want it to be. Clear the check box if you want to turn the account off for the time being.

- **Include When Automatically Checking For New Messages**   Select this check box to have Mail include this account when checking for new messages. This is normally what you want to do.

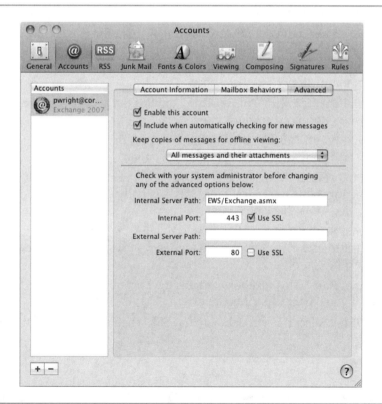

Figure 6-10.   In the Advanced pane of Accounts preferences, make sure the account is enabled. You can also change the server paths and ports.

NOTE To control how often Mail checks for new messages, click the General button on the toolbar of the Preferences dialog box and then choose a setting in the Check For New Messages pop-up menu. The options are Every Minute, Every 5 Minutes, Every 15 Minutes, Every 30 Minutes, Every Hour, and Manually.

- **Keep Copies Of Messages For Offline Viewing** In this pop-up menu, choose which messages and attachments to cache on the Mac so that it can view them offline. These are the options:

  - **All Messages And Their Attachments** Choose this setting for a MacBook that needs full access to e-mail and attachments even when it's not connected to the network.

  - **All Messages, But Omit Attachments** Choose this setting for a MacBook that needs to be able to access messages but not attachments when it's not connected to the network.

  - **Only Messages I've Read** Choose this setting for a MacBook that needs to be able to access only previously read messages when it's not connected to the network.

  - **Don't Keep Copies Of Any Messages** Choose this setting for a Mac that remains connected to the network and will not need offline access to messages or attachments. You can also use this option on a Mac that's running out of hard disk space.

- **Internal Server Path** This text box contains the path to the internal server. You won't normally need to change this.

- **Internal Port** This text box contains the port number on the internal server. You won't normally need to change this either.

- **Use SSL** Select this check box to use Secure Sockets Layer (SSL) when connecting to the internal server. This is usually a good idea, and normally Mail selects this check box when you set up an Exchange account.

- **External Server Path** This text box contains the path to the external server if your setup uses one. If your Exchange setup uses only an internal server, leave this text box empty.

- **External Port** This text box contains the port number on the external server, even if you haven't specified an external server path.

- **Use SSL** Select this check box to use SSL when connecting to the external server.

Saving the Changes to the Mail Settings

When you've finished choosing Mail settings, click another button on the toolbar to display another pane, or click the Close button on the Mail Preferences window. If Mail prompts you to save any unsaved changes, as shown here, click the Save button.

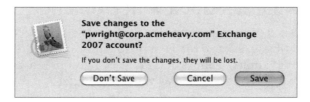

Turning Off Mail's Junk Mail Filtering

If your Exchange setup includes server-based junk mail filtering, and if your network's Macs use only Exchange for e-mail, turn off Mail's junk mail filtering. To do so, click the Junk Mail button on the toolbar to display the Junk Mail pane (see Figure 6-11) and then clear the Enable Junk Mail Filtering check box.

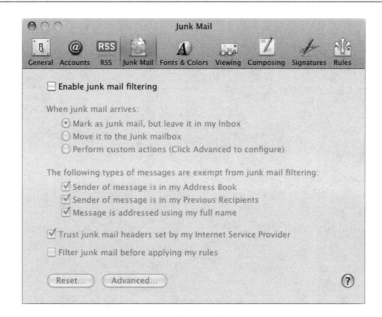

Figure 6-11.   You can turn off Mail's client-side junk mail filtering if your Exchange setup includes server-based filtering for junk mail.

CAUTION   If a user uses Mail to check e-mail on an account other than Exchange and that doesn't provide junk mail filtering, leave Mail's junk mail filtering turned on.

Using iCal and Address Book with Exchange

Once you've established the connection to the Exchange server, the Mac user can simply work with Mail and (if you chose to set them up too) iCal and Address Book. All three applications work pretty much seamlessly with Exchange, but iCal and Address Book have a couple of settings each that you may want to change.

NOTE   Both iCal and Address Book check your Exchange server's digital certificate when they connect to it. If the server is running a self-signed certificate that you haven't told Mac OS X to trust (as described earlier in this chapter), the application displays the Verify Certificate dialog box to warn you of the server's apparent illegitimacy. Click the Connect button to establish the connection anyway.

Using iCal with Exchange

iCal automatically connects to the Exchange server and pulls in the user's calendar and task list, as you can see in Figure 6-12. The user can then work with the Exchange calendar and task list using the same techniques as for their local calendar and task list.

Figure 6-12.   iCal automatically adds the user's calendar and task list from the Exchange server.

You can configure iCal's connection to Exchange by choosing iCal | Preferences, clicking the Accounts button on the toolbar, and then clicking the account in the left pane. The two settings you're most likely to need to change are in the Account Information pane (see Figure 6-13):

- **Description**   In this text box, enter the account name as you want it to appear for the user in the Calendars pane in iCal. The default setting is the e-mail address, but a descriptive name often works better.

- **Refresh Calendars**   In this pop-up menu, choose how frequently to refresh the calendars with the latest data. The options are Every Minute, Every 5 Minutes, Every 15 Minutes, Every 30 Minutes, Every Hour, and Manually.

 NOTE   The user can force a refresh of the calendar data at any time by CTRL-clicking or right-clicking the calendar and in the Calendars list in the left pane and then choosing Refresh from the context menu (or Refresh All to refresh all calendars).

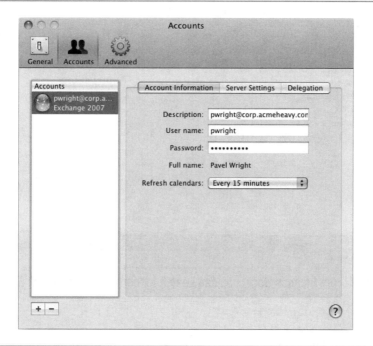

Figure 6-13.   You can configure iCal's connection to Exchange by using Accounts preferences.

Using Address Book with Exchange

Address Book automatically reads the addresses on the Exchange server and makes them available to the user, who can find contact information as usual—for example, by searching, as in Figure 6-14.

To configure Address Book's connection to Exchange, choose Address Book | Preferences, click the Accounts button on the toolbar, and then click the Exchange account in the Accounts list on the left. As with iCal, there are two settings you're most likely to want to change, and they're in the Account Information pane (see Figure 6-15):

■ **Description**   In this text box, enter the account name as you want it to appear for the user in the Group column in Address Book. The default setting is the e-mail address, but a descriptive name is usually easier for the user.

■ **Refresh Contacts**   In this pop-up menu, choose how frequently to refresh Address Book with the latest contact information from the network. The options are Every Minute, Every 5 Minutes, Every 15 Minutes, Every 30 Minutes, Every Hour, and Manually.

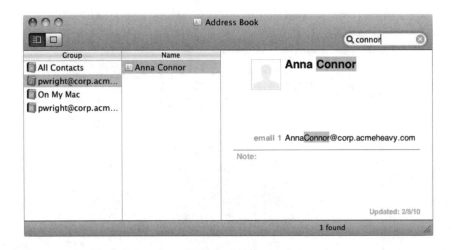

Figure 6-14.   From Address Book, you can search for contact information in Exchange.

Figure 6-15.   In the Account Information pane in Accounts preferences, you can change the description for the Exchange account and the frequency with which Address Book refreshes the information.

CHAPTER 7 | Providing Home Folders and File Services to Macs

W hen a Mac user joins your network, you want him to feel right at home—and that means giving him the type of home folder he needs. Mac OS X offers three options: to give the user a home folder on the Mac, just as if he weren't using the network; to give the user a network home folder that acts just like a local home folder; and to give the user a mobile account that's stored on his Mac but that synchronizes automatically with a network folder. You can also take the mobile account a stage further by letting the user store it as an external account on a portable drive that he can carry anywhere or swallow (or worse) to confound Homeland Security.

Home folders are where the lion's share of the excitement is, but you'll probably also need to provide shared folders that your Macs can access freely to share data with each other. This chapter first discusses how to set up home folders for Macs and then explains how to connect the Macs to shared folders on the network.

NOTE   This chapter assumes that you have already set up your Windows servers to provide file services for your Windows clients, and that you now need to extend those services to your Macs as well. If not, fire up Server Manager, coax the Add Roles Wizard into life, select the File Services check box on the Select Server Roles screen, and follow through the process of setting up file services. Macs are happy working with SMB shares, so you need to select only the File Server check box on the Select Server Roles screen—you don't need any of the more esoteric options.

Providing Home Folders for Mac Users

When you connect a Mac user to Active Directory using Directory Utility, you can give that user one of three different types of home folder: a local home folder, a network home folder, or a mobile account with a portable home directory. The following sections dissect these possibilities.

To control which type of user account the Active Directory plug-in creates, you use the controls in the User Experience pane in the Advanced Options area of the Bind dialog box (see Figure 7-1).

Understanding Local Home Folders and When to Use Them

A local home folder is stored on the Mac, just as if the Mac weren't bound to Active Directory. If you bind a Mac to Active Directory and don't specify a network home folder or portable home folder for the Mac, you get a local home folder. When a user logs in, the Active Directory plug-in creates a folder with the user's short name in the /Users/ folder on the Mac. For example, if the user's short name is zlamb, Mac OS X creates the /Users/zlamb/ folder.

Local home folders tend to be a management nightmare, because the folders are much harder to back up centrally than network folders are. But local home folders are easy for users, who can just keep on saving their files and folders (and making their own regular backups—in your dreams) as usual. There's no need for the user to do anything differently just because the Mac is connected to the network.

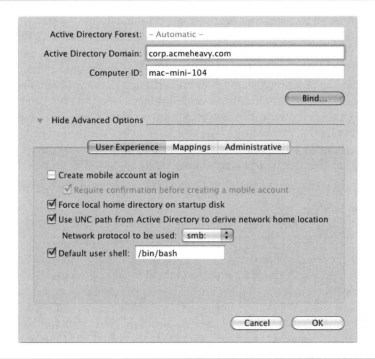

Figure 7-1. Use the controls in the User Experience pane in the Bind dialog box to control which type of home folder the Active Directory plug-in creates during binding.

 CAUTION Mac OS X does not synchronize a user's local home folder with a network home folder, nor does it back up the local home folder unless you've set up Time Machine or another backup application. See Chapter 12 for instructions on backing up users' files.

In most cases, network home folders are a better bet from a management perspective than local home folders, because you can keep them safely backed up and (if you control what users can do with USB devices and the like) you can be sure that your files are stored on the network rather than wandering around the landscape on MacBooks. But in some situations local home folders have advantages over network home folders. Here are a couple examples:

■ **Macs that rarely connect to the network** If you manage Macs that rarely connect to the network—for example, roving salesmen or technicians who are mostly out of the office—local home folders will make more sense than network home folders. Portable home folders may be even better.

■ **Macs that thrash the network**   When you use a network home folder, the Mac stores all its local files and settings on the network—after all, that's the point. If users are just using productivity applications, such as Word or Excel, this is fine. But if they're using applications that store large amounts of data in the home folder, they'll put a strain on the file server and on the network. For example, users who work extensively with hoggish applications—I'm thinking Final Cut, iMovie, Logic, and GarageBand, but you'll have your own *bêtes noires*—may be better off using local home folders. The same goes for other applications that create large files or cache vast quantities of data when you launch them. You can mitigate the backup headache by rigging Time Machine to back up the files to an external hard drive—preferably a capacious one.

Changing an Existing User Account to an Active Directory User Account

If the user of the Mac you're connecting to Active Directory already has a user account on the Mac, he'll already have a home folder. This home folder will conflict with the home folder that the Active Directory plug-in normally creates automatically for the user: The Active Directory plug-in will not create the home folder because the existing folder is there, and the local user account will have ownership of the home folder. This will prevent the user from using the home folder after logging in to Active Directory with the Active Directory account.

Losing access to all documents and settings is a recipe for unhappiness that the user will share enthusiastically with you as soon as he can track you down. So before letting the user log in to Active Directory, you need to remove the local user account without removing the home folder, then change the ownership of the home folder from the local user to the Active Directory user.

Here's what to do:

1. If the user is currently using the Mac, kick him off it. And right off it—none of that Fast User Switching malarkey.

2. Log yourself in on the Mac using an administrator account for that Mac (not an Active Directory administrator account).

3. Open System Preferences. For example, click the System Preferences icon on the Dock.

4. In the System area, click the Accounts icon to open Accounts preferences.

5. Click the padlock icon in the lower-left corner, type your password in the authentication dialog box, and then click the OK button.

6. Click the user's account, and then click the Remove (–) button. Mac OS X gasps in horror and displays the Are You Sure You Want To Delete The User Account? dialog box (shown here).

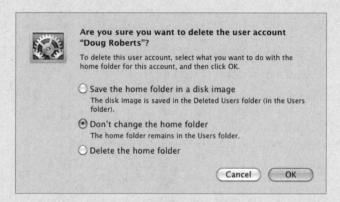

7. Select the Don't Change The Home Folder option button. This setting makes Mac OS X leave the home folder where it is.

8. Click the OK button. Mac OS X closes the dialog box and deletes the user account, which disappears from the list in the Accounts pane in System Preferences.

9. Quit System Preferences (for example, press ⌘-Q) unless you're planning further maneuvers in it.

10. Open a Terminal window. For example, click the Desktop, choose Go | Utilities, and then double-click the Terminal icon.

11. If the user's local account name is different from the Active Directory account name, use the mv command to rename the home folder from the local account name to the Active Directory account name. For example, the following command renames the folder named Doug Roberts (Deleted) to droberts, using double quotation marks because the folder name contains spaces:

```
sudo mv "Users/Doug Roberts (Deleted)" /Users/droberts
```

NOTE   You'll need to use the sudo command to pump yourself up to super-user status to execute the mv command. When sudo reads you Miranda and demands your password, type it in and press RETURN.

12. Now use the chown command with the **–R** parameter to change the ownership of the folder and its contents to the Active Directory user account. The following example uses the username droberts in the CORP\domain users group:

```
sudo chown -R droberts:"CORP\domain users" /Users/droberts
```

13. Quit Terminal. For example, press ⌘-Q.

14. Log out of your administrator account.

15. Have the user log in using his Active Directory credentials. If the user receives the message The System Was Unable To Unlock Your Login Keychain, as shown next, tell him to click the Update Keychain Password button and follow through the procedure of updating the password.

Understanding Network Home Folders and When to Use Them

A *network home folder* is a home folder that is stored on the network—for example, on a Windows server. When the user (let's assume it's you) logs in, Mac OS X mounts the network share in your home folder, so if your user name is Bill Hall, your /Users/ bhall/ folder actually contains the network folder. All the documents you create in this home folder are saved on the network rather than on your Mac. The same goes for the changes you make to your preferences (or at least to those the administrator allows you to change).

A network home folder is the normal arrangement for Mac users who don't need to take their files with them. You'll probably want to use network home folders for Macs that are normally connected to the network—for example, your iMacs, Mac minis, and Mac Pros, which normally don't leave the site.

To create a network home folder for a Mac user, you specify the path to the home folder in Active Directory just as you would for a Windows PC user (see Figure 7-2):

1. Open Active Directory Users And Computers.

2. In the left pane, expand the domain.

3. Click the Users folder to display its contents.

4. Double-click the user to open the Properties dialog box.

5. Click the Profile tab to display its contents.

6. Select the Connect option button, and choose the drive letter (for example, Z:) in the drop-down list next to it.

7. Enter the path to the home folder in the To text box.

8. Click the OK button to close the Properties dialog box.

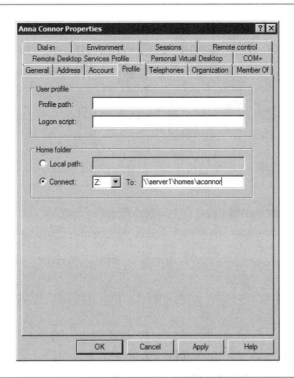

Figure 7-2. Set the path to the user's home folder using the Connect option button on the Profile tab of the Properties dialog box for the user's account.

When binding a Mac, you can cause its users to use network home folders like this:

1. In the Bind dialog box, click the Show Advanced Options disclosure triangle to display the Advanced Options section at the bottom.

2. Make sure the User Experience pane is at the front. If it's not, click the User Experience tab.

3. Clear the Force Local Home Directory On Startup Disk check box.

4. Select the Use UNC Path From Active Directory To Derive Network Home Location check box.

5. Open the Network Protocol To Be Used pop-up menu and choose SMB from it. This pop-up menu also offers AFP, which is a better choice for Macs—but Windows Server doesn't offer AFP.

6. Choose further settings, as needed, and then click the Bind button. As usual, you'll need to provide your Active Directory credentials to commit the Mac to Active Directory bondage.

Understanding Mobile Accounts and Portable Home Directories—and When to Use Them

For your network's portable Macs, you'll probably want to use mobile accounts. A mobile account has both a local home folder that's stored on the Mac itself and a network home folder that's stored on the server. You get to choose which folders in the two home folders to synchronize, and the result is a portable home directory.

A mobile account caches its authentication information on the Mac so that the user can log on using the same credentials even when the Mac isn't connected to the network. The account also caches the user's managed preferences, so that the user sees the same environment whether the Mac is connected to the network or running free.

Setting Up Mobile Accounts in an Extended Active Directory

To set up a mobile account in an extended Active Directory, follow these steps:

1. Open Workgroup Manager, connect to Active Directory, and authenticate yourself.

2. In the left pane, select the user, group, computer, or computer list you want to affect.

3. Click the Preferences button on the toolbar to display the Preferences pane.

4. Click the Mobility icon to display the Mobility pane.

5. In the upper tab bar, click the Account Creation tab to display the Account Creation pane.

6. In the lower tab bar, click the Creation tab to display the Creation pane (shown in Figure 7-3 with settings chosen).

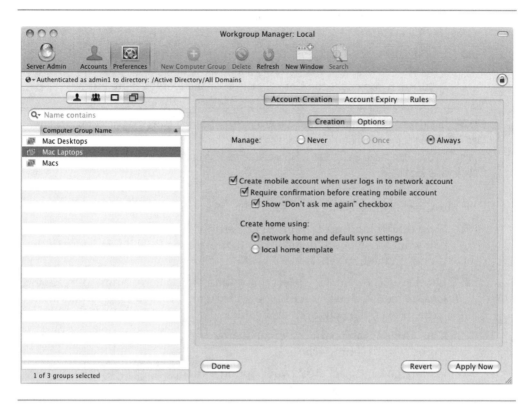

Figure 7-3. Use the Creation pane in Mobility preferences to set up mobile accounts for a user, group, computer, or computer list in an extended Active Directory.

7. In the Manage bar, select the Always option button.

8. Select the Create Mobile Account When User Logs In To Network Account check box. Selecting this check box makes all the other controls in the pane available.

9. Select the Require Confirmation Before Creating Mobile Account check box if you want Mac OS X to offer the user the option of refusing to create the mobile account. The user then sees the Create A Mobile Account? dialog box (shown here with the Don't Ask Me Again check box appearing) when she logs in.

- Normally, it's best to clear this check box, so that the user must create the mobile account.

- If you select this check box, you can select the Show "Don't Ask Me Again" Checkbox check box if you want to allow the user to suppress the prompt in future if she clicks the Cancel button or the Don't Create button.

NOTE If the user selects the Don't Ask Me Again check box and clicks the Don't Create button, Mac OS X logs her in as a network user, doesn't create the mobile account, and doesn't prompt her again. The user can make the Create A Mobile Account? dialog box appear again by holding down Option while logging in.

10. In the Create Home Using area, select the appropriate option button:

- **Network Home And Default Sync Settings** Select this option button if you want the network home folder to replace the local home folder (if there is one) on the first sync.

- **Local Home Template** Select this option button if you want to create the local home folder using the home folder template on the Mac rather than create it from the network home folder.

11. Click the Options tab on the lower tab bar to display the Options pane (shown in Figure 7-4 with settings chosen).

12. In the Manage bar, select the Always option button.

13. If you want to encrypt the mobile account using Mac OS X's FileVault encryption, follow these steps:

    a. Select the Encrypt Contents With FileVault check box.

    b. Select the Use Computer Master Password, If Available option button.

    c. If you want to restrict the local home folder's size, select the Restrict Size check box and then choose either the To Fixed Size option button (and enter the limit in megabytes in the text box) or the To Percentage Of Network Home Quota option button (and enter the percentage in the text box).

NOTE FileVault encrypts the user's home folder by creating an encrypted disk image. When the user logs in, FileVault decrypts the data; when the user logs out, FileVault encrypts the home folder again. Encrypting a mobile account with FileVault is a good idea if the account contains data that's sensitive either for the company or organization or for the individual user. FileVault may slow the Mac down a bit, but the overhead is seldom worth worrying about. Of more concern is that the user may forget the FileVault password and be unable to unencrypt her data.

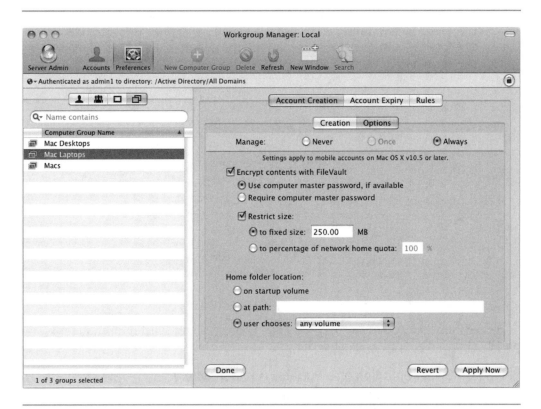

Figure 7-4.   In the Options pane, choose whether to encrypt the mobile account using FileVault, and decide whether to store the account on the startup volume or let the user create an external account on a portable drive.

14. In the Home Folder Location area, choose where to store the local home folder:

   ■ **On Startup Volume**   The startup volume is usually the best place for a mobile account you want to store on a Mac. Mac OS X puts the local home folder in the /Users/ folder under the user's short name (for example, /Users/asmith/).

   ■ **At Path**   Select this option button if you want to force the home folder to a particular path.

   ■ **User Chooses**   Select this option button if you want to allow the user to create an external account on a portable drive. In the pop-up menu, choose which type of volume the user can create the external account on: Any Volume, Any Internal Volume, or Any External Volume. Normally, you'll want to choose the Any External Volume item, which lets the user create the account on a portable drive (for example, a USB stick) without the risk that she'll store it instead on one of the Mac's internal volumes (where it won't do her much good). The user simply selects the drive in the Select The Home Folder's Volume pop-up menu in the Create A Mobile Account With A Portable Home Directory? dialog box (shown here).

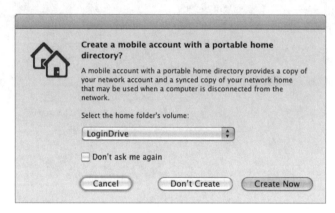

15. Click the Apply Now button to apply your choices.

Leave the Mobility pane displayed so that you can set up synchronization for a portable home directory, as described next.

Setting Up Synchronization on a Portable Home Directory

After setting up a user with a portable home directory, you'll need to decide which folders in the home directory to synchronize.

Understanding Home Sync and Preference Sync

Mac OS X uses two types of synchronization for portable home directories: home sync and preference sync. You can choose different settings for the two in the Home Sync pane and Preference Sync pane in the Rules pane of Mobility preferences, but before you do, it helps to understand the different ways in which the two work.

First, the easy bit. Both home sync and preference sync can take place at four times:

■ **At Login**   Synchronization runs when the user logs in. Logically, this is a great time to make sure files are synchronized, because it helps you avoid working with outdated files. But synchronizing many files at login can make login take a coon's age, which tends to vex users. During synchronization, the user sees the Home Sync Status dialog box (shown here), which shows what's currently happening but doesn't indicate whether the end is imminent or an ice age away.

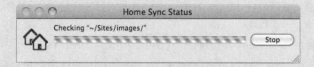

- **At Logout** Synchronization runs when the user logs out. This, too, can be a great time for synchronization, but not if the user is looking to pick up the MacBook and leave the building.

- **In The Background** Synchronization runs automatically in the background using the intervals you specify using the Every slider in the Options pane. Set with a short interval, this is a good option for many users because it lets them log in and log out quickly but ensures that synchronization does take place automatically rather than relying on the user to remember to synchronize.

- **Manually** The user chooses when to synchronize files. This option works well as long as the user remembers to synchronize. The user can run synchronization from the Sync menu on the menu bar or from System Preferences.

Home sync is used for files in the user's home folder but not for files in the ~/Library folder, whereas *preference sync* is used for preference files. Most preference files live in the ~/Library folder, but some applications put them in other folders out of sheer cussedness.

In both types of sync, newer files overwrite older files, as you'd expect. Where things get trickier is when there's a sync conflict—both the file on the Mac and the file on the network have changed, and Mac OS X needs to decide which to keep. Here's how preference sync handles conflicts:

- During login sync, files on the network overwrite conflicting files on the Mac.

- During logout sync, files on the Mac overwrite conflicting files on the network.

- In background sync, Mac OS X synchronizes preference changes from the Mac to the server but not from the server to the Mac—those changes sync only during login sync or logout sync.

To set up synchronization on a portable home directory, take the steps in the following list. If you followed through the previous section and have the Mobility pane open already, jump directly to step 5 without passing Go:

1. Open Workgroup Manager, connect to Active Directory, and then authenticate yourself.

2. In the left pane, select your victim user, group, computer, or computer list.

3. Click the Preferences button on the toolbar to display the Preferences pane.

4. Click the Mobility icon to display the Mobility pane.

5. In the upper tab bar, click the Rules tab to display the Rules pane.

6. In the lower tab bar, click the Preference Sync tab to display the Preference Sync pane (shown in Figure 7-5 with settings chosen).

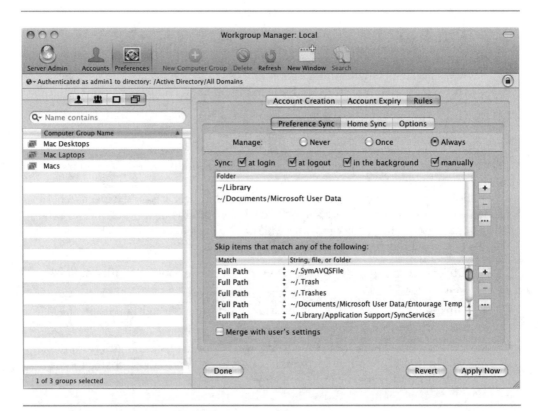

Figure 7-5.   In the Preference Sync pane of the Rules pane in Mobility preferences, choose how to synchronize the preferences files.

7. In the Manage bar, select the Always option button if you want to keep the synchronization under strict management. The alternative is to select the Once option button, which imposes your diktats but then lets the user change them.

8. In the Sync area, select the At Login check box, the At Logout check box, the In The Background check box, and the Manually check box, as needed. (See the sidebar titled "Understanding Home Sync and Preference Sync" for chapter and verse on these options.)

9. In the Sync list box, build the list of preference folders you want to sync:

   - Mac OS X starts you off with the ~/Library folder and any other preferences folders it has identified, such as the ~/Documents/Microsoft User Data folder that Microsoft applications (including Office) use.

   - To add an item, click the Add (+) button and type the folder path in the text box that appears. Alternatively, click the Browse (…) button, use the resulting dialog box to select the folder, and then click the Add (+) button.

   - To remove an item, click it in the list and then click the Remove (–) button.

10. In the Skip Items That Match Any Of The Following list box, add any files or folders that you don't want to synchronize to the list that Mac OS X provides. Use the Add (+) button, Browse (…) button, and Remove (–) button as described above.

11. If you want to add the folders you've chosen for syncing to the folders the user chooses, select the Merge With User's Settings check box.

12. In the lower tab bar, click the Home Sync tab to display the Home Sync pane and then repeat steps 7 through 11 to set home sync options. The Home Sync pane contains the same controls as the Preference Sync pane.

13. In the lower tab bar, click the Options button to display the Options pane (see Figure 7-6).

14. In the Manage bar, select the Always option button or the Once option button, as appropriate.

15. In the Sync In The Background area, select the Every option button and drag the slider to a suitable length of time; the range extends from 5 Minutes to 8 Hours. Normally, you'll want to set a short interval, but you'll need to experiment to find the best balance between keeping files synchronized and keeping the load on your server and network within tolerable limits. You can select the Manually option button instead if you don't want to use automatic background synchronization.

16. Select the Show Status In Menu Bar check box if you want the Homes menu to appear on the menu bar. This menu lets the user quickly check synchronization status, run a sync, and open Mobile Account Preferences, so it's usually useful.

17. Click the Apply Now button to apply your changes.

18. Click the Done button to return to the Preferences pane.

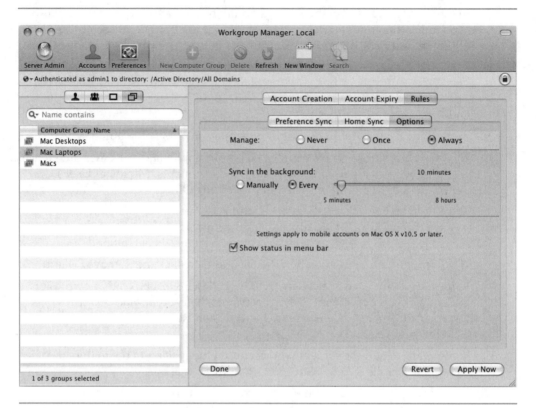

Figure 7-6. In the Options pane of the Rules pane for Mobility preferences, choose how frequently to synchronize in the background and whether to show the status in the menu bar.

Hosting Network Home Folders on Mac OS X with a Magic Triangle

If your network uses a magic triangle, you can choose between hosting the Mac users' network home folders on your Windows server or on your Mac OS X server. Depending on your situation, this may be an easy choice or a tough one.

The main advantage of hosting the folders on Mac OS X is that your Mac OS X server can host the folders via AFP, which gives better performance and security than SMB. Although Macs can use SMB just fine for accessing network home folders on Windows Server, they tend to be much happier with AFP, and your Mac OS X server will be delighted to provide it.

Another advantage to putting the Macs' network home folders on your Mac server is that it means less work for the Windows servers to do. How highly you value this advantage will no doubt depend on whether your Windows servers are in danger of buckling under the load or taking the digital equivalent of an extended latte break interrupted occasionally by chucking the odd file at a user. It'll also depend on

Understanding How Users Control Synchronization

If you allow a user to control parts of synchronization, she can choose which items to synchronize like this:

1. Open the Sync menu on the menu bar and choose Mobile Account Preferences to display the Settings dialog box (shown here). Alternatively, open System Preferences, click the Accounts icon to display the Accounts pane, and then click the Settings button. Which settings are available to the user in the Settings dialog box depend on the policy you've applied. If you've retained total control of synchronization, Mac OS X makes the Settings button unavailable to let the user know she's straight out of luck.

2. In the Sync pop-up menu, choose Automatically, Manually, or one of the time intervals—for example, Every 5 Minutes or Every Hour.

3. Select the At Login check box to synchronize at login. Select the At Logout check box to synchronize at logout.

4. To choose which folders to synchronize, select the Home Folder option button or the Only Selected Folders option button. If the user chooses the latter, she goes to the list box and selects the check box for each folder she wants to synchronize.

5. Select the Show Status In Menu Bar check box to display the Homes menu in the menu bar.

6. Click the OK button to close the Settings dialog box.

   The user can start synchronization by opening the Sync menu on the menu bar and choosing Sync Home Now. If she has opened the Settings dialog box, she can click the Sync Now button in it.

the hardware you're running Mac OS X Server on. If you've got an Xserve eagerly looking for more work, putting the home folders on it may be a no-brainer. But if you've dug up an ageing Mac mini that's fit only for some light authentication tasks, you probably won't want to chain it to the treadmill of file services.

But, as you know, life's seldom a one-way street, and putting the Macs's home folders on a Mac OS X server inevitably has disadvantages too. The main disadvantage is you'll have to back up the home folders on the Mac server separately from those on your regular server.

NOTE   You can also use your Mac OS X server to host home folders for Windows users if you want. Windows PCs connect to the Mac OS X server using SMB rather than AFP (which the Macs use). This book doesn't explore this scenario.

Understanding the Process of Setting Up Home Folders

To set up home folders for your Mac users on your Mac OS X server, you need to take three actions:

- In Server Admin, turn on AFP on your server.
- In Server Admin, set up a share point for the home folders.
- In Workgroup Manager, create the home folders.

Turning On AFP

First, turn on AFP if your Mac OS X server isn't already running it. Follow these steps:

1. Open Server Admin:
   - If you're working on the server, click the Server Admin icon that appears by default on the Dock.
   - If you're working from a client Mac and haven't yet added Server Admin to the Dock, click the desktop and then choose Go | Applications to open the Applications folder. Open the Server folder within it and then double-click the Server Admin icon. Once Server Admin appears in the Dock, CTRL-click or right-click its icon and then choose Options | Keep In Dock if you want to keep it there.
2. If the Servers list in the pane on the left is collapsed, click its disclosure triangle to expand it.
3. Click your server's name to display its configuration panes. The Overview pane appears at first (see Figure 7-7).
4. Look at the Services list and see if the AFP service is running. If it's not, turn it on as described next; if it is, move ahead to step 9 in the list.
5. Click the Settings button on the toolbar to display the Settings pane.
6. Click the Services button on the tab bar to display the Services pane (see Figure 7-8).

Figure 7-7. In the Overview pane for your Mac OS X server, check whether the AFP service is already running.

7. In the Select The Services To Configure On This Server list box, select the AFP check box.

8. Click the Save button to apply the change. Mac OS X Server adds the AFP service to the server's range of skills but doesn't yet turn it on. You need to do that yourself in a moment.

9. In the Servers list on the left, click the disclosure triangle next to your server to expand the list of services below it.

10. In the services list, click the AFP service to display its configuration panes.

11. Click the Start AFP button below the Servers pane. Mac OS X Server starts the AFP service and turns the light next to it green to indicate that systems are go.

Leave Server Admin open so that you can continue with the next section.

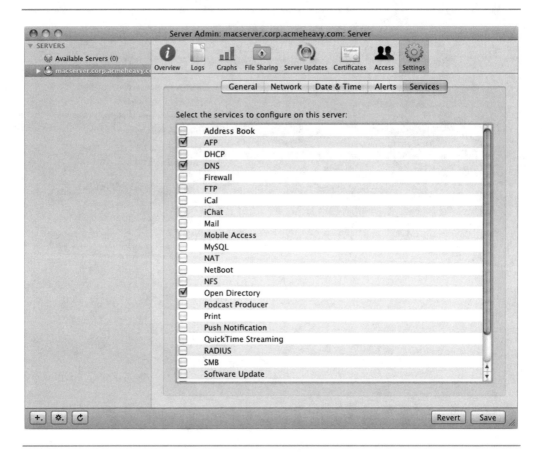

Figure 7-8. If necessary, use the Services pane to turn on the AFP service on your Mac OS X server.

Set Up a Share Point for the Home Folders

Next, you need to set up a share point for the home folders. You do this in Server Admin as well, so you can pick up where you left off in the previous section.

In Server Admin, with the AFP service selected in the Servers pane, click the Share Points button on the toolbar to display the Share Points pane (shown in Figure 7-9 with the list of volumes displayed). This pane shows you the share points for AFP on your server.

As you can see in the figure, this pane has a bar at the top under the toolbar with two pairs of visibility buttons: a Volumes button and a Share Points button, and a List button and a Browse button. There's also a toggle button farther to the right that switches between Share and Unshare, depending on whether the item is currently unshared or shared.

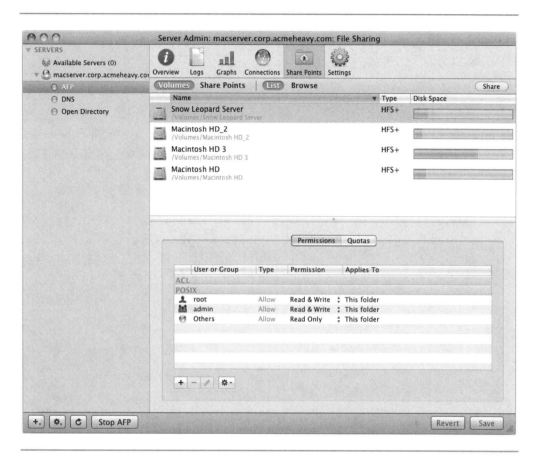

Figure 7-9. The Share Points pane in Server Admin first shows your server's volumes and permissions.

Normally, when you display the File Sharing pane at first, the Volumes button and the List button are selected, so you see the list of volumes. Click the Share Points button to display the list of share points, as in Figure 7-10. Below it is a pane with tab buttons for toggling between showing options for the selected share point and permissions for the selected share point.

These are the share points that are already set up on your server. For a Mac OS X server bound in a magic triangle, you should see three share points that Mac OS X has automatically created:

- **Groups**   This share point is for sharing folders among groups.

- **Public**   This share point is for sharing files and folders with everyone at large on your network. This capability is useful on some networks, but on others you may not need it.

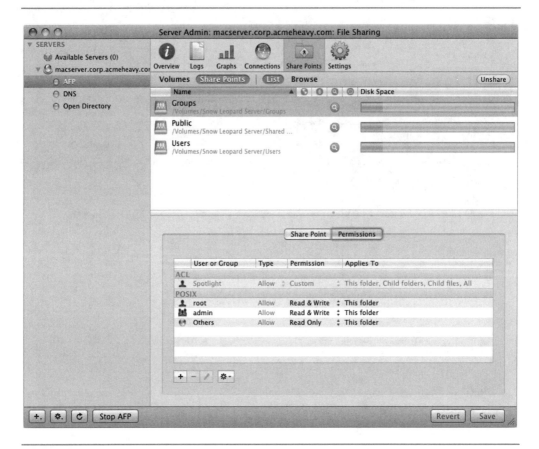

Figure 7-10. Click the Share Points button on the toolbar in Server Admin to display the list of share points.

■ **Users** This share point is for user home folders.

 NOTE If you've set up your Mac OS X server differently, you may see more share points, such as Backups, NetBootsClients0, and NetBootSP0.

The four icons in the Share Points list between the Name column and the Disk Space column provide quick information about the share points. Here's what they mean, looking from right to left:

■ **NetBoot status** The icon appears in the first column if the share point provides NetBoot services for diskless workstations.

■ **Automount status** The icon appears in the second column if the share point is configured to mount automatically.

- **Spotlight status**   The Spotlight icon appears if Spotlight is configured to search the share point.

- **Time Machine**   The Time Machine icon appears if the share point is set up to accept Time Machine backups.

To configure an existing share point, you select it and then use the controls in the Share Point pane or the Permissions pane. Let's look at how you'd configure the Users share point so that users can use it. Follow these steps:

1. Click the Users share in the Share Points list in the Share Points pane in Server Admin. (If the Volumes button is selected, click the Share Points button to display the list of share points.)

2. Make sure the Share Point tab in the lower pane is selected, so that you see the Share Point pane.

3. Set up the share point for automatic mounting so that a Mac automatically mounts the share when a user logs in to the network. This gives the user immediate access to her home folder. Follow these steps:

   a. Select the Enable Automount check box. Mac OS X automatically displays the Configure The Automount For The Selected Share Point dialog box (see Figure 7-11). If Mac OS X doesn't automatically open this dialog box, click the Edit button to display it.

   b. In the Directory pop-up menu, choose the /LDAPv3/127.0.0.1 directory as the directory in which you want the automounting share point to appear.

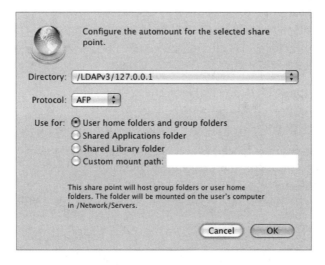

Figure 7-11.   In the Configure The Automount For The Selected Share Point dialog box, you can change the protocols and usage for an automounting share point.

c. In the Protocol pop-up menu, make sure AFP is selected. (AFP should be selected already.)

d. In the Use For area, make sure the Use Home Folders And Group Folders option button is selected. (This option button, too, should be selected already.)

e. Click the OK button to close the Configure The Automount For The Selected Share Point dialog box and apply your choices.

f. If Mac OS X displays the Authenticate dialog box shown here, fill in your directory administrator credentials and click the OK button.

4. If you want Spotlight to search and index the contents of the shared folder, select the Enable Spotlight Searching check box.

5. Make sure the Enable As Time Machine Backup Destination check box is cleared. You don't want Time Machine parking backups in your user folders.

6. Click the Protocol Options button to display the Protocol Options dialog box, which opens with the AFP pane at the front (see Figure 7-12).

7. Make sure the Share This Item Using AFP check box is selected.

8. Clear the Allow AFP Guest Access check box.

9. In the Custom AFP Name text box, change the share point name in AFP if you want. In this case, the default name (Users) works pretty well.

10. Click the SMB tab to display the SMB pane (see Figure 7-13).

11. If Windows users will need to access the shared folder, select the Share This Item Using SMB check box and then change the name as needed in the Custom SMB Name text box. For example, some users may need to access their home folders from either Windows PCs or Macs. Otherwise, clear the Share This Item Using SMB check box.

12. Click the OK button to close the Protocol Options dialog box.

13. Click the Save button in the lower-right corner of the Server Admin window to save the changes you've made to the share point.

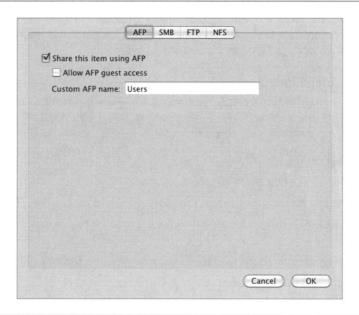

Figure 7-12.   In the AFP pane of the Protocol Options dialog box, make sure AFP sharing is on and that guest access is off.

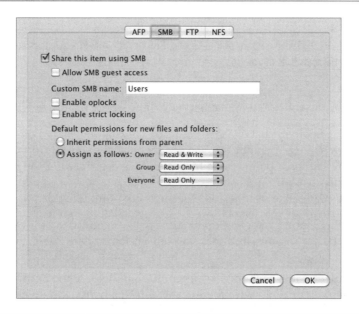

Figure 7-13.   In the SMB pane of the Protocol Options dialog box, turn off the SMB sharing that Mac OS X automatically applies.

NOTE   Mac OS X Server automatically sets the permissions for the Users share point to the permissions you need for home folders, so you don't need to adjust the permissions. For other share points, you may need to adjust the permissions.

Adding Further Share Points

The share points that Mac OS X creates automatically—Users, Groups, and Public—may be all you need for home folders and other sharing. But if you need more share points, you can create them easily by following these steps:

1. Open Server Admin.
2. In the Servers pane on the left, click your server.
3. Click the File Sharing button on the toolbar to display the File Sharing pane.
4. If the Volumes button isn't already selected, click it to display the list of volumes.
5. Choose whether to share the whole volume or just a folder on it:
   - **Share an entire volume**   Click the volume to select it.
   - **Share a folder on the volume**   Click the volume to select it, and then click the Browse button to display the column browser panes (see Figure 7-14). If you want to create a new folder, click the folder in which to create it, click the New Folder button, type the name in the dialog box that appears, and then click the Create button. Otherwise, click an existing folder.
6. Click the Share button to share the volume or folder.

NOTE   When you create a share point like this, Server Admin sets it up for sharing with default options via AFP and SMB. If you don't need to share with SMB clients (such as Windows PCs), turn off the SMB sharing.

7. Click the Save button to make Server Admin apply the change.

If you switch back to the list of share points by clicking the Share Points button, you'll see that your new share point appears. You can then use the controls in the File Sharing pane to configure the share point, using the techniques described for the Share Points pane earlier in this chapter.

You can also change the permissions for the share point like this:

1. In the File Sharing pane in Server Admin, click the share point you want to change. (If the Volumes button is selected, click the Share Points button to display the share points.)
2. In the lower pane, click the Permissions tab to display the Permissions pane (shown in Figure 7-15 with the Users & Groups window displayed).

Figure 7-14.   Use the column browser panes to select the folder you want to share, and then click the Share button.

 NOTE   The root account is the all-powerful system account. The wheel group is an administrative group created automatically by Mac OS X that has lower privileges than the root account but more than user accounts.

3. To add a user or group to the list:

    a. Click the + button to display the Users & Groups window.

    b. Click the Users button or the Groups button, as needed.

    c. Drag the user, group, or multiple items to the ACL list.

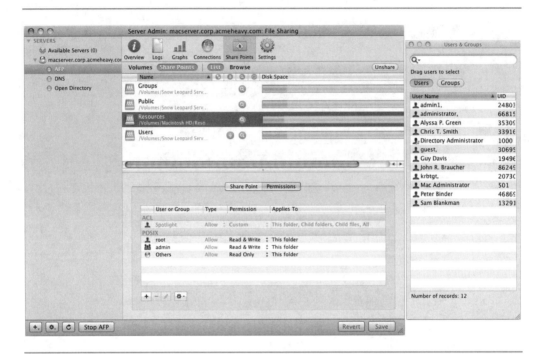

Figure 7-15.   Use the Permissions pane to set permissions for a share point.

    d. In the Type pop-up menu, choose Allow or Deny, as appropriate.

    e. In the Permission pop-up menu, choose the permission level: Full Control, Read & Write, Read, Write, or Custom. If you choose Custom, the dialog box shown in Figure 7-16 opens. Choose the exact permissions you want to apply, and then click the OK button.

4. To remove a user or group from the list, click the entry and then click the – button.

5. To change an existing permission, click it and then choose a different item in the Type pop-up menu or the Permission pop-up menu.

6. When you have finished changing the permissions, click the Save button to apply the changes.

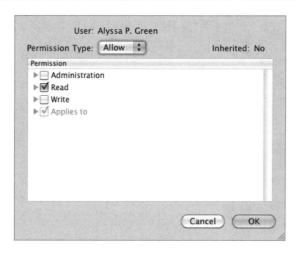

Figure 7-16.   You may sometimes need to set up custom permissions for a user or group.

Assigning a Home Folder to a User Account

After you've set up a share point using Server Admin (as described earlier in this chapter), you use Workgroup Manager to assign a home folder to a user account. Here's what to do:

1. Open Workgroup Manager. For example, click the Workgroup Manager icon in the Dock.

2. Click the Cancel button to suppress the Workgroup Manager Connect dialog box.

3. Press ⌘-D or choose Server | View Directories to connect to the first available directory. If this isn't Active Directory, click the globe icon at the left end of the authentication bar and choose Active Directory from the pop-up menu.

4. Click the lock icon at the right end of the authentication bar to open the Authenticate To Directory dialog box, type your administrator name and password, and then click the Authenticate button.

5. In the left pane, click the user you want to affect.

6. Click the Home tab to display the Home pane (shown in Figure 7-17 with the creation of a Home folder underway).

7. In the list box, click the share point on which you want to create the home folder.

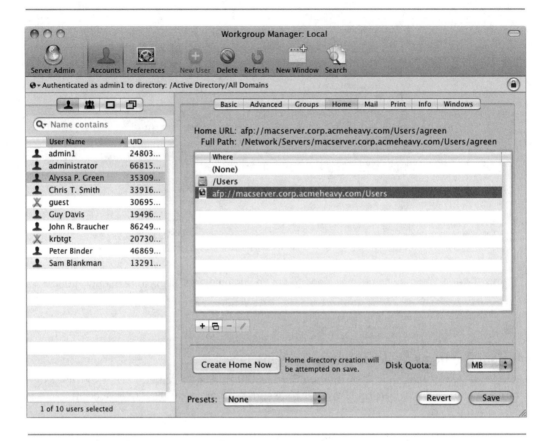

Figure 7-17.   Use the Home pane in Workgroup Manager to assign a home folder to a user account.

8. Click the Create Home Now button. Workgroup Manager displays the message "Home directory creation will be attempted on save" next to the Create Home Now button (as you can see in the figure).

9. If you want to limit the amount of space the user's home folder can devour on the share point, type the appropriate number in the Disk Quota text box and choose GB in the pop-up menu. (You can also set a quota in MB, but that's not enough space for most people these days.)

10. Click the Save button to save your changes. Workgroup Manager now creates the home folder.

Connecting Macs to Network Folders

Home folders are great for keeping a user's files secure and private, but your network's Mac users will certainly want to share some files with each other. Equally certainly, you won't want them to share the files via e-mail—so you'll need to set up network folders for the users.

Setting Up a Network Folder on Windows Server

If you've already set up a shared folder on the network, you're good to connect the Mac users to it. If not, use the Provision A Shared Folder Wizard to set up the folder for sharing and give it the permissions it will need. For example, if you want all users to be able to create and change files in the folder, select the Administrators Have Full Control; All Other Users And Groups Have Only Read Access And Write Access option button on the SMB Permissions screen of the wizard.

Setting Up a Network Folder on Mac OS X Server

To set up a shared folder on Mac OS X server, you use much the same technique you used for setting up network home folders for Mac users earlier in this chapter. See the section "Hosting Network Home Folders on Mac OS X with a Magic Triangle" for details.

You can set a quota by displaying the Home pane, selecting the share point, entering the quota in the Disk Quota text box, and choosing GB or MB (as appropriate) in the pop-up menu.

Connecting Mac Users to Network Folders

Once the folder is ready for use, connect the Mac users to it like this:

1. On a Mac, open Workgroup Manager. For example, click the Workgroup Manager icon in the dock.

2. Click the Cancel button to suppress the Workgroup Manager Connect dialog box.

3. Press ⌘-D or choose Server | View Directories to connect to the first available directory. If this isn't Active Directory, click the globe icon at the left end of the authentication bar and choose Active Directory from the pop-up menu.

4. Click the lock icon at the right end of the authentication bar to open the Authenticate To Directory dialog box, type your administrator name and password, and then click the Authenticate button.

5. In the left pane, select the group or computer list you want to affect. (You can also do this for a user or a Mac, but normally you'll do better to apply the policy at the group or computer list level.)

6. Click the Preferences button to display the Preferences pane.

7. Click the Login button to display the Login pane.

8. In the tab bar, click the Items tab to display the Items pane (shown in Figure 7-18 with a network folder added).

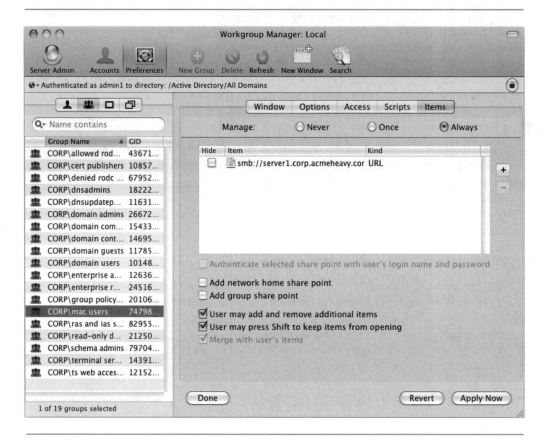

Figure 7-18. Use the Items pane in Login preferences to set up a network folder to mount automatically on login.

9. In the Manage bar, select the Always option button.

10. Click the Add (+) button to the right of the list box to open the dialog box for adding a folder.

11. Select the folder and then click the Add button. The dialog box closes, and the folder name appears in the list box.

12. Click the Apply Now button to apply the change.

CHAPTER 8 | Setting Up Printing on Macs

Unless you've managed to hypnotize or blackmail your network's users into keeping all their documents as bits and bytes, you'll have to put up with them printing out their documents on bits of paper as well. That means diving into the eternal stream of woe that consists of providing printers, feeding them paper, keeping them serviceable, managing print queues, and dealing with printer jams—and being prepared to do so before you've had your first cup of coffee.

If you're reading this chapter, you clearly know all this, but you've still decided to share your Windows network's printers with your Macs. This chapter shows you how to proceed in this generous and benevolent endeavor, starting with the basics—the different ways that Macs can print, and how print jobs get from point Apple to point Output.

NOTE This chapter assumes that you have already set up your Windows servers to provide file services and print services for your Windows clients and that you now need to extend those services to your Macs as well.

Understanding Your Options for Printing from Macs

Like most modern operating systems, Mac OS X enables you to set up printing in a variety of ways. The following list outlines the most common ways:

- **USB printer connected directly to the Mac** The simplest solution for printing is a printer connected directly to the Mac via USB. This is the arrangement you'll normally use on a standalone Mac, such as a Mac used at home. But a USB-connected printer can be a good arrangement in a company or organization for any user who needs exclusive use of a printer—for example, for anyone printing documents so sensitive that anyone unauthorized who sees them must die. The disadvantage—and I can see you've gotten here ahead of me—is that the Mac manages the printer, which removes all the benefits that network management can offer.

NOTE You can also connect an Ethernet printer directly to a Mac's Ethernet port—assuming that the Mac isn't already using the Ethernet port for networking.

- **Ethernet printer connected directly to the network** You can connect an Ethernet printer directly to the network, and then connect the Macs to the printer without using a network print queue. This is the ugliest solution and in most cases a poor choice, because the printer is neither assigned to a single user who can manage it nor embraced in the iron grip of your management—but it's occasionally useful. For example, if you have a small group of Mac users who share an office or area, you could give them their own network printer and let them deal with the jams and the recalcitrant cartridges.

■ **SMB print queues** Windows typically uses SMB to share printers, so in most cases the easiest way to get your Macs printing on Windows printers is to connect them to the existing SMB queues. Generally speaking, this approach works well, although you may have to cross a bridge or two on the way to your destination.

 NOTE This chapter concentrates on printing to SMB print queues because this is the technology you're most likely to need unless you use a vendor-specific printing solution.

■ **Internet Printing Protocol (IPP)** Like Windows boxes, Macs can reach out across the network to a printer that's running IPP, poke it to find out whether it's awake and in a friendly mood, and (if so) send print jobs to it. IPP is useful when you need to print across the Internet or across WAN links. We'll look at connecting Macs to IPP print queues briefly in this chapter—but basically, unless you're sharing printers using IPP for your network's Windows PCs, you shouldn't share printers with IPP just for your Macs.

■ **LPD print queues** You can set up the LPD service on your Windows server so that Macs or UNIX boxes can use the Line Printer Remote (LPR) service to print to the printers. This can be an effective solution, but only if you've got a good reason for not using SMB. This chapter briefly covers adding LPD to your server and connecting Macs to LPD print queues.

■ **Vendor-specific printing solutions** Heavy-duty printer manufacturers make their own heavy-duty printing solutions. If you've implemented one of these printing solutions, you'll probably want to use it to manage your print devices, queues, and jobs.

Understanding How Printing Works for Networked Macs

Mac OS X uses the Common UNIX Printing Solution (CUPS) to organize printing. CUPS includes filters and drivers that enable you to print from a Mac to a wide variety of printers.

Figure 8-1 illustrates the main steps in the process of printing from a Mac to an SMB printer on Active Directory using CUPS. The following sections explain what happens at the different stages.

The Role of the PDF in Mac Printing

If you've worked on Macs, you probably know that Mac OS X uses the Portable Document Format (PDF) as its native metafile format, the format in which it stores graphics internally. And if you've printed from Mac OS X, you know that the Print dialog box offers a PDF button with a pop-up menu that lets you create a PDF file from the document, fax it as a PDF, mail it as a PDF, and so on.

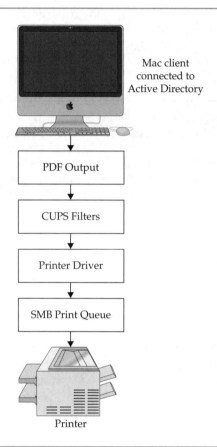

Mac client
connected to
Active Directory

PDF Output

CUPS Filters

Printer Driver

SMB Print Queue

Printer

Figure 8-1.   How CUPS prints from a Mac to an SMB printer on Active Directory.

So it probably won't surprise you to learn that Mac OS X uses PDF technology for as much of the print process as possible. Even when you go ahead and click the Print button rather than digging into the PDF pop-up menu, the Mac creates a print job consisting basically of a PDF and shovels it along toward the printer.

What happens next depends on the printer you're using. If the printer supports direct PDF printing, it simply interprets the PDF data and starts joyfully spraying toner on papyrus. If not, the printer driver needs to turn the PDF into a format the printer can use. For example, if the printer can handle the PostScript page-description language, the printer driver translates the PDF into PostScript and passes the PostScript along to the printer, which rumbles into action.

Most Mac-oriented printers talk either native PDF or PostScript, so printing to a printer connected directly to your Mac is usually pretty straightforward once you've got the right printer driver installed and selected.

Windows handles print jobs differently, so when you print from a Mac to a Windows-based printer, some translation may be needed. If the Windows-based printer is a PostScript printer, all is well, and the print server can just pass the print job on its merry way to the printer. For a non-PostScript printer, the print job will need to be converted to the format the printer needs before being sent along to the printer.

What PostScript Printer Description Files Do and Where You Get Them

To find out which format the printer requires, Mac OS X consults the PostScript Printer Description (PPD) file for the printer. Each printer you can use on Mac OS X has a PPD that describes the printer and its capabilities—monochrome, color, collation, duplexing, different trays, and so on.

When you go to print in Mac OS X, the application you're using reads the printer's PPD so that it can display the right controls in the Print dialog box. For example, the Two-Sided check box appears in the Print dialog box only if the printer offers duplexing.

Mac OS X stores the PPD files in the /Library/Printers/PPDs/ folder. Mac OS X comes with a wide range of PPDs that are included in a default installation (you can remove them if you choose), and Software Update automatically checks for updated PPDs from major manufacturers along with other updates. You can also add new PPDs by downloading them from the printer manufacturer's website or by installing them from the disc included with a new printer you buy.

 NOTE   The PPD files come from the printer manufacturers, although Apple packages and distributes many PPDs to make Mac users' lives easier. The printer manufacturers also create the printer drivers that convert the CUPS output into the exact format a specific printer needs.

How CUPS Uses Filters to Convert Print Jobs

CUPS uses software called *filters* to convert the print job from its original format to the format specified in the PPD.

The filters in CUPS can change a PDF in two main ways:

- **PDF to Raster to Printer-Specific Format**   In this chain, the CUPS filter first converts the PDF to a CUPS-specific raster format. The final filter, which is called the *printer driver* and which comes from the printer manufacturer, converts the raster format to the exact format that the printer requires.

 NOTE   A raster image is a data structure that uses a rectangular grid of pixels to create an image for a particular size and shape of paper—for example, detailing where every pixel on a printable image should be. By contrast, PostScript is a programming language used as a page description language for printing.

- **PDF to PostScript to Printer-Specific Format**   In this chain, the filter first converts the PDF to a PostScript file. The printer driver then converts the PostScript file to the specific format that the printer requires.

Mac OS X stores the printer drivers in the /Library/Printers/ folder, which contains a separate folder for each printer manufacturer—Brother, Canon, EPSON (in caps like that; don't ask, because I can't tell you why), hp (in lowercase; don't ask), Lexmark, Samsung, and so on. These folders also contain utilities for managing printing, everything from the superbly named Brother Status Monitor to the over-solicitous HP Printer Utility.

NOTE   As well as the PPDs, drivers, and utilities supplied by printer manufacturers, Mac OS X includes Gutenprint, a wide-ranging package of free printer drivers that work with CUPS and LPR. If the printer manufacturer doesn't provide a Mac OS X PPD and driver for your printer, you may be able to use a PPD and driver from Gutenprint instead (http://gutenprint.sourceforge.net/). Gutenprint was originally called Gimp-Print, and you'll still see it referred to that way online sometimes.

After the CUPS filter and printer driver have produced a print job in the format the printer needs, CUPS sends the print job to the printer backend specified by the PPD. For example, when you're printing to a printer shared with SMB, the printer backend is a specific SMB share on the server. When the print job lands in the printer backend, the Windows print service takes over and sends the print job along to the printer.

NOTE   Some printer manufacturers also supply custom backends for printing, so that when you print, the job is handled by the custom backend rather than by the SMB print queue.

How Windows Controls Access to the Print Queues

The connection to the print queue can be authenticated either using Kerberos or using NT LAN Manager (NTLM). You should use Kerberos if at all possible because it leverages the single sign-on (SSO) that your Macs should be using for Active Directory at this point. By contrast, if you use NTLM, a user needs to enter their username and password when connecting to the printer for the first time (after that, the user can store the credentials).

We'll look at how to set up the authentication at the end of this chapter.

Putting Printing Essentials in Place

Before you go ahead and set up the printers on your Macs, make sure the printers are where you need them. If you're going to use the LPD service or IPP to make printers available to the Macs, set the service up on your server if it's not already running it. You may also need to install extra printer drivers on your Macs ahead of time.

Deploying Printers for Mac Users

If you've already got your printers in place on your Windows network, you may just want to have the Macs tap into them. If you're going to deploy extra printers specifically for Mac users (for example, to cover high-end color printing or other needs the Mac users have), work out where the printers go, install them in those locations, and then add the printers to Active Directory as usual.

Setting Up Print And Document Services as Needed

If you've already set up Print And Document Services for your network's Windows users, and you've decided to connect your Macs to your SMB print queues, you don't need to perform any further setup.

If you've decided to add either LPD service or Internet Printing service to your server's printing repertoire, run the Add Roles Wizard. On the Select Roles Services screen (see Figure 8-2), select the LPD Service check box or the Internet Printing check box, as needed.

If you select the Internet Printing check box, the wizard may display the Add Role Services dialog box (see Figure 8-3), prompting you to add further role services and features needed for Internet printing. Click the Add Required Role Services button if you want to proceed.

Follow through the rest of the installation procedure, and then restart Windows if you receive a prompt to do so.

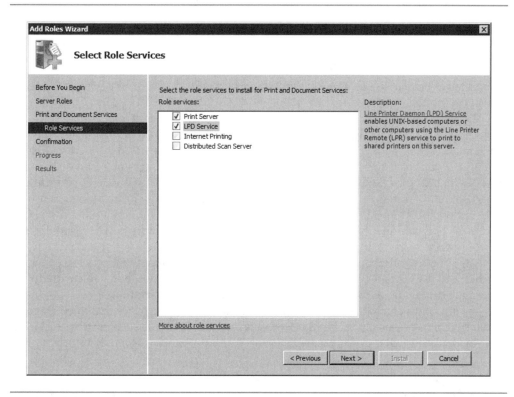

Figure 8-2.   Add the LPD service to Print And Document Services to enable Macs to print to Active Directory printers.

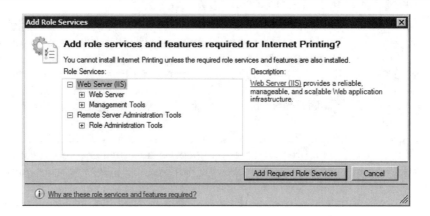

Figure 8-3.   When you add Internet Printing to your server, you also have to add Web Server and Remote Server Administration Tools services and features if your server is not already running them.

Getting the Printer Drivers onto the Macs

For a Mac to be able to use a particular printer, you must install that printer's PPD and driver on the Mac.

The easiest way to get most of the necessary PPDs and drivers onto a Mac is by including them in the image you install. As I mentioned earlier, a default install of Mac OS X includes a large helping of printer drivers that cover many widely used models of printers. If you're customizing your Mac OS X installs by creating your own disk image, you can include exactly the drivers you need—but you'll need to update the disk image if you get new printers or drivers. For example, if your company or organization uses only Canon and HP printers, you could omit the drivers from other manufacturers. Or, if you use only a limited selection of printers, you can slim down Mac OS X's footprint on your Macs by including only the drivers for the actual models you use.

After you've rolled out your Macs, the best way to install new drivers is to push them out to the Macs by using Apple Remote Desktop. This method enables you to install the drivers on as many Macs as you have in a single operation.

The alternative is to install the drivers manually on those Macs that need them, either by going physically to the Macs or by using remote access such as Screen Sharing. This method is much more labor intensive, so you'll probably want to do it only for the occasional Mac that has special needs.

NOTE   Another way to install drivers is to have users install them. The disadvantage is that you'll need to give each user administrator-level privileges for the Mac on which you want them to install the drivers.

Setting Up the Printers on Your Macs

You can set up the printers on your Macs either automatically or manually. Automatic setup usually saves both time and effort, so you'll probably want to use it for most of your printers, reserving manual setup for the occasional printer (or user) that requires (or rewards) special attention.

Adding Printers by Using Policy

Given that you're already managing your Macs through Active Directory, usually the easiest way to add printers to them is by using policy. In this way, you can set the printers up automatically for the users.

You create a group of users or a group of computers that need the same printers, and then assign the printers to them. For example, you could assign a regular set of printers to a group of users, such as Mac Users, and then create a Mac Power Users group or Graphic Artists group and give that group access to the high-end printers.

Adding Printers by Using Policy

To add printers by using policy, follow these steps:

1. Open Workgroup Manager. For example, click the Workgroup Manager icon on the Dock.

2. Click the Cancel button to close the Workgroup Manager Connect dialog box.

3. Press ⌘-D or choose Server | View Directories to open a Workgroup Manager window showing the /Active Directory/All Domains directory.

4. If the authentication bar shows that you're not authenticated, authenticate yourself:

    a. Click the lock icon at the right end of the authentication bar to display the Authenticate To Directory dialog box.

    b. Type your administrator's name in the User Name text box and the corresponding password in the Password text box.

    c. If you want to authenticate automatically next time, select the Remember This Password In My Keychain check box.

    d. Click the Authenticate button.

5. In the left pane, select the item you want to affect. For example, click the Groups tab button and then click the group of users for whom you want to add printers.

NOTE   Normally, you'll want to set printing first for a group of computers or a group of users because this enables you to leverage the power of central control. But you can also set up printers for an individual user or a single computer when you need to. For example, after you have used groups to paint the broad strokes of your printing policy, you can pick up your detail brush and set printers for individual users and computers.

6. Click the Preferences button on the toolbar to display the Preferences pane.

7. Click the Printing icon to display the Printing panes with the Printers pane at the front (shown in Figure 8-4 with settings chosen).

8. In the Manage bar at the top, select the Always option button to turn on everlasting management for printers. This setting means that the user will not be able to change printers and print settings apart from the changes you specifically permit.

9. In the lower tab bar, make sure the Printer List tab is selected so that the Printer List pane is displayed rather than the Access pane.

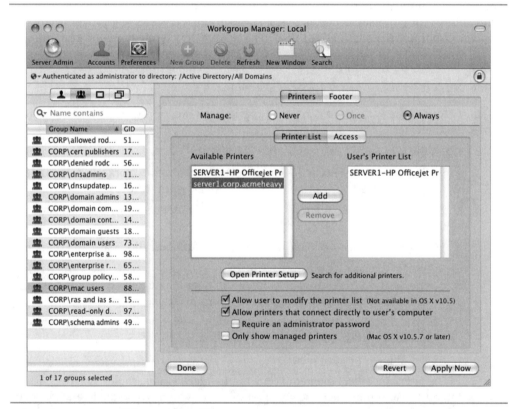

Figure 8-4.   In the Printers pane, set up the printers you want the user group, computer group, or individual user or Mac to use.

10. In the Available Printers list box, select the printer or printers you want to assign to the user, group, or Mac. If the printer you want doesn't appear, follow these steps to add it:

    a. Click the Open Printer Setup button to launch System Preferences and display the Print & Fax pane.

    b. Click the Add (+) button below the Printers list box on the left to display the Add Printer dialog box (shown in Figure 8-5 with settings chosen).

    c. Make sure the Default button is selected in the toolbar so that the dialog box shows the SMB printers available in Active Directory.

NOTE To add an IPP printer or LPR printer, follow the instructions in the section "Connecting a Mac to an LPR or IPP Network Printer Manually," later in this chapter.

    d. In the Printer Name list, click the printer you want. Mac OS X looks up the printer in Active Directory and displays the Location information (assuming Active Directory contains some—this is an optional field) and the model in the Print Using pop-up menu.

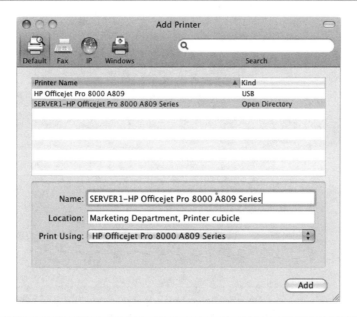

Figure 8-5. Use the Add Printer dialog box to add a network printer to Print & Fax preferences so that you can assign it to a user, group, or Mac in Workgroup Manager.

NOTE You'll see the Kind column in the Add Printer dialog box shows the printer to be of the Open Directory kind rather than the Active Directory kind. This is fine.

    e. Click the Add button to close the Add Printer dialog box. If the printer offers different installable options, Mac OS X displays the Installable Options dialog box (see Figure 8-6).

    f. Select the check box for each option you want to install, and then click the Continue button.

    g. Mac OS X adds the printer to the list in the left pane of Print & Fax preferences (see Figure 8-7).

    h. Add other printers, as needed, and then quit System Preferences. For example, press ⌘-Q.

  11. In Workgroup Manager, click the Add button to add the printer or printers to the User's Printer List box.

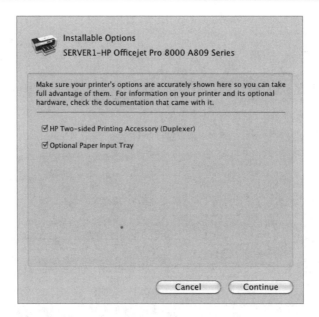

Figure 8-6. If the Installable Options dialog box appears, select the check box for each option you want to make available—for example, two-sided printing.

Figure 8-7.   After adding the printer to Print & Fax preferences, you can apply it to a user, group, or Mac in Workgroup Manager.

12. At the bottom of the Printer List pane, choose options for what the user, group, or Mac can do to your precious printers:

   ■ **Allow User To Modify The Printer List**   Select this check box if you want the user to be able to change the list of printers available to them in Print & Fax preferences. If you're trying to get the user to print on the printers you provide (which isn't monstrously unreasonable), clear this check box.

   ■ **Allow Printers That Connect Directly To User's Computer**   Select this check box if you want the user to be able to connect a printer directly to their Mac and set it up—so usually you'll want to clear this check box. If you do select it, you can select the Require An Administrative Password check box to restrict this privilege to users who have an administrative password or have gained knowledge of one via social engineering.

   ■ **Only Show Managed Printers**   Select this check box if you want to restrict the user, group, or Mac to seeing only managed printers on the network (for example, ones shared through Active Directory) rather than printers that individual users have set up with sharing. If you're keeping a tight rein on your network, select this check box.

13. Click the Access tab in the lower tab bar to display the Access pane (shown in Figure 8-8 with settings chosen).

14. In the User's Printer List box, click the printer you want to make the user's default printer and then click the Make Default button. Workgroup Manager displays a discreet star to its left.

15. If you want to limit a printer's use to users who can provide an administrator's password, click the printer in the User's Printer List box and then select the Require An Administrator Password check box. Workgroup Manager displays Required in the Authentication column for the printer.

16. Click the Apply Now button to apply the changes you've made to the user, group, or Mac.

17. Click the Done button to return to the Preferences pane.

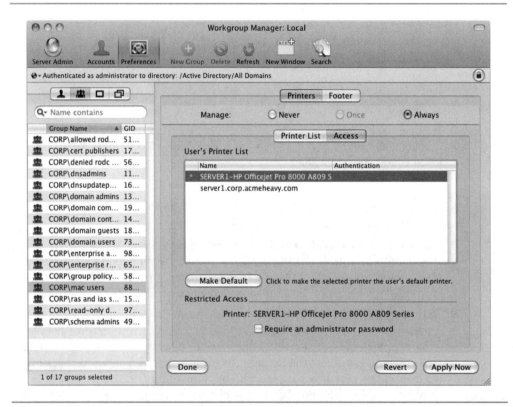

Figure 8-8.   Set the user's default printer in the Access pane. You can also lock down a printer with an administrator password if you're feeling thrifty.

Testing the Printers You've Added

Now check that Mac OS X automatically adds the printer or printers when a managed user or computer logs in. Follow these steps:

1. Log in to a Mac under a user account that's in the managed group, or log in using a Mac that's in the managed group, depending on how you applied the printing policy.

2. Open System Preferences. For example, click the System Preferences icon on the Dock or choose Apple | System Preferences.

Making Sure Users Understand About Restricted Printers

When you apply restrictions to a printer, make sure the affected users know about them. Otherwise, you're setting up support calls for your future entertainment.

When you've applied the Require An Administrator Password restriction to a printer, a discreet little padlock appears to the left of the printer's name in the Printer pop-up menu in the Print dialog box, as shown here.

But if users miss this sign, as they can easily do, the dialog box that prompts them to type an administrator's name and password to allow the application from which they're printing to make changes comes entirely out of left field. The next illustration shows this dialog box for printing from TextEdit (or trying to).

The user can click the disclosure triangle to see the offending component, system .printingmanager, as shown next. But even so, if you haven't conditioned them to expect this, they're likely to pick up the phone and ask you what's going on.

> **Type an administrator's name and password to allow TextEdit to make changes.**
>
> Name: [   ]
>
> Password: [   ]
>
> ▼ Details
>
> Right: system.printingmanager
>
> Application: ☑ TextEdit   ↕
>
> (?)   (Cancel) (OK)

3. Click the Print & Fax icon in the Hardware section to display the Print & Fax pane.

4. Make sure that the printer appears in the Printers list on the left. Also check that any restrictions you applied are in force. For example, if you cleared the Allow User To Modify The Printer List check box, make sure that the Add (+) button and Remove (–) button below the printers list are unavailable.

5. If all is well, quit System Preferences. For example, press ⌘-Q.

Adding Printers to Your Macs Manually

If necessary, you can add printers to your Macs manually, or you can allow any user who has local administrator rights on their Mac to add a printer to it.

Connecting a Mac to an SMB Network Printer Manually

To connect a Mac to a network printer manually, follow these steps:

1. Choose Apple | System Preferences to open the System Preferences window.

2. In the Hardware category, click the Print & Fax icon to display the Print & Fax preferences pane (see Figure 8-9).

3. Click the Add (+) button below the printers pane on the left to display the Add Printer dialog box.

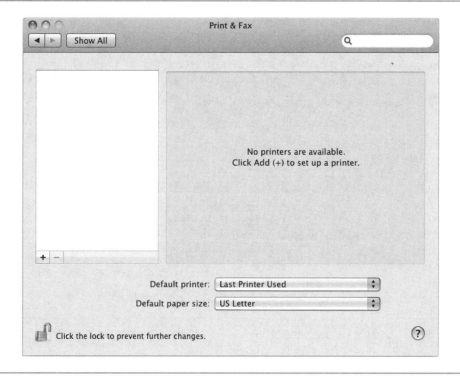

Figure 8-9.   Click the Add (+) button in the Print & Fax preferences pane to start adding a network printer to a Mac.

4. If the Default pane (see Figure 8-10) isn't already displayed, click the Default button on the toolbar to display it. The Default pane shows all the printers that Active Directory is advertising on the network.

5. In the Printer Name list box, select the printer you want to add.

6. If you want, change the default name that appears in the Name text box.

7. Also if you want, edit the location in the Location text box. If you've set a clear description of the location on the shared printer, you shouldn't need to change it.

8. In the Print Using pop-up menu, make sure that Mac OS X has selected the right type of printer. If not, open the menu and choose it yourself.

9. Click the Add button. Mac OS X installs the software needed for the printer and then displays the printer in the Print & Fax pane in System Preferences.

10. Add any other printers you need to add now.

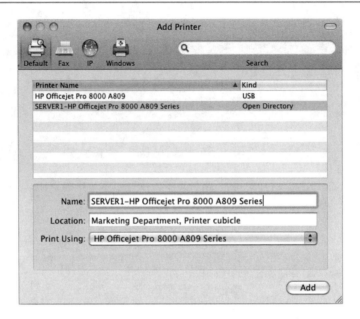

Figure 8-10.   Use the Default pane of the Add Printer dialog box to add to your Mac to a printer that Active Directory is advertising on the network.

11.   In the Default Printer pop-up menu (see Figure 8-11), select the printer you want to use as the default. You can select the Last Printer Used item to use whichever printer you last printed on.

12.   In the Default Paper Size pop-up menu, choose the default paper size to use for printing—for example, US Letter or US Legal.

13.   Quit System Preferences. For example, press ⌘-Q or choose System Preferences | Quit System Preferences.

Connecting a Mac to an LPR or IPP Network Printer Manually

If you need to connect a Mac to a network printer on an LPR print queue or an IPP print queue rather than an SMB print queue, follow these steps:

1.   Choose Apple | System Preferences to open the System Preferences window.

2.   In the Hardware category, click the Print & Fax icon to display the Print & Fax preferences.

3.   Click the Add (+) button below the printers pane on the left to display the Add Printer dialog box.

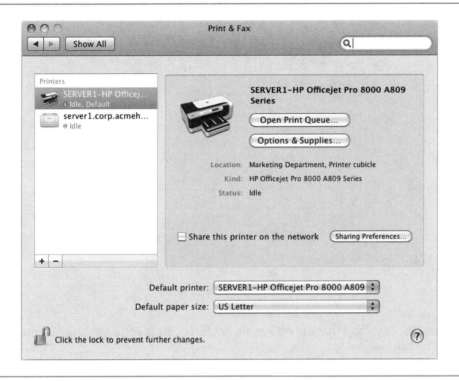

Figure 8-11. After adding one or more printers, choose the user's default printer. You can also set the default paper size.

4. Click the IP button in the toolbar to display the IP pane (shown in Figure 8-12 with settings chosen).

5. In the Protocol pop-up menu, select "Internet Printing Protocol – IPP" for an IPP printer or "Line Printer Daemon – LPD" for an LPR printer.

6. Enter the print server's address in the Address box. You can either open the pop-up menu and choose the address from the list or (if it doesn't appear) type the address into the text box.

7. Mac OS X checks that the address is valid and complete. If so, it displays "valid and complete address" below the Address box to confirm that it has overcome its doubts of you.

8. If you want to use a specific queue on the printer, enter it in the Queue box. Again, you can either pick the queue from the pop-up menu or type it in yourself. If you just want to use the default queue, leave the Queue box blank.

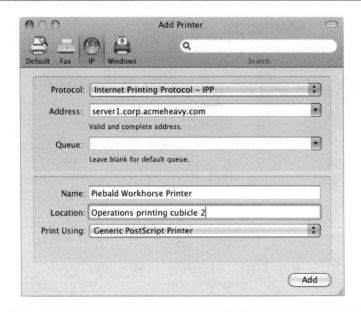

Figure 8-12. Use the IP pane of the Add Printer dialog box to add either an LPR printer or an IPP printer to a Mac.

 TIP Some models of printers require specific queue names, so if you can't print with the settings you've chosen, find out whether the printer manufacturer has imposed this restriction.

9. Edit the printer's name in the Name text box if you want. This is the name you (or the user) will see for the printer, so make it descriptive.

10. In the Location text box, edit the location for the printer as needed. This information is to help the user understand where the printer is.

11. Check Mac OS X's selection in the Print Using pop-up menu. Usually, Generic PostScript Printer works fine here, but you may sometimes need to open the pop-up menu, choose Select Printer Software, and pick the right driver as described earlier in this chapter.

12. Click the Add button to add the printer.

13. Quit System Preferences. For example, press ⌘-Q.

Managing Print Jobs on Your Printers

Normally, once a user has sent a print job to the print queue, the job is beyond the user's recall. You or another administrator can reach into the print queue and give the job a Mickey Finn or a pair of concrete boots, but the user can't touch it.

If you want your users to be able to pause (and resume) and delete print jobs as needed, you need to make the users part of the lpadmin group. The easiest way to do so is to use the dseditgroup command to nest the Active Directory user group in the lpadmin group. Follow these steps:

1. Log in to a Mac that you have bound to Active Directory.

2. Open a Terminal window. For example, click the desktop, choose Go | Utilities, and then double-click the Terminal icon in the Utilities window.

3. Type the **dseditgroup** command with the **–o** parameter, and specify **edit** as the operation you want to perform:

    ```
    dseditgroup -o edit
    ```

4. Add the **–n** parameter and specify the **/Local/Default** directory node as the node that contains the group record, as shown in boldface here:

    ```
    dseditgroup -o edit -n /Local/Default
    ```

5. Add the **–u** parameter and the short name of the user account you've logged on to the Mac with. This example uses the name slonghouse. Follow this with the **–p** parameter, which tells dseditgroup to prompt you for the user account's password so that you don't have to type it into the command:

    ```
    dseditgroup -o edit -n /Local/Default -u slonghouse -p
    ```

6. Add the **–a** parameter and specify the name of the Active Directory group you want to add to the lpadmin group. This example uses the Mac Users group, placing it in double quotation marks because the name contains a space:

    ```
    dseditgroup -o edit -n /Local/Default -u slonghouse -p -a "Mac
    Users"
    ```

7. Finally, add the **–t** parameter and specify **group** as the type of record you want to modify, following this with the group's name (**lpadmin**). You need to enter the following statement all as a single paragraph in Terminal, even if it wraps onto a second line:

    ```
    dseditgroup -o edit -n /Local/Default -u slonghouse -p -a "Mac
    Users" -t group lpadmin
    ```

8. Press RETURN to run the command.

9. When Terminal prompts you for your password, type it in and press RETURN.

10. Quit Terminal. For example, press ⌘-Q.

NOTE You can also add an individual user to the lpadmin group in the same way. Just use the user account's short name after the –a parameter (for example, type **–a csmith**).

Once you've done this, a user will be able to go into the print queue for the printer and delete (or put on hold) their vital print job when they find that a colleague is printing a dozen copies of *War and Peace* on the printer. Mac OS X normally opens the print queue's utility when you print, but you can also open it by selecting the printer in the Print & Fax pane in System Preferences and clicking the Open Print Queue button.

With the print queue opens (see Figure 8-13), you can use the buttons on the toolbar to delete jobs, hold or resume them, and check their information. You can also pause and resume the printer, check its supply levels, or open the Printer Setup utility.

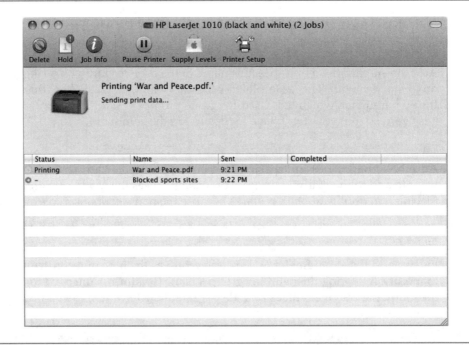

Figure 8-13. If you allow users to manage print jobs, they can open the print queue and lay waste to its contents.

Giving Your Printer Users Single Sign-On for Printers

At this point, you've set your Mac users up to print on the Windows printers, but you haven't given them single sign-on (SSO) for the Windows print queues. Windows print queues usually require authentication either through Kerberos and SSO or through the older NT LAN Manager (NTLM) authentication protocol.

Normally, you'll set up your Active Directory print queues to require Kerberos authentication. In this case, if the user is logged in to Active Directory and so holds a Kerberos ticket (by virtue of having logged in), the ticket gives them passage to use the printer without having to provide authentication separately—they're covered by their Active Directory login.

If you don't set up SSO, when the user tries to print, Mac OS X displays NTLM's prompt for authentication, as shown here.

Unless you've permitted guests to print (which you probably haven't), the user must select the Registered User option button (which will normally be selected by default) and type their password in the Password text box. The user can select the Remember This Password In My Keychain check box to store the password in their keychain. Storing the password will enable them to print without the authentication prompt reappearing for the time being, but if the user changes their Active Directory password, they will need to provide the password afresh to NTLM (and then store it again in the keychain until the next change, and so on).

This is tolerable, but you'll usually want to provide SSO for your Mac users. Here's how to set it up and check that it's working.

1. Log on to the Mac under that user's account.

2. Make sure that the user is set up as an administrator on the Mac. Follow these steps:

   a. Choose Apple | System Preferences to open the System Preferences window.

   b. Choose View | Accounts to display the Accounts pane.

c. See whether "Admin" appears under the user's name in the My Account area of the left pane. If so, go on to step 3; if not, follow through the rest of this sublist.

d. Click the lock icon, and then authenticate yourself in the dialog box that Mac OS X displays to unlock the controls.

e. Click the user's account in the left pane if it's not already selected.

f. Select the Allow User To Administer This Computer check box. Mac OS X double-checks to make sure you know what you're doing, as shown here.

NOTE The Are You Sure You Want To Allow *User* To Administer This Computer? dialog box claims that the user account has parental controls turned on. Don't let this worry you—the restrictions on the account in fact come from the policy you've applied using Workgroup Manager, not from Parental Controls.

g. Click the Yes button.

h. Log the user out (for example, press ⌘-OPTION-SHIFT-Q) and then back in again.

i. Choose Apple | System Preferences to open the System Preferences window.

j. Choose View | Accounts to display the Accounts pane. Verify that "Admin" appears under the user's name in the My Account area of the left pane.

3. Open Terminal. Click the Finder icon on the Dock, choose Go | Utilities, and then double-click the Terminal icon in the Utilities window.

4. Type the lpstat –v command and press RETURN to return the names that CUPS is using for each of the printers currently set up on the Mac. You'll see a list of printers. The following example shows two printers, known as SERVER1_HP_Officejet_Pro_8000_A809 and HP_LaserJet_1010.

```
lpstat -v
device for SERVER1_HP_Officejet_Pro_8000_A809: smb://server1.
corp.acmeheavy.com/HP OfficeJet Pro 8000
device for HP_LaserJet_1010: smb://server1.corp.acmeheavy.com/HP
LaserJet 1010
```

5. Type the **sudo** command followed by the **cupsctl** command with the **User** parameter, specifying the name of the user you're logged on as. This example uses the username pwright:

```
sudo cupsctl User=pwright
```

6. Press RETURN, and then type the user's password when the sudo command prompts you for it.

7. Type the **sudo** command again, this time followed by the **lpadmin** command, the **–p** parameter and the printer name that lpstat gave you, and the **–o** parameter with the value **auth-info-required-none** (all on one line):

```
sudo lpadmin –p SERVER1_HP_Officejet_Pro_8000_A809 –o auth-info-
required-none
```

8. Press RETURN. If the command runs without comment, you got it right.

9. Quit Terminal. For example, press ⌘-Q.

Now open an application and make sure that you (aka the user) can print to the printer without it demanding authentication.

Checking That the User Has a Kerberos Ticket

For SSO to work, the user must hold a valid Kerberos ticket for the Active Directory domain. To check that the user has such a ticket, follow these steps:

1. Click the desktop, choose Go | Utilities, and then display the Keychain Access icon in the Utilities Folder. Keychain Access opens.

2. Choose Keychain Access | Ticket Viewer (or press ⌘-OPTION-K if you like keyboard shortcuts) to open the Ticket Viewer utility (shown here).

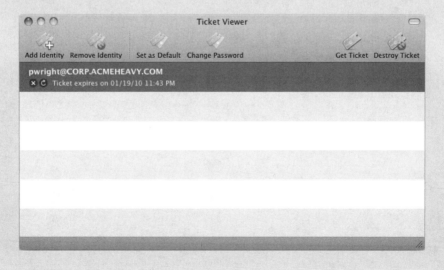

3. Verify that the Ticket Viewer window shows a ticket for the domain and that the ticket is still valid. If not, get a new ticket like this:

    a. Click the Get Ticket button on the toolbar. Ticket Viewer displays a dialog box demanding the user's password, as shown here.

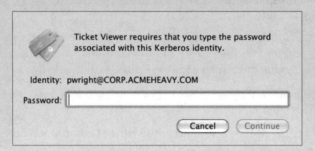

    b. Type the password in the Password text box and click the Continue button. Ticket Viewer requests a new Kerberos ticket and then displays it.

4. Quit Ticket Viewer. For example, press ⌘-Q.

5. Quit Keychain Access. For example, choose Keychain Access | Quit Keychain Access.

CHAPTER 9 | Installing and Updating Software

By this time, you've probably provided your network's Macs with Internet access, e-mail, and home folders and printer access, but you may have left them with no more applications than came with them. If that's Apple's default selection of software, including the iLife application suite, users will be fully equipped for e-mail and chat, browsing the Web, and consuming and creating multimedia content (from songs to movies and DVDs), but they'll be lacking applications to actually process words, crunch data, or create presentations encrusted with enough bling to dazzle a plague of management consultants.

In this case, you'll probably need to install at least some applications on your network's Macs. Ideally, you'll install most of the applications needed on your Macs before you deploy them, but you can also add applications and updates later as needed. Both before and after deployment, you can work either directly on the Macs or by using administration tools. You may also need to restrict the applications that your Mac users can run.

Whichever applications you choose and however you end up installing them, you'll almost certainly want to use Mac OS X's Software Update feature to keep the software on your network's Macs up to date with all the latest fixes, patches, and improvements—so we'll start there.

Keeping Your Macs' Software Up to Date

To keep Mac OS X and all Apple applications up to date on your network's Macs, you'll need to run Software Update. Software Update can automatically check for and download updates, and then shepherd the user through the process of installing them.

Understanding the Options for Getting Software Updates

The normal way for a Mac to get its software updates is by downloading them from Apple's servers and applying them to itself. This method works well for both standalone Macs (such as those used at home) and ones on networks. We'll look at this method first.

For standalone Macs, there's no sensible alternative to getting the updates from Apple, but for Macs on a network that includes a Mac OS X server, there is. You can set your Mac OS X server to provide updates to the Macs on the network. The Mac server itself must download the updates from Apple's servers as usual, but after that, the client Macs can grab them across the network, thus saving Internet bandwidth and time. We'll look at this method second.

Setting Up a Mac to Receive Software Updates the Regular Way

Unless you tweak its configuration, a Mac comes set to check automatically for software updates. To verify or change its settings, follow these steps:

1. Choose Apple | System Preferences to open the System Preferences window.

2. In the System section, click the Software Update icon to open the Software Update pane.

3. If the Scheduled Check tab isn't selected, click it now to bring the Scheduled Check pane to the front (see Figure 9-1).

4. If you want to check automatically for updates, select the Check For Updates check box and then choose either Weekly or Daily in the pop-up menu:

   - Daily updates keep your client Macs safest but put the greatest strain on your server or Internet connection, and the frequent prompts to apply updates may distract users.

   - Weekly updates are often the best balance between constant updating and waiting too long.

   - Monthly updates tend to leave the clients without the benefit of the latest fixes and updates for too long.

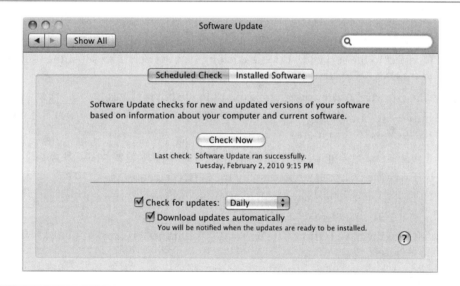

Figure 9-1.   Normally it's a good idea to set Software Update to check for updates either daily or weekly, and to download the available updates automatically.

5. If you select the Check For Updates check box, select the Download Updates Automatically check box if you want the client to download the update files automatically from the server.

NOTE Whether it's a good idea to download updates automatically depends on the speed of your Internet connection and the number of computers sharing it. For a fast broadband connection in a home setup, downloading updates automatically is usually great because the updates are ready to install the moment Software Update notifies you about them. The same goes if you have a Mac OS X server that's grabbing the updates so that it can pass them along to Macs on your network. But if you're looking after a fleet of Macs that download updates individually, you may prefer to clear the Download Updates Automatically check box to prevent the Macs from throttling your Internet connection by all trying to download updates at the same time

6. When you've made your choices, press ⌘-Q to quit System Preferences.

Setting Your Mac OS X Server to Provide Software Updates

If you have a Mac OS X server on your network (for example, in a magic triangle arrangement), you can set up the server to download software updates and then provide them to the other Macs on the network. You then set up the Macs to check your server for updates rather than the Apple servers.

To set up your server to provide software updates, follow these steps on either the server itself or the Mac you use to administer it:

1. Open Server Admin. For example, click the Server Admin icon on the Dock.

2. Connect to the server by double-clicking it in the Servers list. Authenticate yourself if necessary.

3. Click the disclosure triangle to expand the list of services.

4. If the Software Update service doesn't appear in the list of services, follow these steps to turn it on:

   a. Click the Settings button on the toolbar to display the Settings pane.

   b. Click the Services tab to display the Services pane.

   c. In the Select The Services To Configure On This Server list box, select the Software Update check box.

   d. Click the Save button. The Software Update service appears in the list of services.

5. In the list of services, click Software Update.

6. Click the Settings button on the toolbar to display the Settings pane (see Figure 9-2).

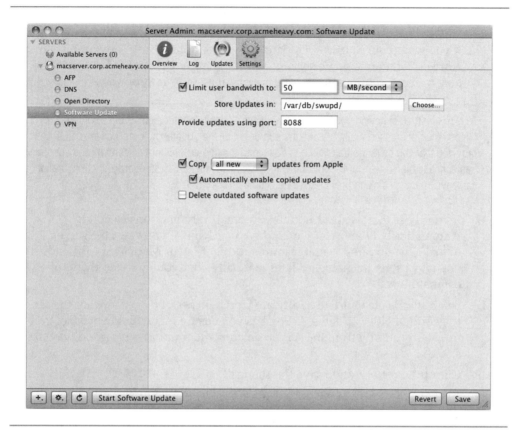

Figure 9-2.   In the Settings pane for the Software Update service, choose which updates to copy and whether to limit the user bandwidth.

7. If you want to limit the amount of bandwidth clients can consume, select the Limit User Bandwidth To check box, type the value in the text box, and then choose KB/second or MB/second in the pop-up menu.

8. In the Store Updates In text box, enter the folder in which to store the updates. The default folder (/var/db/swupd/) is fine unless your system volume is short of space—in which case, click the Choose button, use the Choose A Folder Where You Would Like To Store Software Updates dialog box to pick the folder, and then click the Choose button.

CAUTION   Software updates can take up many gigabytes on your server. Make sure the volume you choose has plenty of free space.

9. In the Provide Updates Using Port text box, enter the port to use. Stick with the default port, 8088, unless you actively prefer a different vintage.

10. If you want your Software Update server to automatically copy updates from Apple's Software Update servers, select the Copy Updates From Apple check box. In the pop-up menu, choose All or All New, as appropriate.

NOTE   Instead of having your server copy all (or all new) updates from Apple's servers, you can choose the updates manually. Having the server get all the updates automatically is usually easiest, provided that you have the bandwidth to download the updates without discomfort and your server has space to store them. But, if your network's Macs have a largely standardized configuration, you can save space by picking only the updates you actually need.

11. If you chose to download updates automatically, you can select the Automatically Enable Copied Updates check box if you want the server to make the updates available automatically to your Mac clients. Instead, you may prefer to enable updates manually after you've tested them for compatibility.

12. Select the Delete Outdated Software Updates check box if you want the server to get rid of older updates. As long as you ensure that your client Macs grab updates promptly from the server, deleting older updates is a good way to save space on the server.

13. Click the Save button to save the changes.

14. Click the Start Software Update button to start using Software Update.

If you selected the Copy Updates From Apple check box, the Software Update service starts downloading available updates. This takes a while, and the Updates pane may seem to show nothing happening beyond a message saying "Sync Started." Don't worry—just give Software Update an hour or two to sort things out.

If you chose not to download updates automatically, choose which updates you want to download. Follow these steps:

1. Click the Updates button on the toolbar to display the Updates pane.

2. Click the Refresh button (the button with the clockwise arrow), just to the left of the Stop Software Update button. Give the Software Update service a while to download the list of available updates (see Figure 9-3).

3. Select each item you want to download, and then click the Copy Now button near the lower-right corner of the Server Admin window.

4. If the Choose Version button is available for an item, click this button to display the Choose Version dialog box (see Figure 9-4). Click the version you want, and then click the Save button.

Figure 9-3. If you've chosen to manage Software Updates manually, select the items you want to download and then click the Copy Now button.

5. When you've downloaded an update, the Copied column shows a blue button next to it. You can then select the Enable check box to make the update available to the Macs on your network.

NOTE If your network has many Mac clients, you can set up multiple Mac OS X servers to provide software updates. You can then set some client Macs to use each of the servers. But at this writing, you can't set your Software Update servers to communicate with each other—for example, for sharing files. Each Software Update server needs to download its own copies of each update file.

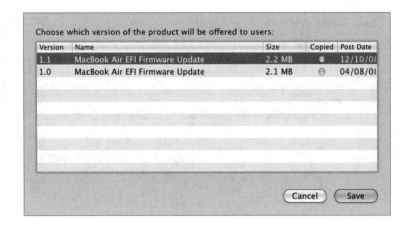

Choose which version of the product will be offered to users:

Version	Name	Size	Copied	Post Date
1.1	MacBook Air EFI Firmware Update	2.2 MB	●	12/10/0!
1.0	MacBook Air EFI Firmware Update	2.1 MB	◐	04/08/0!

Cancel   Save

Figure 9-4.   In the Choose Version dialog box, choose which version of a particular software update you want to make available to your network's Macs.

Setting a Client Mac to Download Updates from Your Update Server

Now you need to tell your Macs to use your Software Update server rather than Apple's Software Update servers. If you're managing the Mac with Workgroup Manager, as you should be for as many of the Macs on your network as possible, follow these steps; if not, see the nearby sidebar "Setting an Unmanaged Client Mac to Use Your Network's Software Update Server."

1. Open Workgroup Manager. For example, click the Workgroup Manager button on the Dock.

2. Connect to the server, authenticating yourself as needed.

3. Click the Computers button to display the Computers pane, or click the Computer Groups button to display the Computer Groups pane, on the left of Workgroup Manager.

 NOTE   You can also apply the Software Update settings to a user account or a group of user accounts. Usually, though, it's more effective to apply them to a computer or group of computers—after all, it's the Macs that need the software updates, not the users. (Your network has users you'd like to upgrade? No, we're not going there.)

4. In the left pane, click the computer or computer group you want to affect.

5. Click the Preferences button to display the Preferences pane for the computer or group.

6. If the Overview pane is not already displayed, click the Overview tab to display it.

7. Click the Software Update icon to display the Software Update pane (shown in Figure 9-5 with settings chosen for an individual Mac).

8. In the Manage box at the top, select the Always option button.

9. In the Software Update Server To Use text box, type the address of your server that is providing software updates. Put the address in this format, providing your server's hostname in place of the *server* placeholder here (for example, **http://macserver.corp.acmeheavy.com:8088/index.sucatalog**):

    ```
    http://server:8088/index.sucatalog
    ```

10. Click the Apply Now button to apply the change.

11. Click the Done button to finish making changes to the Software Update service.

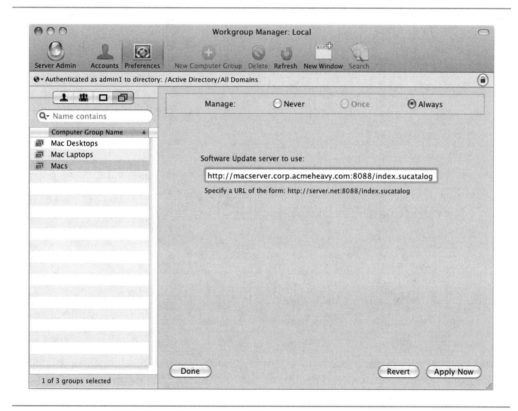

Figure 9-5.   Use the Software Update settings in Workgroup Manager to set a Mac to use your Software Update server.

Setting an Unmanaged Client Mac
to Use Your Network's Software Update Server

If you look after unmanaged Macs as well as ones you manage with Workgroup Manager, you can set them up to use your network's Software Update server—but you need to work directly on the Macs, either logged in locally or through remote access.

To set an unmanaged client Mac to download updates from your Software Update server, follow these steps:

1. Open Terminal. For example, click the Desktop, choose Go | Utilities, and then double-click Terminal in the Utilities folder.

2. Type the appropriate **defaults write** command for the version of Mac OS X the client is running, replacing the placeholder *yourdomain* with your domain name (for example, corp.acmeheavy.com). Each of these is a single command, even though the book shows them wrapped onto a second line:

   ■ **Snow Leopard (10.6)**

   ```
   defaults write ¬
      /Library/Preferences/com.apple.SoftwareUpdate CatalogURL ¬
      http://su.yourdomain:8088/¬
      index-leopard-snowleopard.merged-1.sucatalog
   ```

   ■ **Leopard (10.5)**

   ```
   defaults write ¬
      /Library/Preferences/com.apple.SoftwareUpdate CatalogURL ¬
      http://su.yourdomain:8088/index-leopard.merged-1.sucatalog
   ```

   ■ **Tiger (10.4)**

   ```
   defaults write ¬
      /Library/Preferences/com.apple.SoftwareUpdate CatalogURL ¬
      http://su.yourdomain:8088/index.sucatalog
   ```

3. Press RETURN to apply the command.

4. Quit Terminal (for example, press ⌘-Q) unless you've planned further forays in it.

To check where an unmanaged client is getting its software updates, open Terminal, type a **defaults read** command for the CatalogURL information in the com.apple.SoftwareUpdate preferences, and then press RETURN:

```
defaults read /Library/Preferences/com.apple.SoftwareUpdate ¬
   CatalogURL
```

The terminal displays the server address.

To make an unmanaged client use the Apple Software Update server again instead of your Software Update server, open Terminal, type a **defaults delete** Terminal to delete the CatalogURL information in the com.apple.SoftwareUpdate preferences, and then press RETURN:

```
defaults delete /Library/Preferences/com.apple.SoftwareUpdate ¬
    CatalogURL
```

Installing the Updates

When you've set Software Update to check automatically for updates, it checks surreptitiously, and then prompts you to install any updates it has found (see Figure 9-6). If you prefer to check manually, or you want to supplement the automatic checks with a manual check because you've heard Apple has just released a crucial fix, choose Apple | Software Update to launch Software Update and make it check for updates.

From here, you can simply click the button for proceeding. Depending on what the updates consist of and whether Software Update has already downloaded them, this may be the Continue button (as in the figure), the Install And Relaunch button (to install the updates and restart the Mac), or the Install button (to install the updates if none of them requires the Mac to be restarted afterward).

NOTE If one or more updates require the Mac to be restarted, Software Update first installs those updates that do not require a restart. Software Update then prompts you to restart the Mac, logs you out, and then installs the updates.

Normally, though, you'll want to see what your Mac is getting. To do so, click the Show Details button. The Software Update dialog box expands to show the available updates (see Figure 9-7). A gray circle containing a left-pointing arrow means that the update requires you to restart the Mac.

Figure 9-6. Software Update prompts you to install any updates it has found for your Mac.

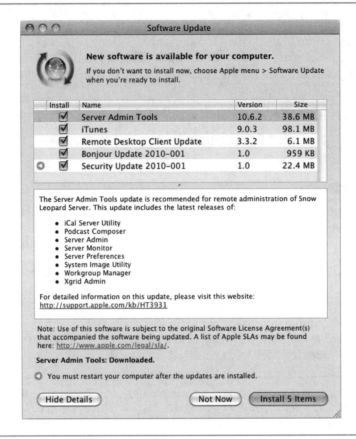

Figure 9-7.   It's a good idea to look through the list of updates in case it includes any you don't want to install.

Clear the check box for any update you do not want to install, and then click the Install Items button (its name includes the number of items—for example, Install 5 Items). If Mac OS X prompts you to restart your Mac to complete the installation, do so as soon as is convenient.

Installing Applications
on Your Client Macs Before Deployment

In many cases, the easiest way to install applications on a Mac is before you deploy it. At this point, the Mac most likely contains a default installation of Mac OS X with its built-in applications (such as Mail, Safari, TextEdit, and iChat), and the iLife applications (iPhoto, iMovie, iWeb, iDVD, and GarageBand), and no user settings or data to complicate things. You can either customize this default installation or replace it entirely with an image that contains what you need.

Understanding Your Options for Installing Applications Before Deployment

Before you deploy a Mac to a workstation in a Windows network, you can add applications to it in three main ways:

- *Install the applications manually.* You can install each application that's needed on the Mac, remove any applications the user doesn't need, and customize the settings. We'll look at this option very briefly.

- *Have someone else set up the Mac for you.* If you buy your Macs customized the way your network needs them, you can roll them straight out. You'll save time, but most likely spend more money both on the software and having it set up for you. We won't discuss this possibility further.

- *Set up the Mac with a disk image.* You can create a custom disk image that contains the software and settings you need, and then use the disk image to install Mac OS X, the applications, and the settings on the Macs. This feature is called NetInstall, and this section of the chapter examines it in detail. You'll need a Mac OS X server for this approach.

 NOTE A fourth way to set up a Mac is to boot it off the network by pulling a disk image from a Mac OS X server and then loading it on the Mac. This feature is called NetBoot, and we won't examine it in this chapter. See Apple's *System Imaging and Software Update Administration* document (from http://support.apple.com) or *Mac OS X System Administration* (McGraw-Hill, 2010) for more information on NetBoot.

Setting Up a Mac Manually

If you have only a few Macs to add to your network, you may want to set them up manually rather than bothering with one of the automated means of setup. This is easy enough for a small number of Macs, especially if you have space to line them up in a row in your lab and install the applications on them all at the same time, moving from keyboard to keyboard as needed. This approach also works well if you need to give each Mac a custom setup—for example, with different applications or different settings—rather than rolling out a standard configuration to all the Macs.

For larger numbers of Macs, you'll probably want to automate setup to save time and effort.

Setting Up a Mac Using a Disk Image

To set up a Mac automatically, you can create a disk image by using System Image Utility, an application that comes with Mac OS X Server or as part of the Server Admin Tools package. You set up the disk image with the software and settings the Macs need, and then copy the disk image to the Macs.

You can create an image in two main ways:

■ Start from the Mac OS X installation DVD and add applications as needed.

■ Set up a Mac the way you want it and then create an image from the disk.

We'll look at each of these approaches in turn.

NOTE   A disk image of Mac OS X and applications usually takes 10GB–20GB of space, so make sure the Mac you're using has plenty of free space.

Starting to Create a Disk Image

Follow these steps to start creating a disk image:

1. Insert the Mac OS X Install DVD that you will use to create the image.

TIP   You can also use a disk image file of the Mac OS X Install DVD.

2. Launch System Image Utility (see Figure 9-8):

   ■ **Mac OS X Server**   Click the System Image Utility icon on the Dock.

   ■ **Mac OS X client**   Click the desktop, choose Go | Applications, double-click the Server folder in the Applications folder, and then double-click the System Image Utility icon. (Alternatively, open the Spotlight field and type **image** into it, then click the System Image Utility hit.)

3. In the Sources list on the left, make sure that System Image Utility has selected your Mac OS X Install DVD. If not, click it.

NOTE   If you don't insert the DVD before launching System Image Utility, the NetInstall Image option button is unavailable.

4. Select the NetInstall Image option button.

From here, you can either create an image of the Mac OS X Install DVD as it is or customize the installation. Let's look at each option in turn.

Creating a Disk Image of Just the Mac OS X Files

The simpler option is to create a disk image—one that contains only the contents of the Mac OS X install DVD, with no extra software and no customized settings. This is occasionally useful, but normally you'll want to customize the disk image to save time.

To create a vanilla disk image, click the Continue button in the System Image Utility window. System Image Utility then displays the Image Settings screen shown in Figure 9-9.

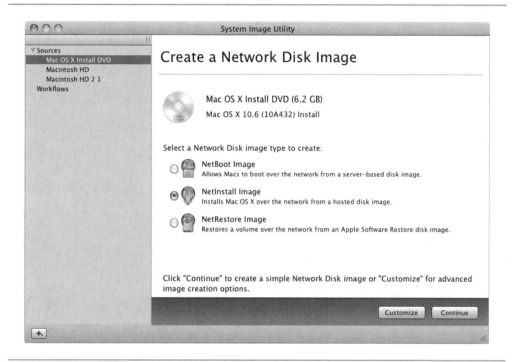

Figure 9-8.   On the opening screen of System Image Utility, select the NetInstall Image option button to start creating a disk image for installing on a Mac.

Change the text in the Network Disk text box as needed. This is the name you'll see for the disk image on the server. Similarly, change the default description as needed to help you identify the disk image easily and beyond doubt.

If you will put this disk image on two or more servers, select the Image Will Be Served From More Than One Server check box. This setting makes System Image Utility add an index ID to the disk image that the servers can use for load balancing.

Click the Create button. Up comes a Save As dialog box that lets you specify the name for the disk image and choose where to save it. Make your choices, and then click the Save button.

NOTE   To use the disk image with NetBoot, you must put it in the /Library/NetBoot/NetBootSP0/ folder on your server's hard disk. You can either put the disk image there when you create it or move it there later.

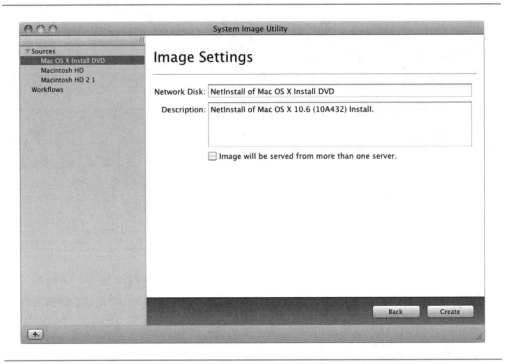

Figure 9-9.   To create a vanilla disk image, edit the name and description on the Image Settings screen as needed and then click the Create button.

System Image Utility then creates the disk image, keeping you updated on its progress as it does so (see Figure 9-10). This involves several gigabytes of data, so it takes a while, depending on the speed of the Mac you're using.

When System Image Utility displays the Done button, click it. System Image Utility then displays its first screen, from which you can either choose to create another disk image or simply quit System Image Utility (press ⌘-Q as usual).

Creating a Customized Disk Image

When you're creating a disk image, you'll normally want to customize it so that it contains exactly the software your Macs need. For example, you will likely want to add application software to the Macs and apply network settings to them. You may also want to strip out some items included in the default Mac OS X install that you don't want the Macs to have.

To create a customized disk image, pick your disk image type on the opening screen of System Image Utility and then click the Customize button. System Image Utility

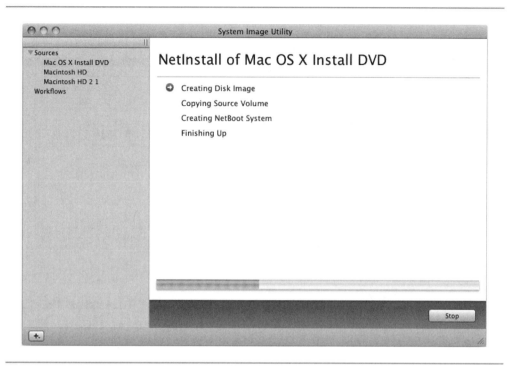

Figure 9-10.   System Image Utility creates the disk image.

displays the Automator Library window (which you'll meet in a moment) and adds the two default actions to the System Image Utility window, as shown in Figure 9-11.

If you've used the Mac OS X Automator, you'll be right at home when you see the Automator Library window. If you haven't used Automator, it may take you a moment to get your bearings. Here's a guide to what's happening in the System Image Utility window:

- The whole thing is called a *workflow*. A workflow consists of a series of actions, or steps. You build the workflow by adding the actions you want, setting options for them, and putting them in the order in which you want them to run.

- Two actions appear in the System Image Utility window: the Define Image Source action at the top, and the Create Image action below it.

- Each action is a self-contained unit. You can click the disclosure triangle to the left of the action's name to collapse or expand it.

- Each action has various settings. For example, the Define Image Source action has the Source pop-up menu, in which you choose the source image for the image file you're creating. (If you've been following along, you've chosen the source image already.)

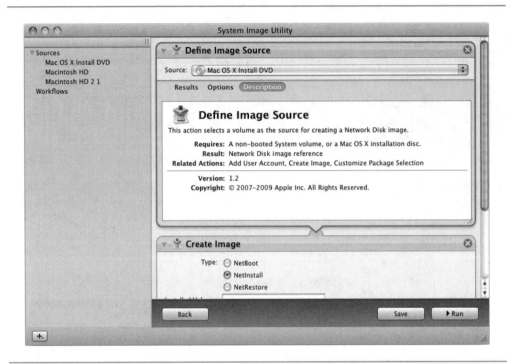

Figure 9-11.   Click one of the three visibility buttons in an action to display the results, options, or description (shown here).

- Each action has three visibility buttons at the bottom—Results, Options, and Description—that you can click to show the action's results, options, and description, respectively, in an area below the buttons. For example, if you click the Description button in the Define Image Source action, you see the description shown in Figure 9-11; if you click the Options button, you see the few options shown in Figure 9-12. Click the same button again (for example, the Description button or the Options button) to hide the area again.

- To remove an action, click the X button to the right of it.

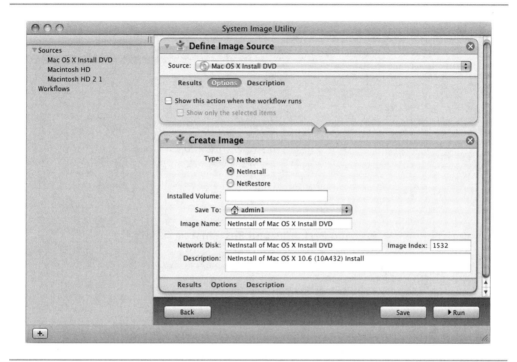

Figure 9-12.   Build the list of actions in the System Image Utility window.

■ To rearrange the order in which actions occur, you can drag an action up or down the right pane of System Image Utility by grabbing its title bar. Rearranging is easier if you collapse all the actions first.

The Automator Library window (see Figure 9-13) shows a list of actions and variables you can add to the workflow to make it do what you want—in this case, create a custom installation of Mac OS X. The Automator Library window shows either actions or variables; you can switch between the two by clicking the Actions visibility button or the Variables visibility button.

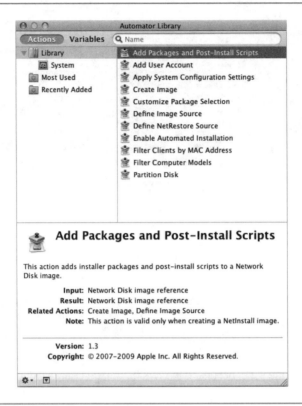

Figure 9-13. The Automator Library window provides a list of actions and variables that you can drag to the System Image Utility window.

Follow these steps to customize the disk image:

1. From the Automator Library window, drag the Custom Package Selection item to the System Image Utility window and drop it between the Define Image Source item and the Create Image item. System Image Utility adds the Custom Package Selection item between these items, as shown in Figure 9-14.

2. Click the disclosure triangle next to the Mac OS X item to display its contents.

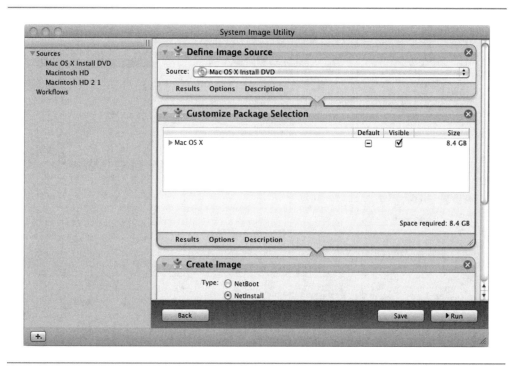

Figure 9-14. Add the Custom Package Selection item to the workflow so that you can choose which Mac OS X packages to install.

3. Drag the sizing handle at the lower-right corner of the Customize Package Selection box downward to give yourself more space to work in.

4. Choose which packages to include and which to remove, as in the example in Figure 9-15:

   ■ **Default column** Select this check box to install an item by default.

   ■ **Visible column** Select this check box to make an item available to whoever sets up the Mac.

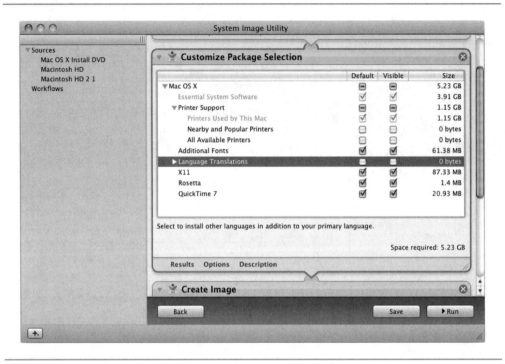

Figure 9-15.   Clear the Default check boxes for items you do not want to install. Clear the Visible check boxes for icons you do not want to be visible.

5. Click the disclosure triangle to the left of Customize Package Selection to collapse the box and give yourself more space.

6. From the Automator Library window, drag the Add Packages And Post-Install Scripts item to the System Image Utility window and drop it between the Customize Package Selection item and the Create Image item. The Add Packages And Post-Install Scripts item appears in the System Image Utility window, as shown in Figure 9-16.

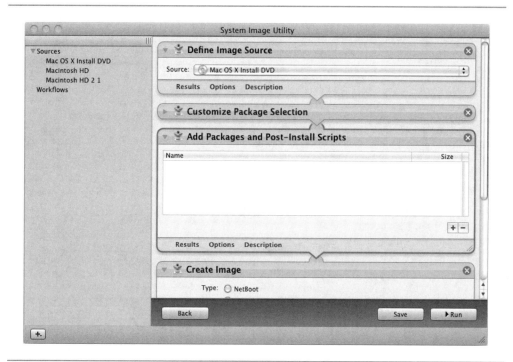

Figure 9-16.   Drag in the Add Packages And Post-Install Scripts item to enable yourself to add further software packages to the disk image you're creating.

7. Click the + button near the lower-right corner of the Add Packages And Post-Install Scripts box to open a dialog box for adding packages. Select the package or script you want, and then click the Open button. The package or script appears in the Add Packages And Post-Install Scripts box (see Figure 9-17).

TIP   You can add a folder full of packages or scripts if necessary. See the section "Creating Your Own Package Files," later in this chapter, for instructions on creating custom package files for your network's needs.

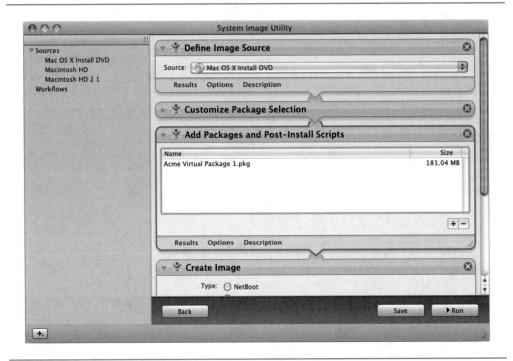

Figure 9-17. Add the software packages to the Add Packages And Post-Install Scripts box.

8. Repeat step 7 to add other packages or scripts as needed.

NOTE   Don't try to insert the Add User Account action in a NetInstall image—this action works only for NetBoot images, which you use for automatically booting a Mac from a server on the network.

9. If you want to perform automated installations on your client Macs, drag the Enable Automated Installation action to the System Image Utility window and drop it after the Add Packages And Post-Install Scripts action. Figure 9-18 shows the Enable Automated Installation action in place.

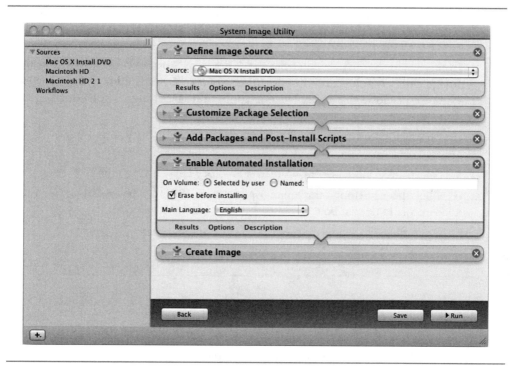

Figure 9-18. The Enable Automated Installation action lets you create NetInstall and NetRestore images that install automatically on client Macs.

10. On the On Volume line, select the Selected By User option button if you want the user to be able to choose the drive on which to install Mac OS X. Otherwise, select the Named option button and type the name of the volume to use—for example, **Macintosh HD**.

TIP You can use the Partition Disk action before the Enable Automated Installation action to partition the disk and name the volumes. With this action, you can partition the disk into different volumes as needed, but you can also create a single partition—partitioning does mean dividing, but not necessarily by a number greater than one.

11. Select the Erase Before Installing check box if you want to erase the disk before installing Mac OS X. Erasing is usually a good idea—you want to level the building site before you start construction.

12. In the Main Language pop-up menu, select the language to set as the main language for the installation—for example, English or Spanish.

13. If you want to automatically configure the system, drag the Apply System Configuration Settings action from the Automator Library window to the System Image Utility window and drop it after the Enable Automated Installation action. Figure 9-19 shows the Apply System Configuration Settings action added to the workflow.

14. If you want to automatically bind each client to a directory server, follow these steps:

    a. Select the Connect Computers To Directory Servers check box.

    b. Click the + button at the lower-right corner of the list box to add a line of controls to the list box.

    c. Open the Server pop-up menu and choose the directory server.

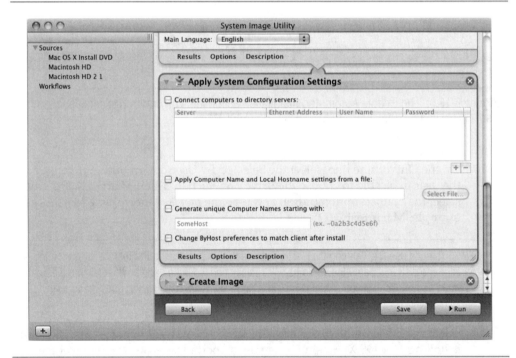

Figure 9-19. Use the Apply System Configuration Settings action when you need to configure the client Mac automatically.

  d. If you want to apply these settings to a particular Mac, click in the Ethernet box and type the MAC address of the Mac's network card—for example, **00:26:4a:02:e6:9e**. Leave the Ethernet box at its default setting, Any Computer, if you want the settings to apply to any Mac.

  e. Click in the User Name box and type the administrator's account name for the directory server. This is optional, but if you don't enter it here, you'll need to enter it on the client.

  f. Click in the Password box and type the administrator's password for the directory server. Again, this is optional, but you'll need to enter it later if you don't enter it here.

15. If you want the client to pick up a computer name and hostname from a file, select the Apply Computer Name And Local Hostname Settings From A File check box. Click the Select File button, use the resulting dialog box to select the file, and then click the Open button.

16. If you will use this image to set up multiple Macs, select the Generate Unique Computer Names Starting With check box and then type the base name in the text box.

17. If you want the Mac you're setting up to acquire the preferences of the Mac you're building the image on, select the Change ByHost Preferences To Match Client After Install check box.

18. Double-check that the Create Image action appears at the end of your workflow, and then click the Save button. System Image Utility displays a Save As dialog box for saving the workflow you have created.

19. Type a name for the workflow in the Save As text box.

20. Choose the folder in which to save the workflow.

21. Click the Save button. The Save As dialog box closes, and System Image Utility adds the workflow to the Workflows list on the left side of the window.

22. Now click the Run button to start running the workflow. Type your password when System Image Utility prompts you to authenticate yourself.

After the workflow finishes running, your disk image is ready for use. Press ⌘-Q if you're ready to quit System Image Utility, or press ⌘-N if you want to create another disk image.

Creating an Image from a Mac You've Set Up

If you're not familiar with Automator, you may prefer to create a disk image the easier way: by setting up a Mac the way you want it and then cloning the Mac's disk.

  The advantage of cloning a Mac's disk is that you get to make sure the Mac is working exactly the way it should be, and that all the applications and settings are in place. The disadvantage is that you can't perform the cloning operation while the Mac is booted from the disk you want to clone. You need to use one of these two approaches instead:

- Use two partitions.

    1. Set up the Mac with two partitions.

    2. Put Mac OS X on each partition.

    3. Set up the first partition the way you want your disk image.

    4. Boot from the second partition.

    5. Use Disk Utility to create a disk image from the first partition.

    6. Run System Image Utility and specify the disk image as the source for the installation.

- Use Target Disk mode.

    1. Connect the Mac you will clone to the cloning computer via a FireWire cable.

    2. Boot the Mac in Target Disk mode so that it shows up as a drive on the cloning computer.

    3. Run Disk Utility on the cloning computer and make the image.

    4. Eject the drive that represents the target Mac, and turn its power off before disconnecting it.

NOTE   The easiest way to boot a Mac in Target Disk mode is to press т during startup. You can also go into Startup Disk Preferences and click the Target Disk Mode button.

Once you've booted from the other partition, or you've connected the Mac in Target Disk mode, create an image in Disk Utility like this:

1. Open Disk Utility. For example, click the Desktop, choose Go | Utilities, and then double-click the Disk Utility icon.

2. Select the disk you want to close. For example, in Figure 9-20, the Mac to be closed is connected in Target Disk mode, so it shows up as a FireWire drive called AAPL FireWire Target Media.

3. Choose File | New | Disk Image From (the command shows the name of the disk). Disk Utility displays the Save As dialog box (see Figure 9-21).

4. Type a name for the disk image, and choose the folder in which to save it. To use the disk image, you must put it in the /Library/NetBoot/NetBootSP0/ folder on your server's hard disk, but you don't necessarily have to put it there when you're creating it—you can move it there later.

5. In the Image Format pop-up menu, choose Compressed.

6. In the Encryption pop-up menu, choose None.

Figure 9-20. Use Disk Utility to create a disk image from a Mac that's already configured the way you want it. The selected AAPL FireWire Target Media disk is a Mac in Target Disk mode.

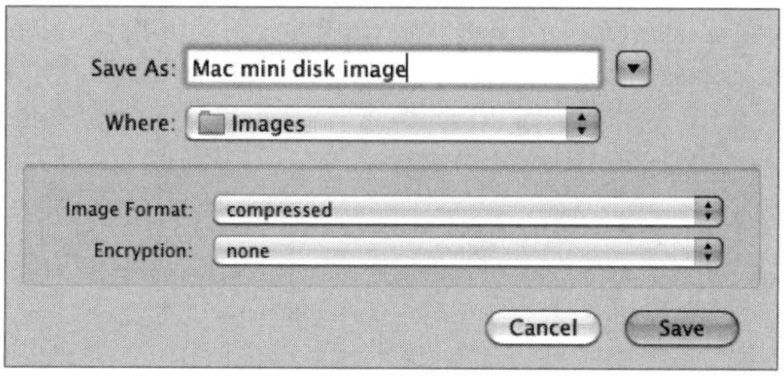

Figure 9-21. Choose to save the disk image in compressed format with no encryption.

7. Click the Save button, and then give Disk Utility some breathing space to create the disk image. Depending on how much stuff you've loaded on the Mac, it may take a while.

8. When Disk Utility has finished creating the disk image, press ⌘-Q or choose Disk Utility | Quit Disk Utility to quit the application.

Now switch to System Image Utility, select the disk image you've created, and follow through the procedure described earlier in this chapter to create a NetInstall disk.

Turning On and Setting Up the NetBoot Service to Make NetInstall Images Available

Your next step is to set up the NetBoot service to make your NetInstall images available on the network. You need to do this before the client Macs can find them.

Follow these steps to turn NetBoot on and make it do your bidding:

1. Open Server Admin. For example, click the Server Admin icon on the Dock.

2. In the Servers list, double-click the server.

3. Check or enter your credentials in the login dialog box, and then click the Connect button.

4. Click the Settings tab to display its contents.

5. Click the Settings button to display the list of services.

6. Select the NetBoot check box.

7. Click the Save button. Mac OS X Server turns on the NetBoot service and adds it to the list of services running under the server.

8. Click the NetBoot item under the server in the Servers pane to display the NetBoot screens.

9. Click the Settings button on the toolbar to display the Settings screen.

10. Click the General tab to display the General pane (see Figure 9-22).

11. In the Enable NetBoot On At Least One Port list box, select the Enable check box for the port on which to enable NetBoot—for example, the Ethernet port.

12. In the Select Where To Put Images And Client Data list box, select the appropriate check box in the Images column to indicate the disk on which you've stored the images. Ignore the Client Data column—this is for NetBoot images rather than NetInstall images.

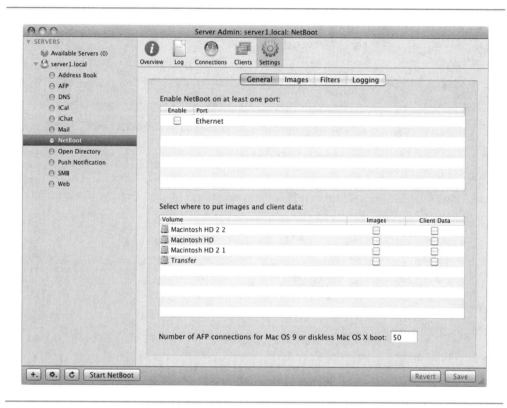

Figure 9-22. In the General pane, select the port on which to enable NetBoot.

13. Click the Images tab to display the Images pane (see Figure 9-23). The main list box shows a list of the images Server Admin has found in the /Library/ NetBoot/NetBootSP0/ folder on your server's hard disk.

14. In the Default column, select the option button for the image you want to use as the default.

15. In the Enable column, select the check box for each disk image you want to enable. You must enable the disk image you've marked as the default.

16. In the Diskless column, clear the check box. (You'd select it if you were using NetBoot to fire up diskless workstations.)

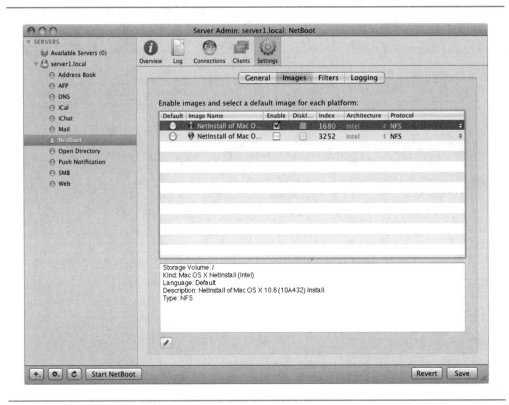

Figure 9-23. In the Images pane, enable the NetInstall images you want to use.

17. If your disk image contains both Intel and PowerPC code, as in Leopard (10.5) and earlier versions of Mac OS X, you can open the pop-up menu in the Architecture column and choose which to use. If your disk image is Snow Leopard (Mac OS X 10.6), only Intel will be available, because Apple took the PowerPC code out to make my sturdy old PowerBooks obsolete.

18. In the Protocol column, open the pop-up menu and choose the network protocol you want to use for delivering the disk image to the workstation. Normally, you'll want to use NFS; the alternative is HTTP.

19. If you need to protect your disk images against unauthorized Macs using them, click the Filters tab to display the Filters pane (see Figure 9-24). Here, you can select the Enable NetBoot/DHCP Filtering check box, choose between the Allow Only Clients Listed Below (Deny Others) option button and the Deny Only Clients Listed Below (Allow Others) option button, and then build a list of the Macs that you're allowing access or denying access, depending on the choice you made. You identify the Macs by the hardware (MAC) address of their network cards, which provides fairly solid authentication (although a malefactor can spoof a MAC address).

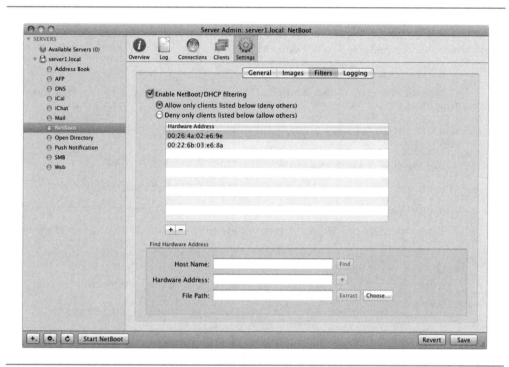

Figure 9-24.   The Filters pane enables you to set up a list of Macs that are allowed—or are not permitted—to use your NetBoot images.

20. Click the Logging tab to display the Logging pane, open the Log Level pop-up menu, and choose the level of logging you want for NetBoot:

   ■ **High (All Events)**   Use this level when you are getting started with NetBoot and will find it helpful to be able to track everything that happens.

   ■ **Medium (Errors And Warnings)**   Use this level when you're getting more confident with NetBoot but you still want to see every alert that crops up.

   ■ **Low (Errors Only)**   Use this level when NetBoot is configured to your satisfaction and working well.

21. Click the Save button to save the changes you've made to NetBoot.

22. Click the Start NetBoot button at the bottom the pane. The NetBoot light on the left glows green, and you can quit Server Admin if you're ready to.

Setting a Mac Client to Install from a NetInstall Image

Now that you've created your NetInstall images and set the NetBoot service to make them available, you just need to tell your Mac clients to boot from the network. To do so, follow these steps:

1. On the Mac client, open System Preferences. For example, click the System Preferences icon on the Dock, or choose Apple | System Preferences.

2. Click the Startup Disk icon in the System area to display the Startup Disk preferences pane (see Figure 9-25).

3. Select the Network Startup icon.

4. Click the Restart button. Mac OS X displays a confirmation dialog box.

5. Click the Restart button and wait for Mac OS X to find the server on the network.

6. Follow any prompts required to complete the setup.

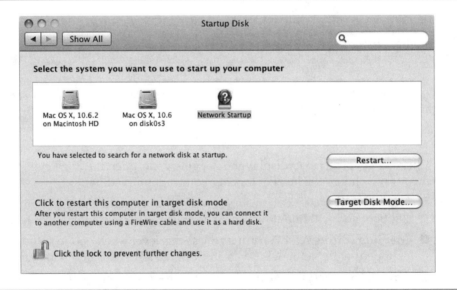

Figure 9-25.   Choose Network Startup in the Startup Disk preferences pane.

Creating Your Own Package Files

To add software to a disk image or to create your own package files for distribution, you use the PackageMaker tool. You'll find PackageMaker in the Utilities folder in the Server Administration Tools disk image. Drag PackageMaker from there to the /Applications/ Server/ folder or another convenient folder (for example, your Utilities folder), and then double-click the PackageMaker icon to run the application.

When you open PackageMaker, you'll see an Untitled window. In front of this window, PackageMaker automatically displays the Install Properties dialog box (see Figure 9-26).

Type your organization's name in the Organization text box. You need to create the name in the form com.*example*—for example, com.acmeheavy or org .sleepyparentsoftoddlers—so that Mac OS X can generate suitable package identifiers for the components in the package.

Next, open the Minimum Target pop-up menu and choose the lowest version of Mac OS X your clients will run—for example, Mac OS X v10.5 Leopard.

Click the OK button to close the Install Properties dialog box. You can then see the whole of the PackageMaker window (see Figure 9-27).

Saving Your Package Description Document

In PackageMaker, you create a package description document in the .pmdoc format that specifies the contents of the package. This document is tiny—just a few kilobytes—because all it contains is a list of what you want the package to contain. When the description is finished, you build the package to create the file in the .pkg format that you add to your installation workflow. This file contains all the files, so it's much bigger—roughly the size of all the files plus some packaging.

Press ⌘-S (or choose File | Save) to display the Save As dialog box, and then save the description document in a convenient location and under a descriptive name.

Figure 9-26.   In the Install Properties dialog box, type your organization name and choose the minimum version of Mac OS X your clients will run.

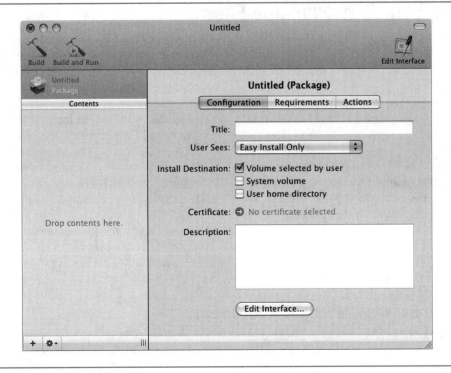

Figure 9-27. PackageMaker is the tool for creating custom packages to include in your automated installations of Mac OS X.

Setting the Title and Options for the Package Description Document

After you save the file, the package file at the top of the Contents pane is still called Untitled. With this item selected (click it if it's not selected), click the Configuration tab (see Figure 9-28) and type a title in the Title box.

The package title is the only required item, but you can also do the following in the Configuration pane:

- *Choose which installation types are available to the user.* Open the User Sees pop-up menu, and then choose Easy And Custom Install, Custom Install Only, or Easy Install Only. Easy Install Only is the best choice if you can set up a standardized configuration for all users.

- *Choose where the user can install the package.* In the Install Destination area, select the appropriate check boxes:

  - **Volume Selected By User** Select this check box to let the user decide where to install the package.

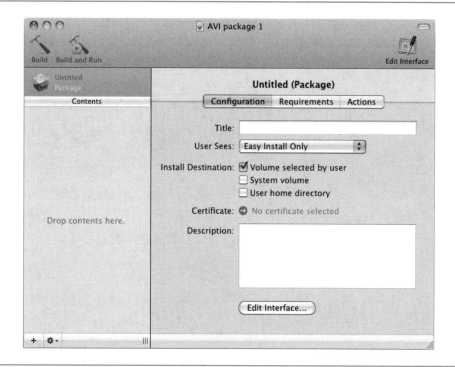

Figure 9-28.   Name your package by typing in the Title text box in the Configuration pane.

- ■ **System Volume**   Select this check box if you want to get the package's contents onto the Mac.
- ■ **User Home Directory**   Select this check box if you want to get the package's contents into the user's home directory (wherever it is).
- ■ *Choose which certificate to use to sign the package.* Click the arrow button, pick the certificate in the Choose A Certificate To Be Used For Signing The Package dialog box, and click the Choose button.
- ■ *Add a description to the package.* Type the description in the Description text box so that you can easily identify the package afterward.

NOTE   You can also edit the Installer interface for the package by clicking the Edit Interface button. For example, you can add a readme file to the Installer.

If you need to set any hardware or software requirements for the package, click the Requirements tab and work in the Requirements pane (shown in Figure 9-29 with a requirement added).

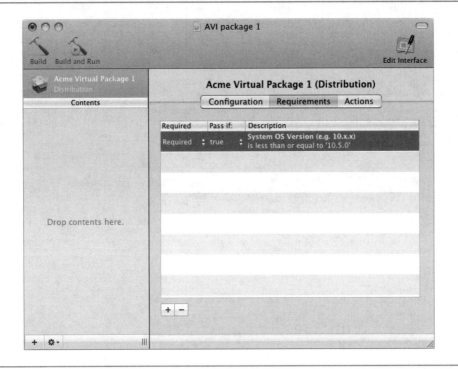

Figure 9-29. In the Requirements pane, set any hardware or software requirements for the package.

To add a requirement, follow these steps:

1. Click the + button to display the dialog box shown in Figure 9-30.

2. In the upper area, put together the condition.

   a. Open the If pop-up menu and choose the item—for example, System OS Version.

   b. Open the Is pop-up menu and choose the comparison—for example, <= (is less than or equal to).

   c. In the text box, type the value—for example, **10.5.0** for Mac OS X version 10.5 (Leopard).

3. In the Failure message area, type a message title and message text to display if the system fails the requirement.

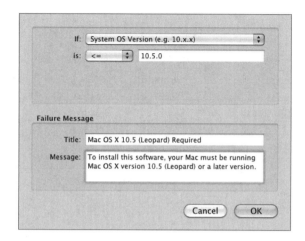

Figure 9-30.   Use this dialog box to create a requirement for a software package.

4. Click the OK button. PackageMaker closes the dialog box and adds the requirement to the list.

5. If necessary, click the Required pop-up menu in the Required column and choose Optional instead.

6. Also if necessary, click the True item in the Pass If column and choose False instead.

As well as hardware and software requirements, you can add actions to your package. You can create actions that run before the installation, after the installation, or both.

To add actions, click the Actions button and work in the Actions pane (shown in Figure 9-31 with an action added). There's a Preinstall Actions list box for actions to run before the installation, a Postinstall Actions list box for actions to run after installation, and a pair of Edit buttons, one for setting up each list of actions.

To edit one of the lists of actions, click its Edit button and then work in the dialog box that PackageMaker displays (see Figure 9-32). As you'll notice at once, this is an Automator workflow, so you drag the actions you want from the left pane to the workflow, choose options in them, and arrange them into the order in which you want them to occur. Click the Save button when you're done, and the list appears in the Actions pane in PackageMaker.

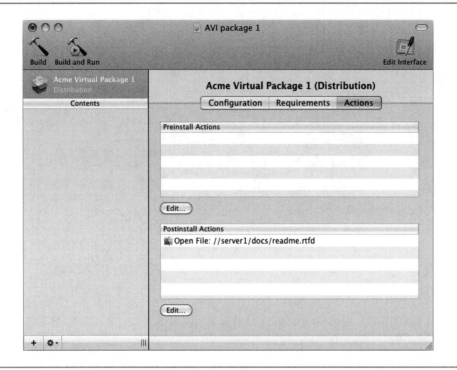

Figure 9-31. Use the Actions pane to set up preinstall actions or postinstall actions for the package.

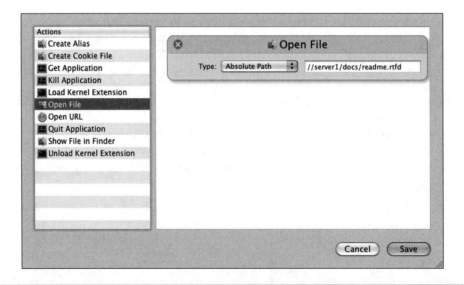

Figure 9-32. Set up the list of preinstall actions or postinstall actions in this dialog box.

Adding Files to the Package Description Document

Now that you've named your package description document and chosen options for it, you're ready to add files to the package.

The easiest way to add files is to open a Finder window to the folder that contains the files, and then drag them to the Contents pane on the left side of the PackageMaker window. Alternatively, you can click the + button in the lower-left corner of the PackageMaker window, use the resulting dialog box to pick the file, and then click the Choose button to add it.

When you've added one or more files to the package, each file appears as a collapsible choice in the contents pane. You can then set options both for the choice and for the package.

Setting Options for the Choice

To set options for the choice, click the choice and work in the Configuration pane (see Figure 9-33).

You can make the following changes in the Configuration pane:

- **Choice Name** In this text box, type the name the user will see in the Customization pane of the Installer.

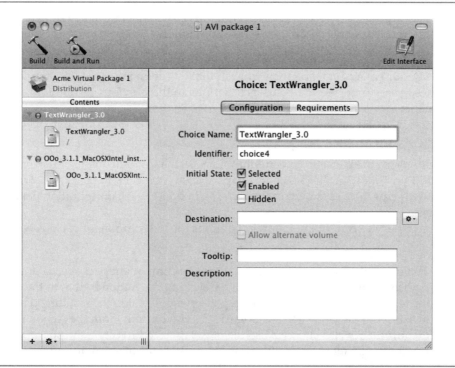

Figure 9-33. In the Configuration pane, you can name the choice, set its initial state and destination, and add a tooltip and description.

- **Identifier**   In this text box, type the text that identifies the choice inside the package.

- **Initial State**   In this area, choose how the item should appear in the Customization pane. Select the Selected check box to have the choice's check box appear already selected; select the Enabled check box if you want the user to be able to select or clear the check box; and select the Hidden check box if you want to hide the choice from the user.

- **Destination**   Choose the folder in which to install the components of the choice. Click the Action button to the right of the text box, click Choose on the pop-up menu, select the folder in the resulting dialog box, and then click the Choose button. Click the Action button again, and then choose Absolute or Relative To Project on the pop-up menu, putting a check mark next to the item you want. Absolute means you're setting an absolute path in the file system; Relative To Project means you're setting a path that's relative to where the project files go.

NOTE   After setting the destination, select the Allow Alternate Volume check box if you want to let the user install the choice on a different volume.

- **Tooltip**   Type a short message—up to a dozen words or so—for the Installer to display in a tooltip when the user puts the mouse pointer over the choice.

- **Description**   Type a longer description for display in the Customization pane in the Installer when the user selects the choice.

If necessary, you can set hardware and software requirements for the choice. Click the Requirements tab, and then work in the Requirements pane. Use the same techniques to set up the requirements as described in the previous section for setting requirements for the package as a whole.

Setting Options for the Package

To set options for the package, expand the choice in the Contents pane of the System Image Utility window (if the choice is collapsed) and then click the package. You'll see a screen with four tabs, as shown in Figure 9-34, in which the Configuration pane takes center stage.

In this pane, you can set the following options for the component package you've selected:

- **Install**   This text box shows the path to the component package. Change the path as needed, either by typing or by clicking the Action button to the right of the text box, clicking Choose on the pop-up menu, using the resulting dialog box to select the file, and then clicking the Choose button. From the Action pop-up menu, you can also choose Absolute or Relative To Project on the pop-up menu if necessary. (Chances are you'll normally install from an absolute path.)

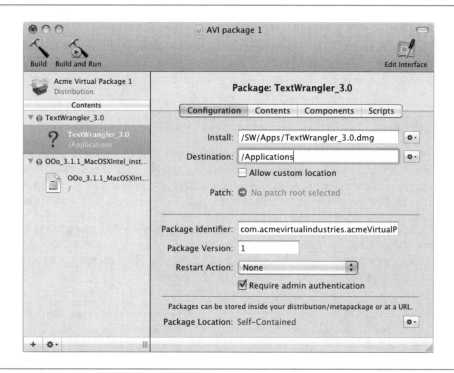

Figure 9-34.   The Configuration pane includes options for choosing where to install the component package and whether to restart the Mac.

- **Destination**   Enter the folder to which you want to install the component package. For example, if this is an application, you may want to choose the Applications folder. Again, you can type in the path or click the Action button and then click Choose; the Action button also offers the choice of an absolute path or a relative path. You can select the Allow Custom Location check box if you want the user to be able to override the location you chose.

NOTE   If the application will patch an earlier version of the application, click the arrow next to Patch. In the Configure Patch Package dialog box that opens, specify the older version of the application by clicking the Action button, clicking Choose, and then using the Open dialog box to pick the application. Click the Save button to close the Configure Patch Package dialog box.

- **Package Identifier**   This is a Uniform Type Identifier (UTI) that uniquely identifies the package—for example, com.mycompany.apps1.customapp .pkg—so that Mac OS X is certain which package you're referring to and can register it properly.

- **Package Version**   A positive integer that identifies the version of the package. Usually it's easiest to start with 1.

- **Restart Action**   In this pop-up menu, choose whether the user needs to log out, restart, or shut down after installation. Your choices are None, Require Logout, Require Restart, and Require Shutdown.

- **Require Admin Authentication**   Select this check box if you want to force the user to authenticate as an administrator for the Mac before running the installation.

- **Package Location**   Normally, the readout says Self-Contained, because the package you added contains the files. You can also click the Action button and choose another option: Same Level, Custom Path, HTTP URL, or Removable Media. For the last three, you enter the path to the package in a text box.

Next, click the Contents tab to display the Contents pane (see Figure 9-35). Here, depending on the files you're installing, you can choose to omit certain files, either by clearing their check boxes in the list box or by clicking the File Filters button and using the resulting dialog box to specify a list of filters to apply.

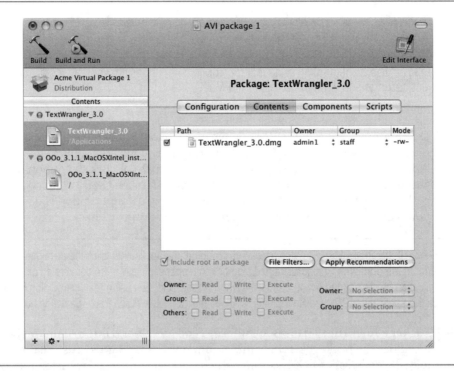

Figure 9-35.   In the Contents pane, you can choose whether to omit files from the component package.

Click the Components tab to display the Components pane (see Figure 9-36). Here, you can make two decisions for any component listed:

- **Whether the user may relocate it**   Select the check box in the Allow Relocation column if the user may relocate the component.

- **Whether the component can be replaced with an earlier version during an install**   Select the check box in the Allow Downgrade column.

Finally, click the Scripts tab to display the Scripts pane (see Figure 9-37). Here, you can designate the scripts directory and choose scripts to run before and after install, as needed.

You've now finished setting up the first component package. Repeat the procedure for each other component package you want to include in the overall package.

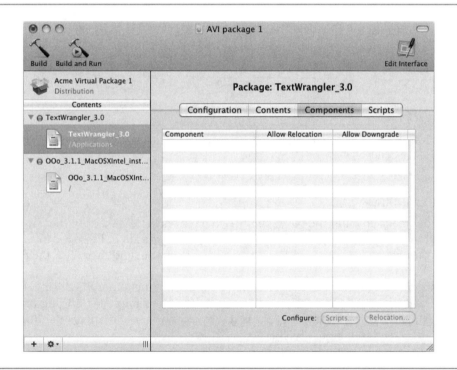

Figure 9-36.   In the Components pane, choose whether to allow relocation or downgrading for components of the package.

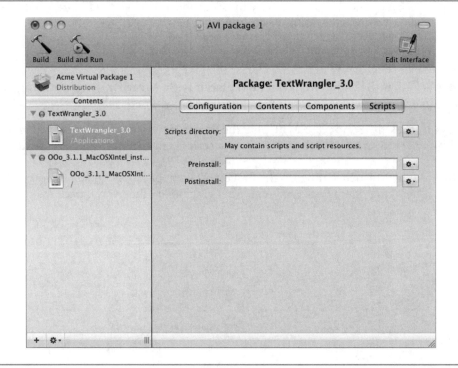

Figure 9-37. Specify the scripts directory and set up any preinstall or postinstall script needed in the Scripts pane.

Building the Package File

You're now ready to build the package file—to have PackageMaker put the package file together using the components and settings you've specified. Press ⌘-s to save the changes you've made to the package description document, and then click the Build button on the toolbar.

PackageMaker displays a Save As dialog box. Choose the folder in which you want to save the package file, and then click the Save button to start the building process. PackageMaker shows you its progress as it works, and then it displays the Build Succeeded! screen (see Figure 9-38).

From here you have three choices:

■ Click the Open In Installer button to open the package in Installer. This is a good way of finding out if the package works the way you intended.

■ Click the View in Finder button to open a Finder window showing the package—for example, so that you can copy it to another disk.

■ Click the Return To Editing button to return to editing the package in PackageMaker.

Figure 9-38. From the Build Succeeded! screen, you can open the package in Installer, view it in the Finder, or return to editing in PackageMaker.

Installing Applications on Your Client Macs After Deployment

Apart from any applications you install with Mac OS X itself, you have three main options for installing applications on your client Macs:

- *Install the applications directly.* You can go to the Mac, log yourself in, and install the application from a CD, DVD, USB stick, or network drive. This approach works fine for small networks—say, one to three handfuls of Macs—but involves too much labor and legwork for any network larger than that.

NOTE Alternatively, you can have the users install the applications on their Macs for you. This can save you any amount of time, but you must trust the users enough to give them administrative privileges—otherwise, they can't usually install the applications.

■   *Install the applications remotely via Screen Sharing.* If you don't have Apple's Remote Desktop software (discussed next), you can use Screen Sharing to take control of a remote Mac and install applications on it. You're limited to working on a single Mac at a time, so installing the applications will take a while, but at least you're spared the trek to the other Mac, and you can perform other tasks on your local Mac while Installer chugs along.

■   *Install the applications through Apple Remote Desktop.* If you have Apple Remote Desktop, you can use it to install applications on multiple Macs at the same time from the comfort of your aerie. This is the fastest and most convenient method—as long as you have Apple Remote Desktop.

 NOTE   You can buy Apple Remote Desktop from the Apple Store (http://store.apple.com) or—often for less—from other online retailers such as Amazon.com. For intimate networks, get the ten-client version priced at $299; for larger gatherings of Macs, get the unlimited-client version priced at $499.

Installing the applications directly is straightforward if time-consuming. The following sections discuss the other two approaches.

Deploying Applications Through Screen Sharing

Mac OS X's Screen Sharing feature lets you view another Mac's screen remotely or take control of it. Screen Sharing is great for helping users remotely, and you can also use it for installing software. The disadvantage is that you can work on only one Mac at a time, which makes installing software a lengthy process.

If this is enough for your network's needs, proceed as described in this section. You'll need first to turn on Screen Sharing on each Mac that you want to access remotely. Once you've done that, you can connect to the Mac via Screen Sharing in moments.

Turning On Screen Sharing for a Client Mac

First, set up Screen Sharing on the client Mac like this:

1. Open System Preferences. For example, click the System Preferences icon in the Dock, or choose Apple | System Preferences.

2. In the Internet & Wireless section, click the Sharing icon to display the Sharing pane (shown in Figure 9-39 with settings chosen).

3. In the list box on the left, select the Screen Sharing check box.

4. Click the Computer Settings button to display the Computer Settings dialog box (see Figure 9-40) and then choose settings as needed.

5. If you want anyone to be able to ask for permission to control the screen, select the Anyone May Request Permission To Control Screen check box. Normally, you'll want to clear this check box.

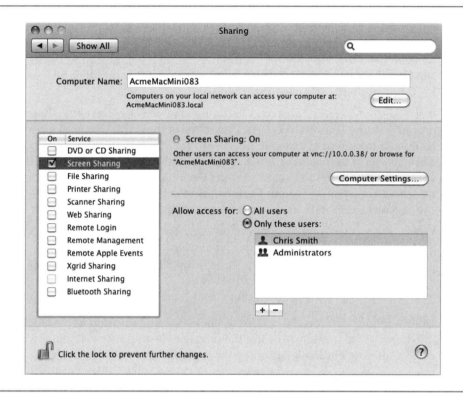

Figure 9-39.   Turn on Screen Sharing in the Sharing pane in System Preferences to give yourself remote control of a Mac.

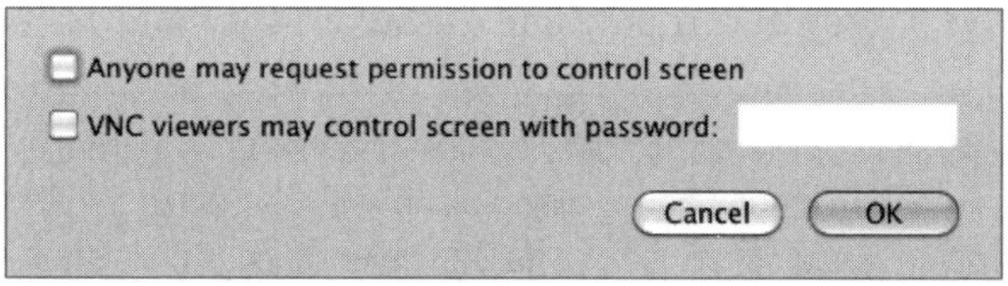

Figure 9-40.   Choose whether anyone can request control of the screen via Screen Sharing and whether VNC users can connect as well.

6. If you want users of Virtual Network Computing (VNC) to be able to control the screen, select the VNC Viewers May Control Screen With Password check box and then type the password in the text box. VNC is great when you yourself need to access another computer remotely—for example, when you need to take control of a Mac from a PC. If you don't want other people using VNC on your network, clear this check box.

7. In the Allow Access For area, you'll usually want to select the Only These Users option button rather than the All Users option button. Also, make sure the Administrators item appears in the list box. If it doesn't, click the + button, select Administrators in the dialog box that opens, and then click the Select button. (If you want to set yourself in a privileged position over other administrators, use the – button to remove Administrators from the list box. Then click the + button, choose your account in the dialog box, and click that Select button.)

8. When you're done, quit System Preferences. For example, press ⌘-Q or choose System Preferences | Quit System Preferences.

Connecting to a Client Mac via Screen Sharing

To connect to a client Mac via Screen Sharing, follow these steps:

1. Open a Finder window. For example, click the Finder button in the Dock, click the desktop and press ⌘-N, or use the mouse to lasso an already open window that's cantering aimlessly around your desktop.

2. In the sidebar, double-click the Shared category to expand it if it's currently collapsed. The list of accessible computers on your network appears.

3. Click the Mac to which you want to connect.

4. Click the Share Screen button. In the Finder's column view, the Share Screen button appears handily in the second column. In any of the three other views, it appears in the gray bar below the Search box.

5. The Screen Sharing application opens, contacts the remote Mac, and then prompts you for your username and password for that Mac (see Figure 9-41).

NOTE The By Asking For Permission option button and the As A Registered User option button appear only in the Screen Sharing dialog box if you've selected the Anyone May Request Permission To Control Screen check box in the Computer Settings dialog box. Otherwise, you can connect only as a registered user.

6. In the Connect area, select the As A Registered User option button.

NOTE To connect by asking for permission, select the By Asking For Permission option button and then click the Connect button. The user sees a Control Request dialog box. If they click the Share Screen button, you're in; if they click the Cancel button, you get an Authentication Failed message. This seems ambiguous, but the small print spells it out by telling you that the user declined your request.

Figure 9-41.   Normally you'll want to connect to the remote Mac as a registered user rather than by asking for permission.

7. Type your username for the remote Mac in the Name text box and your password in the Password text box.

8. Select the Remember This Password In My Keychain check box if you want Mac OS X to store the password for future use.

9. Click the Connect button. Screen Sharing establishes a connection to the remote Mac and displays a window showing whatever is happening on its desktop.

You now have control of the remote Mac, and can install software on it as if you were sitting at it.

Deploying Applications Through Apple Remote Desktop

If you have Apple Remote Desktop, you can manage your Macs not just singly, but in groups—even managing every single Mac on the network at the same time.

 NOTE   You can install Apple Remote Desktop either on a Mac OS X server or on a Mac client—for example, the Mac you use for administration.

Once you've installed Apple Remote Desktop, run it from the Applications folder like any other application. If you plan to use it frequently—and chances are that you will—CTRL-click or right-click the icon in the Dock and choose Options | Keep In Dock to anchor it there for eternity.

Turning On Remote Management for a Client Mac

To manage your client Macs via Apple Remote Desktop, the Remote Management feature in Sharing preferences needs to be turned on. If you've already turned this feature on during setup, you're riding high. If not, follow these steps on each client Mac to turn on Remote Management:

1. Open System Preferences. For example, click the System Preferences icon in the Dock, or choose Apple | System Preferences.

2. In the Internet & Wireless section, click the Sharing icon to display the Sharing pane (shown in Figure 9-42 with settings chosen).

3. In the list box on the left, select the Remote Management check box.

4. Click the Computer Settings button to display the Computer Settings dialog box (see Figure 9-43) and then choose settings as needed:

   ■ **Show Remote Management Status In Menu Bar**   Select this check box if you want to display a Remote Management menu in the client Mac's menu bar. From this menu, the user can send a message to the administrator and can directly open Sharing Preferences.

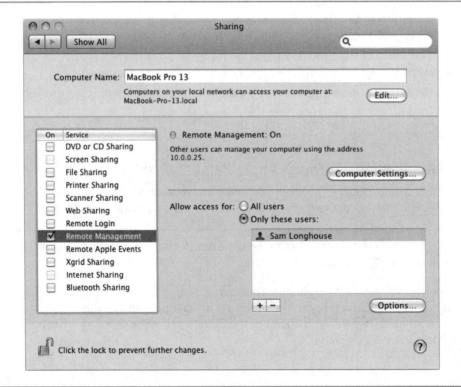

Figure 9-42.   Turn on Remote Management in the Sharing pane in System Preferences to make a Mac manageable with Apple Remote Desktop.

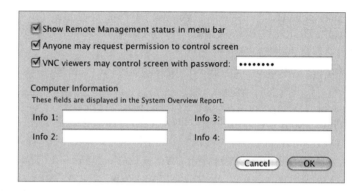

Figure 9-43.   In the Computer Settings dialog box, choose whether to display a Remote Management menu in the menu bar and whether to allow VNC access.

- ■ **Anyone May Request Permission To Control Screen**   Select this check box only if you want screen sharing to be available to other, non-administrator users too. Normally, you'll want to clear this check box.

NOTE   The Anyone May Request Permission To Control Screen feature and VNC Viewers May Control Screen With Password feature are primarily used for Screen Sharing, which is based on the same technology as Apple Remote Desktop.

- ■ **VNC Viewers May Control Screen With Password**   Select this check box if you want to allow Virtual Network Computing (VNC) clients to connect to Screen Sharing, and then type a tough-to-guess password in the text box. Normally, you will not want to do this—it's better to use Screen Sharing and keep VNC safely shut off.

- ■ **Computer Information**   Add to the four Info fields (named Info 1 through Info 4) any information that you want to make available to Apple Remote Desktop's System Overview Report feature.

5. Click the OK button to close the Computer Settings dialog box.

6. In the Allow Access For area, choose which users may access the Mac remotely. Rather than select the All Users option button as Mac OS X suggests, you will typically want to select the Only These Users option button, click the + button, choose yourself in the dialog box that opens, and then click the Select button. When you do so, Mac OS X displays the Options dialog box, discussed next, so that you can decide which powers to bestow on yourself.

7. To choose options for all users (if the All Users option button is selected) or a listed user selected in the Allow Access list box, click the Options button. The Options dialog box (see Figure 9-44) offers the following options, most of which you'll probably want to turn on:

   ■ **Observe** Select this check box to let yourself view the Mac's screen via Apple Remote Desktop.

   ■ **Control** When you've selected the Observe check box, you can select this check box to allow yourself to take control of the Mac without consulting the user.

   ■ **Show When Being Observed** When you've selected the Observe check box, you can select this check box to give the user a visual cue when you're observing the Mac. The Remote Management menu icon changes from a pair of binoculars to a monitor showing a pair of binoculars, and the item at the top of the menu changes from Ready Mode to Controlled Mode.

CAUTION Even when you turn it on, Apple Remote Desktop's visual cue that you're observing the screen is subtle enough for many users to miss. Unless you're in an environment where monitoring is expected, such as in a lab during a computer training class, it's a good idea to warn the user with a text message that you are about to observe their screen.

   ■ **Generate Reports** Select this check box to allow Apple Remote Desktop to generate reports including this Mac.

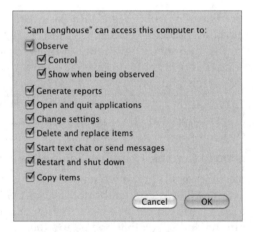

Figure 9-44. You'll probably want to grant yourself a full set of powers in the Options dialog box for Remote Management.

- ■ **Open And Quit Applications**   Select this check box to give yourself control over applications—useful when you will use Apple Remote Desktop to update them.

- ■ **Change Settings**   Select this check box to enable yourself to change settings such as system preferences.

- ■ **Delete And Replace Items**   Select this check box to allow yourself to delete files and folders and to replace existing items. This capability is useful for upgrades, but tread carefully over the user's loved-and-wanted files.

- ■ **Start Text Chat Or Send Messages**   Select this check box to enable Apple Remote Desktop to chat with the Mac or send messages to it. Both capabilities are highly useful.

- ■ **Restart And Shut Down**   Select this check box to give yourself the power to restart the Mac or shut it down. Restarting is regrettably often necessary for software upgrades.

- ■ **Copy Items**   Select this check box to let yourself copy items from the Mac.

8. Quit System Preferences. For example, press ⌘-Q or choose System Preferences | Quit System Preferences.

Connecting to Client Macs Using Apple Remote Desktop

After you've set up the Remote Management service, you can connect to the client Macs quickly with Apple Remote Desktop.

Launch Apple Remote Desktop if it's not running, and then select the computers in the All Computers list (shown in Figure 9-45) or the Scanner list.

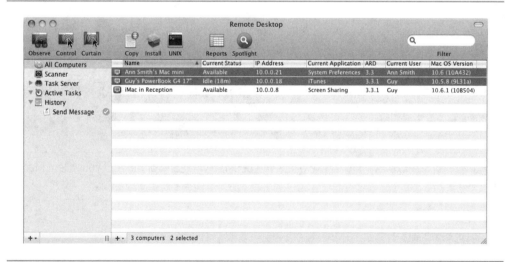

Figure 9-45.   In Apple Remote Desktop, select the client Macs you want to affect.

You can then click the Observe button on the toolbar to see what the Macs are doing. In Figure 9-46, the left Mac is researching life sciences on Wikipedia, while the right Mac is running its screen saver. In other words, both are ripe for an installation—though you'll probably want to warn the users first.

To take control of a Mac, click it and then click the Control button on the toolbar. To keep the hemispheres of your brain from detaching themselves in disgust, you can take control of only one Mac at a time.

Installing Software via Apple Remote Desktop

Once you've taken control, you can configure the Mac as if you were sitting at it. For example, you can change System Preferences manually, drag an application to the Trash, or take any other action you're permitted to take directly on it.

NOTE   To install software via Apple Remote Desktop, you need package files. If the software is not already in a package file, use PackageMaker as described earlier in this chapter to create your own custom package files.

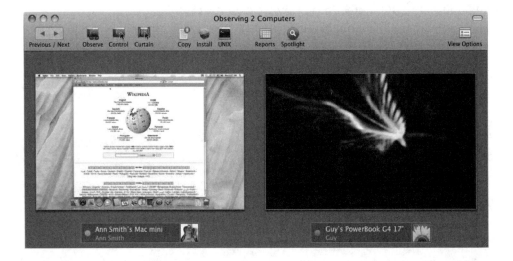

Figure 9-46.   Apple Remote Desktop lets you observe what one or more of your client Macs are doing.

Rather than configure a Mac by taking control of it, however, what you'll often want to do is use Apple Remote Desktop's feature for installing software on multiple Macs at the same time. To do so, follow these steps:

1. In the Remote Desktop window, select the Macs on which you want to install the software.

NOTE   You can also start installing software from the Observing window in which you're observing one or more Macs. Just click the Install button on the toolbar to get started.

2. Click the Install button on the toolbar to display the Install Packages dialog box (see Figure 9-47).

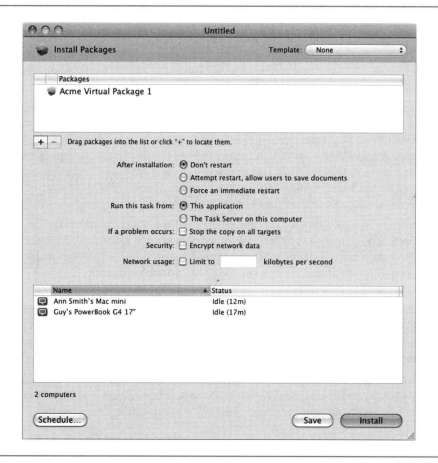

Figure 9-47.   In the Install Packages dialog box, set up the list of packages you want to install and choose options for installing them.

3. Add packages to the Packages list at the top of the Install Packages dialog box. Either drag in packages from a Finder window or click the + button, select the package or packages in the resulting dialog box, and then click the Open button.

4. In the After Installation area, select the appropriate option button:

   ■ **Don't Restart**   As long as the software you're installing doesn't require Mac OS X to be restarted afterward, this is always the best choice. If the user is at the Mac, they'll notice the Mac slow down somewhat while the installation runs.

   ■ **Attempt Restart, Allow Users To Save Documents**   Select this option button if the software requires Mac OS X to be restarted, but you want to give the users the chance to save any unsaved changes to documents they've been working on. Users may grumble about having to let the Mac restart itself, but it's better than losing them any unsaved changes they've been hoarding.

   ■ **Force An Immediate Restart**   Select this option button if you absolutely need to restart the Macs straightaway, without even giving the users the chance to save unsaved changes. Normally, you'd use this approach only when installing a hyper-critical update or patch.

5. In the Run This Task From area, select the This Application option button to run the installation from Remote Desktop. This is the normal way to run the installation, but it requires all the Macs that you're installing on to be online now. The alternative is to select the other option button, The Task Server On This Computer, which lets you use a designated Task Server to run the installation for computers that are currently offline. (Using a Task Server is a more advanced use that we won't get into here.)

6. On the If A Problem Occurs line, select the Stop The Copy On All Targets check box if you want to stop the copy operation if any of the Macs can't take the update for whatever reason. Leave this check box cleared to make the installation go ahead on as many Macs as possible—usually the best choice.

7. On the Security line, select the Encrypt Network Data check box if it's vital to keep the installation data secure as it passes across your network. Performance suffers when you encrypt the data, so don't encrypt it unless you have a good reason. If you have a wired network, and you're installing applications that aren't top secret, you probably don't need encryption.

8. On the Network Usage line, select the Limit To *NN* Kilobytes Per Second check box and then type a suitable value in the text box, if you want to prevent the installation from hogging your network's bandwidth.

NOTE   If you want to install the software later, click the Schedule button and use the resulting dialog box to choose when to install it.

9. Click the Install button. Apple Remote Desktop closes the Install Packages dialog box and starts installing the software.

Controlling the Applications and Widgets a User Can Run

For the managed Macs on your network, you can decide which applications the users can run. For any user you trust to be responsible (you may be the only candidate here) or who genuinely needs complete freedom of action (likewise), you can simply leave the user free to run any applications they choose. But for other users, you may want to put some applications off limits, or you may want to restrict them to running only those few applications that management has approved.

Getting Ready to Restrict the Applications and Widgets

To restrict the applications and widgets a user can run, you use Workgroup Manager, running it on a Mac that contains the applications you want to restrict. This is because Workgroup Manager needs to be able to read the digital signatures of those applications to help it identify exactly which applications to lock down.

If you've got a Mac client that has both the applications and the Server Administration Tools already installed, use that. Otherwise, download the Server Administration Tools from the Apple website (http://support.apple.com/downloads/; search for "Server Admin Tools" and grab the latest version) and install them on one of your client Macs.

NOTE   If you have a Mac OS X server, and you've installed on it all the applications you need to restrict, you can perform these maneuvers on the server instead.

To get ready to restrict the applications and widgets, take these steps to launch Workgroup Manager and get to the Applications pane:

1. Log in to a Mac that has all the applications you want to permit, plus the Server Administration Software.

2. Click the Workgroup Manager icon on the Dock to open Workgroup Manager.

3. Connect to your directory server.

4. Authenticate yourself as directory administrator if Workgroup Manager doesn't do this for you automatically.

5. Click the user or group you want to affect.

6. Click the Preferences button to display the Preferences pane.

7. In the Overview pane, click the Applications icon to display the Applications pane.

NOTE   You can also control applications for a Mac or a group of Macs in Workgroup Manager. For example, if you provide Macs that can be used by anyone who can physically access them (for instance, in a library setting), you may want to restrict the applications they can run.

You're now ready to set restrictions for the user as discussed in the following sections.

Restricting the Applications the User Can Run

You can restrict the applications a user can run in three ways:

- **By allowing only specific applications**   You can draw up a list of the applications the user is allowed to run.
- **By blocking applications in specific folders**   You can prevent the user from running applications in one or more folders.
- **By allowing applications in specific folders**   You can tell Mac OS X that applications in one or more particular folders are okay, even if you don't know which applications are actually there.

You can use one, two, or all three of these approaches to control what the user can run. For example, you can allow only specific applications but also allow the user to run any application that's in a folder you approve.

TIP   When you restrict the applications a user can run, it's a good idea to customize the Dock and remove the icons for the applications they're not allowed to use. Also tell the user about the restrictions. Otherwise, you'll get help calls asking why the user receives the message "You don't have permission to use the application 'Preview'" or whichever restricted application they've tried to run.

Allowing Only Specific Applications

To choose the applications the user can run, follow these steps:

1. In Workgroup Manager, click the Applications tab to display the Applications pane.
2. In the Manage bar, click the Always option button to activate the other controls. Figure 9-48 shows the Applications pane open with a list of permitted applications underway.
3. Select the Restrict Which Applications Are Allowed To Launch check box.
4. With the lower Applications tab selected, add the permitted applications to the Always Allow These Applications list box like this:
   a. Click the + button to open a dialog box for adding applications.
   b. Select the application or applications. SHIFT-click or ⌘-click to select multiple applications at once.
   c. Click the Add button.

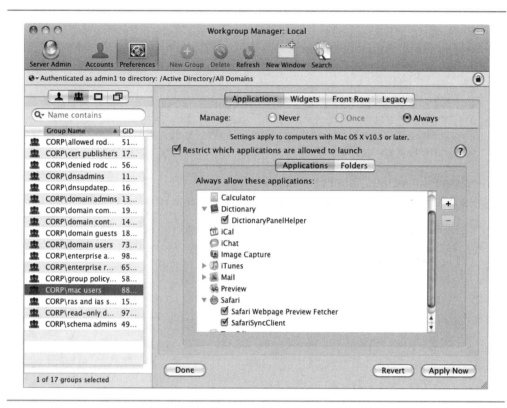

Figure 9-48. Set up a list of approved applications in the Applications pane.

  d. If the application has a digital signature applied to it, Workgroup Manager protects it using the digital signature. If the application doesn't have a digital signature, Workgroup Manager prompts you to add one (see Figure 9-49). Normally, you'll want to click the Sign button. This prevents users from renaming a restricted application as one of the applications you've allowed and running it under the radar.

Figure 9-49. Workgroup Manager prompts you to add a digital signature to an application that lacks one.

5. If a disclosure triangle appears to the left an application you add, the application has helper applications that you can disable. To do this, click the disclosure triangle to display the helper applications and then clear the check box for each one you want to disable.

CAUTION Normally it's best to leave the helper applications enabled unless you know users can use them to take actions you don't want. Disabling a helper application may make the application behave differently or become unstable—so if you do decide to disable helper applications, make sure you test the applications they help to make sure they run okay without them.

Setting Up Allowed and Blocked Folders

To set up allowed and blocked folders of applications, follow these steps:

1. In Workgroup Manager, with the Applications tab selected on the upper tab bar, click Folders on the lower tab bar to display the Folders pane (shown in Figure 9-50 with folders added).

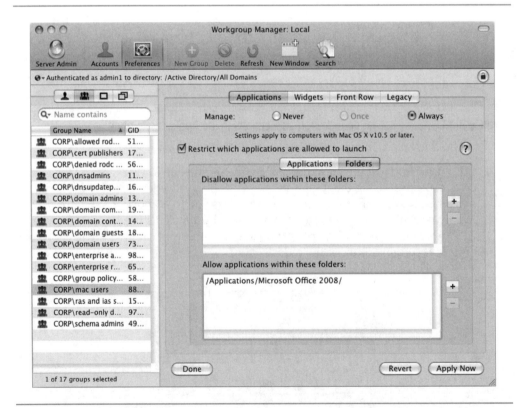

Figure 9-50. In the Folders pane, you can specify folders of blocked applications and folders of permitted applications.

2. To bar applications in one or more folders, follow these steps:

   a. Click the + button to the right of the Disallow Applications Within These Folders list box.

   b. In the dialog box that opens, select the folder that contains the applications you want to block.

   c. Click the Add button.

   d. Repeat these steps to add other blocked folders as needed.

3. To allow applications in one or more folders, follow these steps:

   a. Click the + button to the right of the Allow Applications Within These Folders list box.

   b. In the dialog box that opens, select the folder that contains the applications you want to permit the user to run.

   c. Click the Add button.

   d. Repeat these steps to add other allowed folders as needed.

4. If you've finished making changes to the software the user can run, click the Apply Now button. If you're going to change the settings for widgets, Front Row, or legacy applications, you may prefer to wait until you've finished changing the settings before you apply the changes.

Choosing Which Widgets the User Can Run

Depending on what the user is doing, widgets can be essential to a productive working day or another means of frittering away your company's precious time. To reduce distractions, you may want to lock down the selection of widgets that users can run—or prevent them from running any widgets at all.

To control which widgets the user can run, follow these steps:

1. Click the Widgets tab in the upper tab bar in the Applications pane to display the Widgets pane.

2. In the Manage bar, select the Always option button to enable the controls in the lower pane (shown in Figure 9-51 with some business-useless widgets pruned out).

3. Select the Allow Only The Following Dashboard Widgets To Run check box.

4. In the list box, select each widget that you want to prevent the user from running. As usual, click to select a single item, click the first item and then SHIFT-click the last item to select a contiguous range of items, or click the first item and then ⌘-click each other item to select separate items.

5. Click the – button to remove the selected items from the list.

6. If you need to add widgets to the list, click the + button, select the widget or widgets in the dialog box that opens, and then click the Add button.

7. If you've finished making changes to the software the user can run, click the Apply Now button. Otherwise, follow through the next section.

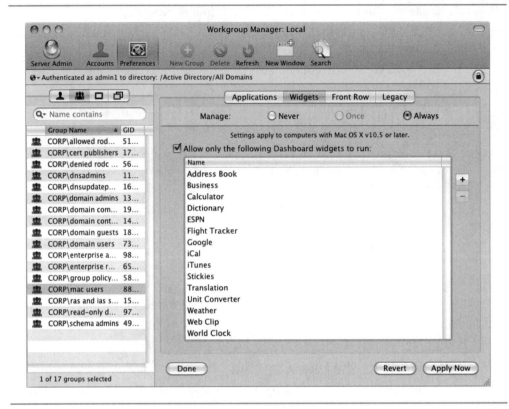

Figure 9-51. You can also choose which widgets to allow the user to run.

Choosing Whether the User Can Run Front Row

Front Row tends to be used for home entertainment rather than work, so Workgroup Manager provides a separate pane for turning it off easily. If you want to disable Front Row, follow these steps:

1. Click the Front Row tab in the upper tab bar to display the Front Row tab.

2. In the Manage bar, select the Always option button.

3. In the main part of the pane, clear the Allow Front Row check box.

Again, you can click the Apply Now button to apply the change immediately.

NOTE The Legacy pane in Workgroup Manager lets you control applications for Macs that are still running Mac OS X 10.4 (Tiger). If you need to add older Macs to your Windows network, look into these options—but also see whether you can upgrade the Macs to Mac OS X 10.6 (Snow Leopard) to make them more manageable. If a Mac has a PowerPC processor, Mac OS X 10.5 (Leopard) will be as far as you can go, but even Leopard is a hefty improvement on Tiger.

CHAPTER 10 | Run Windows Programs on Macs

or many of your network's Mac users, the best bet may be a pure play—to use only native Mac OS X applications or UNIX applications that you can run under the X11 windowing system. But other Mac users may need to run Windows programs as well, either for full-on compatibility with the Windows users or because no Mac application (or no adequate Mac application) is available.

This chapter starts by discussing your options for running Windows programs on Macs. It then shows you how to use each approach.

Understanding the Options for Running Windows Programs on Macs

Any Intel-based Mac can run Windows programs in three ways:

- **Remote Desktop Connection** Remote Desktop Connection enables a Mac to run one or more Windows programs across a network or the Internet. On your Windows server, you use the Remote Desktop Services feature in a similar way to how you use it for Windows PCs: You turn on Remote Desktop Services if you're not already running it, set up virtual machines, and then set up the programs that users may run remotely. Once the user has established a connection using Remote Desktop connection, they can run the programs much as if they were running them locally.

 NOTE You can also use Remote Desktop Connection to control a Windows PC across the network. This capability can be useful for administering servers remotely (even from a Mac rather than from a PC). You can also connect remotely to a PC running Windows XP Professional; Windows Vista Business, Ultimate, or Professional; or Windows 7 Professional, Ultimate, or Enterprise. We won't examine this capability in detail in the chapter, but you'll find it works in much the same way as Remote Desktop Services.

- **Virtual machine** You install a virtual-machine application and run it to create a fake PC running within Mac OS X. You can then install Windows on the virtual machine and run whichever Windows programs you need. (You can also install other operating systems, such as Linux.)

 NOTE Some virtual-machine applications can run a Boot Camp installation of Windows, which lets you use your Boot Camp Windows from inside Mac OS X as well as on its own.

- **Boot Camp** You create a separate partition on a Mac's hard drive and install Windows on it. You can then boot the Mac either to Mac OS X or to Windows.

 NOTE Macs with PowerPC processors can't use Boot Camp, but they can use either Remote Desktop Connection or Microsoft's geriatric virtual-machine emulation application, Virtual PC.

Which Means of Running Windows Programs Is the Best for Your Network?

Here are quick points for deciding which way of running Windows programs is best for your network:

- Given that you have a Windows Server (or perhaps whole server farms of the beasts), start by looking at Remote Desktop Connection. This may not provide the performance you need, or it may add too grievously to the burden on your server. But in many cases it's a neat and highly manageable solution for light to moderate use of Windows programs.

- If your users need to run Windows programs right alongside Mac applications, use a virtual machine.

- If any users need high-performance Windows workstations, use Boot Camp. (Or give each user a PC as well as a Mac.)

You'll find more details on the pros and cons of the different approaches in the following sections.

Running Windows Programs Using Remote Desktop Connection

In a Windows Server network, the best way of running Windows programs on Macs is by using Remote Desktop Connection to control a virtual Windows PC hosted by Remote Desktop Services. The virtual PC runs the programs, and you control it—and them—from the Mac.

Like most Microsoft technologies, Remote Desktop Services works better and offers far more options for Windows PCs (preferably running Windows 7) than for the Mac. But Microsoft's Remote Desktop Connection for Mac is still a powerful and effective piece of software that gives you an easy way to access a Windows PC and run Windows programs from the Mac.

Setting Up Remote Desktop Services for Macs

On the assumption that you know your way around Windows Server, I'm not going to tell you how to set up Remote Desktop Services. But there are two points to keep in mind.

First, for your Macs to be able to use Remote Desktop Services, you must set Remote Desktop Services to not require Network Level Authentication:

- If you're setting up Remote Desktop Services on a server, select the Do Not Require Network Level Authentication option button on the Specify Authentication Method For Remote Desktop Session Host screen.

- If you've already set up Remote Desktop Services, follow these steps:

    1. In Server Manager, expand the Remote Desktop Services node under the Roles node.

    2. Click the Remote Desktop Session Host Configuration node to display its screens.

    3. In the Connections box, right-click the RDP-Tcp connection and choose Properties from the context menu. On the General tab of the RDP-Tcp Properties dialog box, make sure the Allow Connections Only From Computers Running Remote Desktop With Network Level Authentication check box is cleared. Click the OK button to close the dialog box.

Second, Macs can't connect through RemoteApp, so you need to provide complete virtual PCs for them to connect to rather than just programs.

Installing Remote Desktop Connection on the Mac

Next, download the Remote Desktop Connection client from the Mactopia zone on the Microsoft website (www.microsoft.com/mac/). Click the Downloads link, click Remote Desktop in the Products section (down toward the bottom of the page), and then click the link for the latest version of Microsoft Remote Desktop Connection Client for Mac in the language you want. You get a choice of languages, from English and Spanish through to Dutch, Swedish, and Japanese.

Open the disk image file if Safari doesn't open it automatically for you, and then double-click the Remote Desktop Connection package file it contains. Follow through the rest of the installation. There are no tricky choices, but if you're running any of the Microsoft Office 2004 or Office 2008 applications, Installer prompts you to quit them in order to continue.

Connecting via Remote Desktop Connection

After installing Remote Desktop Connection, launch it from the Applications folder. At first, you'll see a minimalist window that shows only the Computer text box and the Connect button. Figure 10-1 shows the Remote Desktop Connection window with a remote host's address entered.

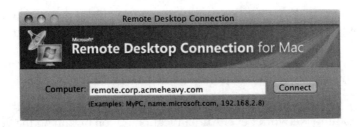

Figure 10-1. Remote Desktop Connection first opens as a small window like this.

NOTE   As with any other application, CTRL-CLICK or RIGHT-CLICK Remote Desktop Connection's Dock icon and choose Options | Keep In Dock if you plan to use Remote Desktop Connection frequently.

Connecting Quickly via Remote Desktop Connection

If you need to connect to a Remote Desktop host only once, type the host's name (for example, **remote.corp.acmeheavy.com**) or IP address (for example, **10.0.0.5**) in the Computer text box and click the Connect button. But if you'll use the host in the future, as is usually the case, create a connection with the host's details and save it in a file. You can then open the connection file just like any other file.

Creating and Saving a Connection File for Remote Desktop Connection

The connection file includes the computer's name or IP address, your logon details for the computer (optionally), and settings that control how the connection behaves.

Remote Desktop Connection confusingly uses preferences (which are normally for an application) instead of settings to configure each connection, so it may take you a moment to get the hang of where things are. Here's what you do:

- Create a new connection.
- Open the Preferences window (which is for the connection) and choose settings in it.
- Close the Preferences window.
- Save the connection.

Here's a walkthrough of what you actually do:

1. If you've just opened Remote Desktop Connection for the first time, you'll have an empty connection open named Default.rdp (you won't see the name, but Remote Desktop Connection creates this connection automatically). If you've used Remote Desktop Connection before, press ⌘-N or choose File | New Connection to create a new connection. Again, you get the little Remote Desktop Connection window shown in Figure 10-1.

2. Type the computer's name or IP address. (You need to enter this information before Remote Desktop Connection will let you save a connection.)

3. Press ⌘-SHIFT-S or choose File | Save As to display the Save As dialog box.

NOTE   If you've got the Default.rdp file open, you need to press ⌘-SHIFT-S rather than plain ⌘-S to display the Save As dialog box. Pressing ⌘-S simply saves the changes to Default.rdp, which may not be what you want to do.

4. Type a descriptive name for the connection, and then click the Save button to save it and close the dialog box.

NOTE   Remote Desktop Connection automatically saves your connections in a folder called RDC Connections in your Documents folder (~/Documents/RDC Connections/). This is usually a good place to keep the connections, but you can choose a different folder if you prefer.

5. Press ⌘-COMMA or choose Remote Desktop Connection | Preferences to open the Preferences window.

6. If the Login pane (see Figure 10-2) doesn't appear at the front, click the Login button.

7. Type the username, password, and domain (if necessary) for the Remote Desktop Services host.

8. Select the Add User Information To Your Keychain check box if you want to store the details in the keychain. This move saves time, but it gives less security than typing the user name and password each time.

9. Select the Reconnect Automatically If Disconnected check box if you want Remote Desktop Connection to automatically reestablish the connection if it gets disconnected. Usually this setting is helpful, too.

10. Click the Display button to open the Display pane (see Figure 10-3).

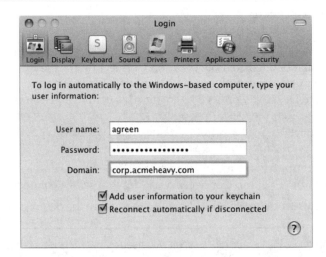

Figure 10-2.   Enter the login information for the Remote Desktop Services host on the Login pane of Remote Desktop Connection's Preferences window.

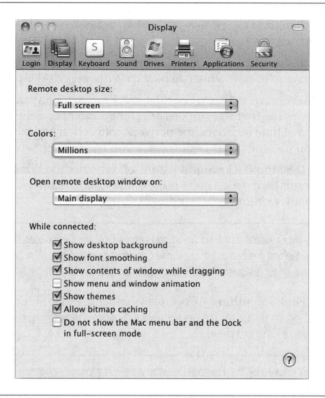

Figure 10-3. Use the Display preferences pane to set the remote desktop's size and number of colors and to choose performance options.

11. In the Remote Desktop Size pop-up menu, choose the window size to use. You get a full range of resolutions from 640×400 (useful for some mobile devices, but too small for Macs) up to the highest resolution the Mac's screen can handle. Choose Full Screen if you want the Windows desktop to appear full screen. This is often a good choice if the user will be working exclusively on the remote desktop because it saves them from clicking outside the Windows box unintentionally.

12. In the Colors pop-up up menu, choose the number of colors to use:

   ■ **256 Colors** Use this setting for dial-up connections only. All the colors will look horrible.

   ■ **Thousands** Use this setting when connecting over the Internet or if your network is usually busy. If the Windows programs the user runs don't involve graphics, thousands of colors is usually plenty to make them look okay.

- **Millions**　Use this setting to see the display at full quality over a LAN connection (don't try it over an Internet connection). For working with graphics on the Windows box, this is the best setting for seeing the details.

13. If the Mac has multiple displays, use the Open Remote Desktop Window On pop-up menu to choose which display the Windows desktop appears on.

14. In the While Connected area, clear the check boxes for any options the user doesn't need. The first five options affect the amount of data that Remote Desktop must transfer across the network connection to the Mac, so the fewer options you use, the better performance you'll get—at the cost of looks.

- **Show Desktop Background**　Controls whether the Windows desktop background appears. This is useless other than helping sustain the illusion of actually working on a Windows PC.

NOTE　If the network across which you're using Remote Desktop Connection has plenty of bandwidth, it's fine to turn on the first five options in the While Connected area to give Windows a better look. Turn some or all of them off for a slower network connection or for a fast but congested network.

- **Show Font Smoothing**　Controls whether the Mac shows the fonts smoothed or in all their jagged glory. You can safely turn off font smoothing unless working on designs.

NOTE　Settings chosen by the Remote Desktop administrator may override the choices you make in Remote Desktop Connection preferences. For example, if the Remote Desktop administrator has turned font smoothing off, your selecting the Show Font Smoothing check box will have no effect. If you are the Remote Desktop administrator, you can resolve these issues by having an argument with yourself.

- **Show Contents Of Window When Dragging**　Controls whether a window shows its contents when dragged or whether it appears as an empty frame. Turning off this setting is generally a good idea.

- **Show Menu And Window Animation**　Controls whether the Mac displays Windows' animations on menus and windows. You can easily dispense with these.

- **Show Themes**　Controls whether the Mac displays Windows' themes—the graphical looks and rounded corners on Windows. If you turn off themes, you get better performance and the square-cornered Windows 2000 look—functional enough, but a bit industrial for some tastes.

- **Allow Bitmap Caching**　Controls whether the Mac stores partial screen pictures to help it redraw the screen more quickly. Caching improves performance but is technically a security threat, because someone could hack into the Mac and retrieve the bitmaps to see what you had been doing. For desktop Macs kept inside a company or organization, this threat isn't worth worrying about, so select this check box. For MacBooks that venture beyond the premises, decide depending on how sensitive your company or organization's data is.

■ **Do Not Show The Mac Menu Bar And The Dock In Full-Screen Mode** Controls whether the menu bar and the Dock appear when Remote Desktop Connection is running full screen.

15. Click the Keyboard button to display the Keyboard pane (see Figure 10-4). Here, you can choose which Mac keys to use in place of Windows keys, such as the Windows key. For most users, the Secondary Mouse Button, the Alt Key, and the Windows Start Key are the most important settings.

■ To turn off a shortcut, clear its check box.

■ To change a shortcut, click to select it, click in the Mac column, and then press the key or key combination you want to use.

16. Click the Sound button to display the Sound pane (see Figure 10-5).

17. Select the appropriate option button for dealing with the sound:

■ **On The Macintosh Computer Only** Select this option button if you want to bring the sound to the Mac's speakers. This takes more network bandwidth but is vital for any Windows program that depends on sounds.

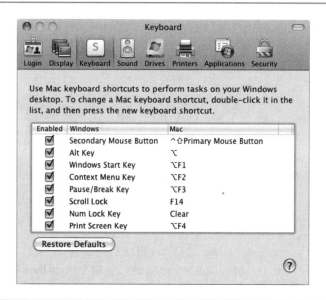

Figure 10-4. Use the Keyboard pane to configure how to map the Mac's keyboard to the Windows keyboard.

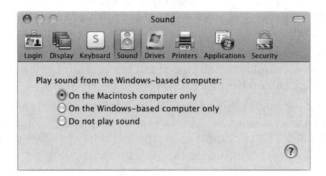

Figure 10-5. The Sound pane lets you bring the remote PC's sound to the Mac, play it on the remote host or PC, or suppress it.

- **On The Windows-Based Computer Only** Don't select this option button because the Remote Desktop host won't have any interest in playing sounds from the virtual PC. (This option button is for using Remote Desktop Connection to control a physical Windows PC.)

- **Do Not Play Sound** Select this option button to turn off sound altogether. This helps reduce Remote Desktop Connection's use of the network.

18. Click the Drives button to display the Drives pane (see Figure 10-6).

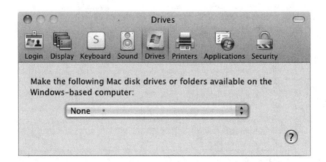

Figure 10-6. The Drives pane enables you to share one or more of the Mac's drives or folders with the Windows host.

19. If you want to share one or more of the Mac's drives or folders with the Windows PC, open the pop-up menu and make the appropriate choice (the default setting is None). For example, choose All Disk Drives to share all disk drives. Sharing a drive like this creates a potential security risk to the Mac and is not normally a good idea, but you may need to use it sometimes to let the user transfer files easily between the Windows PC and the Mac.

20. Click the Printers button to display the Printers pane (see Figure 10-7).

21. If you want to be able to print from the Windows PC to a printer connected to the Mac, select the Use A Printer That Is Connected To The Mac check box and then pick the printer in the pop-up menu.

22. Click the Applications button to display the Applications pane (see Figure 10-8).

23. If you want Windows to launch an application automatically when the user connects via Remote Desktop Connection, select the Start Only The Following Windows-Based Application When You Log In To The Remote Computer check box. Type the application's path and filename into the Application Path And File Name text box, and then type in the application's working directory in the Working Directory text box.

24. Click the Security button to display the Security pane (see Figure 10-9).

25. Select the appropriate option button for your company or organization's security needs:

   ■ **Always Connect, Even If Authentication Fails**   Select this option button if your priority is on connecting and you're confident the user won't connect to an imposter. If you've set up the network, this may be a reasonable assumption.

Figure 10-7.   You can also print from the Windows PC to a printer connected to the Mac.

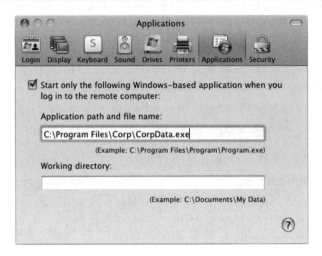

Figure 10-8. The Applications pane lets you set an application to run automatically when you connect to the Windows PC via Remote Desktop Connection.

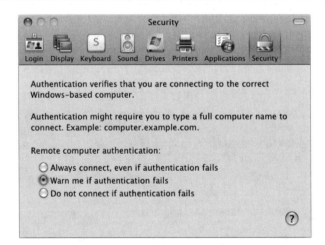

Figure 10-9. In the Security pane, decide whether to require authentication to make sure the user is connecting to the right remote computer.

■ **Warn Me If Authentication Fails**   Select this option button to have Remote Desktop Connection warn about authentication problems and allow the user to decide whether to go ahead with the connection. This is usually the most practical setting.

■ **Do Not Connect If Authentication Fails**   Select this option button to have Remote Desktop Connection refuse any connection that fails authentication. This is the safest setting.

26. Click the Close button (the red button on the title bar) to close the Preferences window.

27. Press ⌘-s or choose File | Save to save the changes you've made to the connection.

The connection is now ready for use.

Connecting Using a Saved Connection

If you've just created a connection as described in the previous section, all you need do to connect to the Windows PC is click the Connect button.

Otherwise, open the connection in one of these ways:

■ Choose File | Open A Recent Connection, and then click the connection on the submenu. Remote Desktop Connection automatically starts connecting for you.

■ Choose File | Open A Saved Connection (or press ⌘-o), click the connection in the Open RDC dialog box, and click the Open button. Then click the Connect button in the Remote Desktop Connection window.

If you chose not to store your username or password (or both) in the connection, Remote Desktop Connection prompts you to provide them (see Figure 10-10).

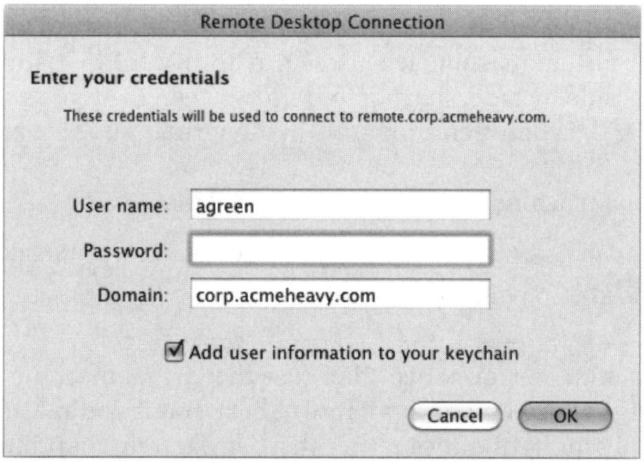

Figure 10-10.   Enter your credentials for the connection if Remote Desktop Connection prompts you.

Type your credentials, and select the Add User Information To Your Keychain check box if you want to save them for future use. Then click the OK button.

Working on the Remote Windows Box

Once you've connected to the remote Windows box, the Remote Desktop Connection window shows the PC's screen (or, if you chose to use Remote Desktop Connection full screen, the Windows desktop takes over your whole screen).

You can now work much as if you were sitting at a Windows PC. Use the keyboard shortcuts you chose in the Keyboard pane to issue keyboard commands, and wield your mouse as usual.

If you chose to share a printer with the PC, you'll find it in the Printers folder or Printers And Faxes folder (depending on the version of Windows). If you chose to share one or more drives or folders, you'll find them in Computer or My Computer (again, depending on the version of Windows) in the Other Drives category.

NOTE   When you're using Remote Desktop Connection full screen, press ⌘-TAB to switch to another Mac application. Unless you've selected the Do Not Show The Mac Menu Bar And The Dock In Full-Screen Mode check box, you can display the menu bar by moving the mouse pointer to the top of the screen and display the Dock by moving the mouse pointer to the bottom of the screen or whichever side you've parked it on.

Logging Off from the Remote Desktop Host

When you have finished using the remote desktop, log off to stop using it. Click the Start menu, and then click the Log Off button.

Running Windows Programs Using a Virtual Machine

If Remote Desktop Connection isn't a practical solution to your users' Windows needs, consider running a virtual-machine application on the Mac instead and installing Windows on it. The virtual machine lets users run both Mac OS X applications and Windows programs side by side, sharing folders between the two as needed and copying and pasting data between programs in the virtual machine and the Mac's native applications.

Running a virtual machine has three main disadvantages:

- **Cost**   You will need to pay for a copy of Windows for the virtual machine. You may also need to pay for the virtual-machine application itself. (More on this in a moment.)

- **Virtual-machine performance**   Because the virtual machine is emulating a PC, its performance will be moderate at best. But if you're using the virtual machine only for light duties rather than, say, terrain mapping, this may be enough.

- **Mac performance**   Running the virtual machine may also slow down the Mac.

Choosing a Virtual-Machine Application

At this writing, there are three main virtual-machine applications for Mac OS X:

- **VMWare Fusion**   VMWare Fusion, from VMWare, Inc., costs around $80 per workstation. VMWare Fusion lets you run most versions of Windows and many other operating systems; it can also run Mac OS X Server on top of Mac OS X (though it cannot run the client version of Mac OS X). You can run a virtual machine either inside a VMWare Fusion window or have its applications appear in Mac-like windows directly on the Mac desktop (not contained by a VMWare Fusion window), a feature called Unity.

- **Parallels Desktop for Mac**   Parallels Desktop for Mac, from Parallels, costs around $80 per workstation. Parallels Desktop can run most versions of Windows and many versions of UNIX and Linux, but it cannot run Mac OS X. Parallels Desktop can import virtual machines from VMWare and VirtualBox, which is a neat trick. You can run a virtual machine either in a Parallels window or have each application appear in its own Mac-like window directly on the Mac desktop, which Parallels calls Coherence mode.

- **VirtualBox**   VirtualBox from Sun Microsystems (www.virtualbox.org) is a free open-source virtualization application. VirtualBox runs all current versions of Windows—Windows 7, Windows Vista, and Windows XP; Windows Server 2008 and Windows Server 2003—and many versions of UNIX and Linux. VirtualBox does not run Mac OS X.

If you're just getting started with virtual machines, VirtualBox is well worth looking at first. Apart from the price being right, it's easy to use and generally works pretty well. But its performance seems to lag behind that of VMWare Fusion and Parallels Desktop.

VMWare Fusion and Parallels Desktop are pretty much neck and neck for features, so choosing between them can be tough. Both VMWare, Inc., and Parallels offer a free trial version, so you can check them out thoroughly. This section shows screens from VMWare Fusion.

 NOTE   VMWare Fusion and Parallels Desktop both can create a virtual machine based on a Boot Camp partition. This capability lets you run the same copy of Windows in either a virtual machine or directly on the Mac's hardware, which gives you much more flexibility in using Windows.

Installing the Virtual-Machine Application

Once you've downloaded the full version or the trial version of the virtual-machine application, you can install it in minutes. For example, Figure 10-11 shows the disk image for VMWare Fusion. Double-click the Install VMWare Fusion icon, and you're in business. You get to accept the license agreement, you can change the default installation location if you so choose, and you must authenticate yourself; but that's the full extent of the excitement.

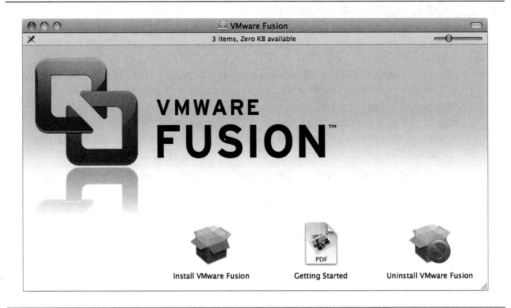

Figure 10-11. Double-click the Install VMWare Fusion icon on the disk image to launch Installer.

 NOTE Keep the virtual-machine application's disk image. You will need it again if you want to uninstall the virtual-machine application.

Creating a Virtual Machine

After installing the virtual-machine application, you create a virtual machine so that you can then install Windows on it. Each of the applications walks you through the process of setting up the virtual machine, making it as easy as possible. For example, VMWare Fusion offers an Easy Install feature (see Figure 10-12) that lets you preload the account name, password, and Windows product key, so that you can just leave the installation to run while you go off and find better entertainment.

You'll usually want to select the option for customizing the virtual machine, as shown for VMWare in Figure 10-13, so that you can adjust key elements such as the amounts of disk space and RAM the virtual machine has and which of the Mac's network interfaces it uses.

Depending on the Mac you're using and the virtual-machine application, you can also choose the number of processors to give the virtual machine (see Figure 10-14).

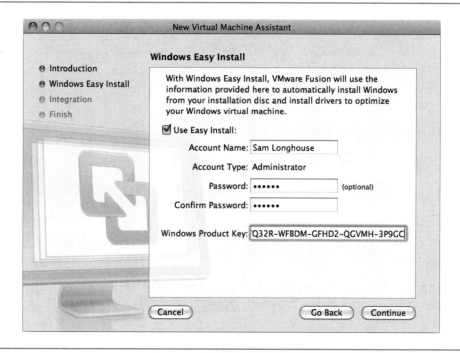

Figure 10-12. VMWare offers an Easy Install feature in which you supply all the information needed to run the installation without your further intervention.

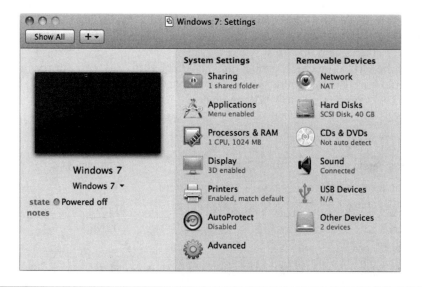

Figure 10-13. To customize the virtual machine, open the Settings dialog box.

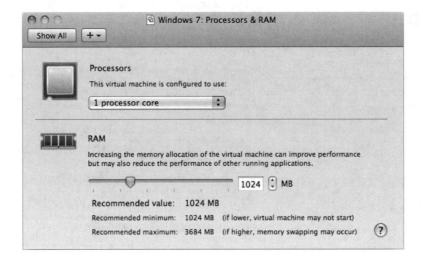

Figure 10-14.   Setting the number of CPUs and the amount of RAM for a virtual machine in VMWare Fusion. You can change these settings later if necessary.

Table 10-1 suggests how much disk space and RAM to use for virtual machines running the most widely used versions of Windows. The RAM amounts are minimums, so if the Mac has plenty of RAM to spare, give the virtual machine more. The amounts of disk space shown in the table are plenty for the operating system itself plus conventional numbers of Windows programs, but they assume that you will store most of the data files on the network. If you will store them on the virtual hard disk inside the virtual machine, you'll need more space. Generally, though, it's better to keep the files on a real disk from which you can back them up easily.

Each of the virtual-machine applications uses a slightly different approach to setting up the virtual hard disks, but the general principles are the same. Figure 10-15 shows the Virtual Disks preferences in VMWare Fusion.

Windows Version	Disk Space	Minimum RAM
Windows 7	16GB	1GB
Windows Vista	16GB	1GB
Windows XP	8GB	512MB

Table 10-1.   Disk Space and RAM for Windows in Virtual Machines

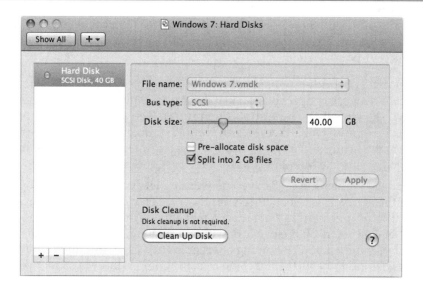

Figure 10-15. Choosing settings for the virtual hard disk for a virtual machine in VMWare Fusion.

The terminology varies among the various applications, but there are three main choices to make here:

- **How big to make the virtual hard disk**   Again, Table 10-1 offers some suggestions. If the Mac has plenty of disk space to spare, you can give the virtual machine a bigger cage.

- **Whether to split the virtual hard disk into 2GB files**   Creating 2GB files makes it easier to back up the virtual hard disk onto a DVD. If you're planning to back up the virtual hard disk onto a huge external hard drive, or if you're not planning to back it up, you don't need to select this option.

- **Whether to create an expanding disk or a plain disk**   An *expanding disk* is a file that takes up only as much space on the Mac's hard disk as it actually needs, while pretending to the virtual machine it has all the gigabytes you allocated to the virtual hard disk. A *plain disk* is a file that actually grabs that amount of space on the Mac's hard disk and devotes it to the virtual machine, whether the VM uses it or not. A plain disk gives better performance, as long as the Mac can spare all those genuine gigabytes. Create an expanding disk if the Mac is short of disk space.

 NOTE   In VMWare Fusion, you create a plain disk by selecting the Pre-Allocate Disk Space check box in Hard Disk preferences. Clear this check box to create an expanding disk.

Choosing How to Handle Networking

Your other main choice is how to handle networking for the virtual machine. You typically have four choices, as you see in Figure 10-16, which shows the Network preferences in VMWare Fusion:

■ **Shared Networking** Shared networking lets the virtual machine tap into the Mac's network connections, so that it can access the network just as the Mac can. The virtual-machine application runs a Network Address Translation service (a mini DHCP server, as it were) that doles out IP addresses to the virtual machines. This gives you the greatest integration between the virtual machine and the Mac and is usually the best option to choose.

■ **Bridged Networking** Bridged networking lets your virtual machine appear on the network as a separate computer with its own IP address. The advantage of this arrangement is that you can make the virtual machine accessible to other computers on the network without involving the host machine (the Mac). This is handy if you're running a server in the virtual machine, but it's usually less helpful if the virtual machine is just running Windows so that you can run Windows programs.

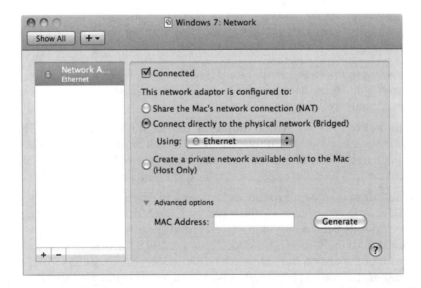

Figure 10-16. Choose among shared networking, bridged networking, and host-only networking, or turn off networking to prevent your virtual machine from contacting the outside world.

- **Host-Only Networking** Host-only networking gives the virtual machine access to the Mac but not to the rest of the network. Use this option when you're running two or more virtual machines as their own network on top of the Mac—for example, when testing software.

- **No Networking** This option runs the virtual machine in glorious isolation.

When you've made your choice, follow through the remaining screens to finish creating the virtual machine. Then start the virtual machine to kick the installation process into life.

 NOTE Depending on the virtual-machine application you're using, you may need to tell the virtual machine to boot from the Windows DVD. In VMWare Fusion, you typically identify the DVD earlier in the process, so the virtual machine knows where it is.

If you've set the virtual machine for an easy install, you can simply leave it to run. If you've chosen to do things the hard way, you'll get the chance to choose installation options as usual—for example, whether to perform a custom installation or an upgrade. (Clue: Unless this virtual machine already contains a version of Windows, you'll want the custom installation, which installs a fresh copy of Windows.)

 TIP The Easy Install options can be a great timesaver, but be aware that they tend to leave Windows 7 or Windows Vista set to activate itself immediately the moment you log on. If you're running a Windows network, you'll know that activation ties the product key to this installation of Windows—which you probably don't want until you've checked out how well Windows runs on the virtual machine. On the other hand, if you have a site license for Windows, this may be less of a concern than if you're paying through the nose for each additional copy of Microsoft's finest code.

Installing the Virtual Machine Tools or Additions

After you get Windows running, you need to install the virtual machine "tools" or "additions" that make the virtual machine run better on Mac OS X. Normally, the most immediate benefit of these tools is gaining seamless movement of the mouse pointer between the virtual machine and Mac OS X rather than having to press a key combination to release the focus from the virtual machine. The tools also drop a turbo in the graphics performance and reduce the amount of processor power the virtual machine demands—so make sure you install them the moment you get the chance.

To install the virtual machine tools or additions, use these commands:

- **VMWare Fusion** Choose Virtual Machine | Install VMWare Tools.
- **Parallels Desktop** Choose Virtual Machine | Install Parallels Tools.
- **VirtualBox** Choose Devices | Install Guest Additions.

Each of the virtual-machine applications prompts you to install the tools or additions until you give in or kill the prompting—so there's no chance that you'll pass up this vital step in the long run.

Installing Antivirus Software on the Virtual Machine

Installing the tools or additions gives the virtual machine a welcome speed boost—but in this relentlessly warming but heartless world, you need to take away some of that boost immediately by installing antivirus software.

 CAUTION Don't skip installing antivirus software on a Windows virtual machine. If you've seen the movie *Aliens,* you may remember the android Bishop saying, "I may be synthetic, but I'm not stupid." Well, your Windows PC may be synthetic in that it's virtual, but it's certainly stupid enough to catch any of the Windows-themed malware on the Internet unless you protect it. (The one time when you're pretty much safe without using antivirus software is when you've created a virtual machine with no network connection—and you never share documents between it and your network-connected computers.)

The virtual-machine applications are convincing enough these days that very few antivirus programs can detect that they're running on bytes rather than genuine hardware. That means you can use pretty much any of the standard Windows antivirus programs to protect your virtual machine.

VMWare Fusion comes with a complimentary 12-month subscription to McAfee VirusScan Plus. This is a nice touch from VMWare, because you can protect your virtual PC at the click of a button. If you find VirusScan Plus a weightier antivirus package than you want to burden your virtual PC with, or if you're using a different virtual-machine application, look at the free antivirus applications from the likes of Avast (www.avast.com) or AVG (http://free.avg.com). These provide the essential protection that your network's users likely need but don't assume the users' knuckles are dragging close enough to the ground to require a full metal jacket against phishing messages.

Updating Windows with the Latest Service Pack and Patches

After hardening your virtual Windows box with antivirus software, update Windows with the latest Service Pack and then slather on all the patches that have been released since it.

Run Windows Update by choosing Start | All Programs | Windows Update, and then do something productive or amusing (or both) while Windows Update downloads all the updates. Install them, restart Windows as many times as it insists, and your virtual machine will be ready for installing the applications that you actually want to run on it.

 NOTE You may need to reinstall your virtual machine's tools or additions after installing a Windows Service Pack. This is because Service Packs can include severe enough changes to break the tools or additions.

Installing and Running Programs

When you have protected and updated Windows on your virtual machine, install the programs that you actually want to run. Installation should be a breeze—it works the same on the virtual machine as on a real machine.

To run a program, launch it from the Start menu as normal, or use one of Windows' other ways of launching it (for example, use the Quick Launch toolbar).

Most virtual-machine applications give you the choice of running the Windows programs either in the virtual-machine window or integrated into Mac OS X. Using the virtual-machine window (see Figure 10-17, which uses VMWare Fusion) helps you keep Windows and Mac apart and gives you a separate Windows desktop to work on, but integrating the windows (see Figure 10-18, again starring VMWare Fusion) is usually easier when you need to switch from a Mac application to a Windows program, or vice versa.

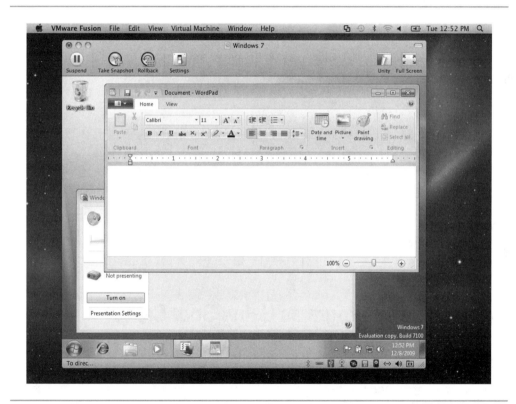

Figure 10-17. Running a Windows program in the virtual machine's window gives you an almost genuine Windows desktop.

Figure 10-18. Running a Windows program integrated into Mac OS X makes switching among applications easier.

Running Windows Programs Using Boot Camp

The third way of running Windows programs on a Mac is to use the Boot Camp feature that Apple builds in. Boot Camp lets you install Windows alongside Mac OS X so that you can boot a Mac in either Mac OS X or Windows, with no virtualization needed.

In a company or organization, you should normally use Boot Camp only for users who have special needs for Windows. When a user genuinely needs better performance than Remote Desktop Connection or a virtual machine can provide, Boot Camp can provide a solution—but it's not a solution you'll normally want to use for regular users.

Boot Camp has three main disadvantages:

■ *You must create a separate partition for Windows on the Mac's hard disk.* You must install Windows on its own partition so that the Mac can boot from it. Boot Camp Assistant makes this easy enough to do, so this disadvantage isn't much of a problem.

- ◼ *You must reboot to switch between Mac OS X and Windows.* You can't use both operating systems, or their applications, at the same time. If what you really need is integration between Mac OS X and Windows, Boot Camp isn't the solution.

- ◼ *You must buy a full, licensed copy of whichever version of Windows you want to run.* You need a copy of Windows for a virtual machine as well, so this disadvantage isn't too severe either.

Understanding the Process of Setting Up Boot Camp

To set up Boot Camp, you perform three main steps:

- ◼ *Create a new partition for Windows.* To do this, you use Boot Camp Assistant.

- ◼ *Install Windows on the new partition.* Boot Camp Assistant automatically launches the installation after creating the new partition.

- ◼ *Install the Windows drivers for the Mac's hardware.* After starting Windows, you need to install the Windows drivers to tell Windows what the Mac's hardware items are and how they work.

TIP   You can install Windows using Boot Camp and then run it through VMWare Fusion or Parallels Desktop. This neat solution can give you the best of both worlds.

Using Boot Camp Assistant to Create a New Partition

First, create a new partition with Boot Camp Assistant like this:

1. Click the desktop to activate the Finder, then open the Utilities folder by pressing ⌘-SHIFT-U or choosing Go | Utilities.

2. Double-click the Boot Camp Assistant icon to launch Boot Camp Assistant. The Assistant displays its Introduction screen.

3. Click the Print Installation & Setup Guide button to print out a hard copy of the Boot Camp Installation & Setup Guide, or print it to a PDF that you can open on another computer.

4. Click the Continue button. The Create A Partition For Windows screen appears (see Figure 10-19).

5. Choose how big a Windows partition to create:

   - ◼ Drag the divider bar to set a custom amount of space for each partition.

   - ◼ Click the Divide Equally button to divide the space equally between Mac OS X and Windows. Unless this Mac has a small disk, this will probably give Windows more space than it really needs.

   - ◼ Click the Use 32 GB button to create a 32GB partition for Windows. This is plenty of space for Windows 7 or Windows Vista, so it's a fair choice.

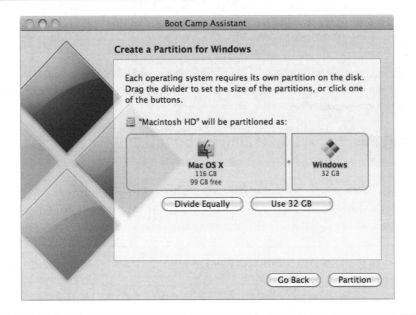

Figure 10-19. On the Create A Partition For Windows screen, drag the divider bar or click one of the buttons to tell Boot Camp Assistant how big a Windows partition to create.

6. Click the Partition button. Boot Camp Assistant partitions the disk as you commanded without damaging your existing Mac OS X data. Boot Camp Assistant then displays the Start Windows Installation screen.

7. Feed the Windows CD or DVD into the Mac's optical drive and click the Start Installation button.

8. The Mac restarts and launches the Windows installation.

9. Follow through the Windows installation, typing in your product key when prompted, and then accepting the license terms.

NOTE   When you enter the license key, clear the Automatically Activate Windows When I'm Online check box to prevent Windows from locking itself to the Mac. Check that Windows runs properly, and that you want to keep using Boot Camp, before you activate Windows. You have a 14-day or 30-day grace period, depending on the version of Windows, so there's plenty of time to assess the performance.

10. On the Where Do You Want To Install Windows? screen, click the partition marked BOOTCAMP.

11. If you're installing Windows Vista or Windows 7, you'll see a warning saying "Windows cannot be installed to Disk 0 Partition 3." When you click the Show Details link, you'll see the message "Windows cannot be installed to this hard disk space. Windows must be installed to a partition formatted as NTFS." This message appears because Boot Camp Assistant has formatted the disk space as FAT32. To convert the partition, follow these steps:

    a. Click the Drive Options (Advanced) link to display a row of controls toward the bottom of the window.

    b. With the BOOTCAMP partition still selected, click the Format link. Windows displays an Install Windows dialog box warning that you're about to wipe out all the data on the partition.

    c. Click the OK button. Windows formats the partition and removes the warning message.

12. With the BOOTCAMP partition still selected, click the Next button to start the installation.

13. After Windows copies and expands the files, follow through the setup screens to create your initial user account, set a password, and pick a user account picture and desktop background.

Installing the Mac Hardware Drivers

Once you've logged on, you'll find Windows using a low resolution that probably makes the Mac's screen look blurry. This is simply because Windows doesn't yet have the right driver for the Mac's graphics card.

Choose Start | Computer to open a Computer window. (In Windows XP, choose Start | My Computer to open a My Computer window.)

Now CRTL-click or right-click the optical drive, and then click Eject on the shortcut menu to eject the Windows disc. Remove it and insert your Mac OS X installation DVD.

Up pops an AutoPlay dialog box for the WindowsSupport disc (see Figure 10-20).

Click the Run Setup.Exe button, and then follow through the steps of Boot Camp Installer. Apart from accepting the license agreement, the only choice you have to make is whether to install the Apple Software Update For Windows. Normally, this is a good idea.

After you've clicked through the screens, the Installer gets to work. It typically takes several minutes to install all the drivers, so take the time to knock a couple of quick tasks off your to-do list.

Figure 10-20. Insert your Snow Leopard install DVD and accept the offer to run the setup .exe application.

When Installer completes its tasks and you click the Finish button, you see the Boot Camp dialog box shown in Figure 10-21, telling you that you must restart the Mac. Click the Yes button to clear up all of Windows' hardware problems.

After Windows restarts, and you log on, your desktop appears at the correct resolution, and all the Mac's hardware should be present and correct.

Installing Antivirus Software

Before you go online to get Windows updates, install antivirus software to protect Windows (and the Mac) from both local and Internet threats.

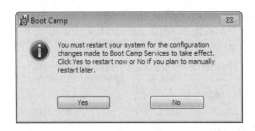

Figure 10-21. After installing the drivers, you'll need to restart Windows.

Because Windows is running directly on the Mac's hardware, you don't have the same performance concerns as for Windows running on a virtual machine, so you can safely load a full antivirus, antispyware, and antiphishing package if the user will need it. To keep Windows running as fast as possible, however, you may prefer to use a less wide-ranging antivirus program.

Updating Windows with the Latest Service Pack and Patches

Next, update Windows with the latest service pack (if there is one) and every relevant patch Microsoft has released since it.

Run Windows Update by choosing Start | All Programs | Windows Update, tell Windows to download everything it says is important, and then give it time to do so. Install all the updates, restart Windows when it prompts you, and you'll be ready to install the programs.

Installing the Programs You Need

Now install the programs you need to run in Windows. Check for updates to the programs to make sure you've got the latest fixes.

Returning to Mac OS X from Windows

To return to Mac OS X from Windows, you can either quickly restart from the Boot Camp icon in the system tray or use the Boot Camp Control Panel to set the startup disk to the Mac OS X installation.

Restarting from the Boot Camp Icon

When you need to restart straight into Mac OS X, click the Boot Camp icon in the system tray (the gray diamond-shaped icon) and click Restart In Mac OS X on the pop-up menu (see Figure 10-22). In the Boot Camp dialog box that opens, click the OK button.

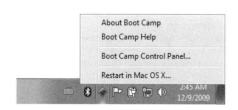

Figure 10-22.   The quick way to return to Mac OS X is to use the Boot Camp icon in the system tray.

Using the Boot Camp Control Panel to Set the Startup Disk

If you want the Mac to start in Mac OS X the next time you boot it, rather than restart it now, use the Boot Camp Control Panel to change the startup disk. Follow these steps:

1. Click the Boot Camp icon in the system tray (the gray diamond-shaped icon), and then click Boot Camp Control Panel.

2. If the User Account Control dialog box opens, make sure it says Boot Camp and then click the Continue button.

3. In the Boot Camp Control Panel (see Figure 10-23), click the Mac OS X item on the Startup Disk tab. This item has the name of the Mac's hard disk partition—for example, Macintosh HD.

4. Click the Restart button. Boot Camp displays a confirmation dialog box.

5. Click the OK button. The Mac restarts into Mac OS X.

NOTE   To get back into Windows, choose Apple | System Preferences and click the Startup Disk icon. Click the Windows On BOOTCAMP icon, and then click the Restart button. Click the Restart button again in the confirmation dialog box that Mac OS X displays. Alternatively, restart the Mac, hold down OPTION at the startup chime, and then select the boot disk.

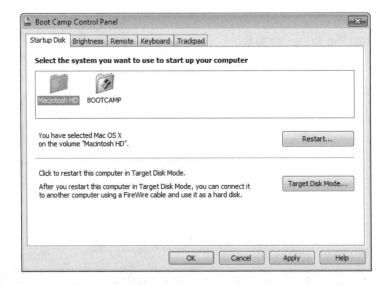

Figure 10-23.   Use the Boot Camp Control Panel to change your startup disk to the Mac's Mac OS X partition.

CHAPTER 11 | Providing Remote Access for and to Macs

These days, working on the road or working from home is an inescapable fact of life for many of the lucky people who still have jobs. And if you run a network, you may positively welcome the freedom to connect to the network remotely rather than having to drive to the office in the middle of the night to discover that a sensitive server has started hyperventilating again and to persuade it to calm down and breathe normally.

So it's likely that you'll need to provide your network's Mac users with remote access via virtual private networking. You can do this either by patching the Macs into your existing virtual private network or by setting up a custom arrangement for the Macs. For example, you can set up virtual private networking on a Mac OS X server connected in a magic triangle to enable your remote Macs to connect to the network.

You may also need to make certain Macs on the network available for connections from outside the network—for example, so that you yourself can reach out from home to grab vital files you've left on your thundering Mac Pro at work, or so that your company's knowledge workers can take remote control of their Macs from outside the office. We'll look briefly at how you can do this as well.

Giving Mac Users Access to Your Windows VPN

If you've already set up a VPN using the Routing And Remote Access (RRAS) service on a Windows server, and you're using conventional VPN authentication rather than Direct Access, you can add the Macs into that VPN along with the Windows users.

You can do this in the same way as for Windows users:

1. Open Active Directory Users And Computers.
2. Click the Users folder to display its contents.
3. Double-click the user to open the Properties dialog box.
4. Click the Dial-in tab to display its contents (see Figure 11-1).
5. In the Network Access Permission group box, select the Allow Access option button if you're not using NPS Network Policy. If you are using NPS Network Policy, select the Control Access Through NPS Network Policy option button.

NOTE   If you need to assign a static IP address to the user, select the Assign Static IP Addresses check box. When Windows Server opens the Static IP Addresses dialog box automatically, select the Assign A Static IPv4 Address check box, type the address, and then click the OK button. (If you're using IPv6, select the Assign A Static IPv6 Address check box, type the address, and provide the prefix and interface ID information if needed.) Similarly, if you need the user to use static routes, select the Apply Static Routes check box and then use the Static Routes dialog box (which opens automatically) to define them.

6. Click the OK button to close the Properties dialog box for the user account.

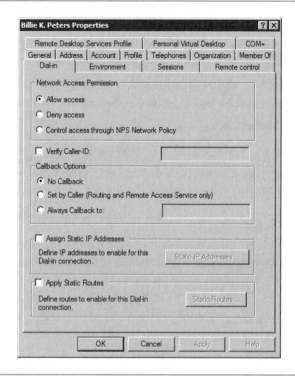

Figure 11-1. Use the Dial-in tab of the Properties dialog box for a user account to allow a user VPN access.

Adding a Mac OS X Server VPN to Your Windows Network

If you use Windows Server 2008's Direct Access feature instead of a VPN, and you have a Mac OS X server running in a magic triangle setup, you may prefer not to set up a Windows-based VPN for your Mac clients. Instead, you can set up the Mac OS X server as the VPN server and have the Macs connect to the network through it.

To set up a VPN on your Mac OS X server, you need to turn on the VPN service (if it's not already running) and configure it (if it's not configured). You can then start the service and choose the users you will allow to connect to it.

Turning On the VPN Service

Start by seeing if the VPN service is running, and turning it on if it isn't. Follow these steps:

1. Open Server Admin. For example, click the Server Admin icon in the Dock.

2. In the Servers list on the left, double-click the server to which you want to connect.

3. Type your username and password if you haven't told your Mac to remember them, and then click the Connect button.

4. In the Servers pane on the left, double-click the server to display the list of services. If the VPN service appears in the list, skip the remaining steps in this list.

5. Click the Settings button on the toolbar to display the Settings pane.

6. Click the Services tab to display the Services pane.

7. Select the VPN check box.

8. Click the Save button to apply the change.

The VPN service appears in the list of services in the Servers pane. Keep Server Admin open so that you can configure the VPN service, as described next.

Configuring the VPN Service

Next, configure the VPN service as described in the following subsections. You first choose settings in the L2TP pane or in the PPTP pane. You then use the Client Information pane to set DNS, search, and routing information for the VPN clients, and finally you choose whether you want your logging to be verbose or terse.

Choosing Between L2TP and PPTP for a Mac OS X Server VPN

When you're setting up a VPN on Mac OS X Server, you can use either L2TP Over IPSec or PPTP:

■ **L2TP Over IPSec** Layer 2 Tunneling Protocol (L2TP) over IP Security (IPSec) is usually the best choice for VPNs on Mac networks. This type of VPN uses strong encryption derived either from a signed digital certificate or from a *shared secret*, a sort of password. Use L2TP Over IPSec for your VPN unless you have a compelling reason to use PPTP. This section shows L2TP in its examples because L2TP is the VPN technology you're most likely to use for a Mac OS X Server VPN.

■ **PPTP** Point-to-Point Tunneling Protocol (PPTP) is an older tunneling protocol that is much less secure than L2TP Over IPSec. PPTP is secured by a password and uses either 128-bit encryption (which is fine) or 40-bit encryption (which is much too weak). At this writing, the only reason to use PPTP for a Mac OS X Server–based VPN is if some of your clients are running Mac OS X version 10.2 (Jaguar)—which they shouldn't be even in these straitened times.

Setting Up an L2TP VPN

To set up an L2TP VPN, follow these steps:

1. In the Servers pane in Server Admin, click the VPN service in the list of services under the server to display the VPN screens.

2. Click the Settings button to display the Settings pane.

3. Click the L2TP tab to display the L2TP pane (see Figure 11-2).

 NOTE   To set up a PPTP VPN, click the PPTP tab instead of the L2TP tab. The PPTP pane has fewer settings than the L2TP pane, but most of the settings it does have are similar to those in the L2TP pane, so you'll have no trouble figuring them out from the instructions here. The one setting that deserves mention is the Allow 40-Bit Encryption Keys In Addition To 128-Bit check box. Make sure this check box is cleared unless you are compelled to accept connections with 40-bit encryption, which is too weak to be safe.

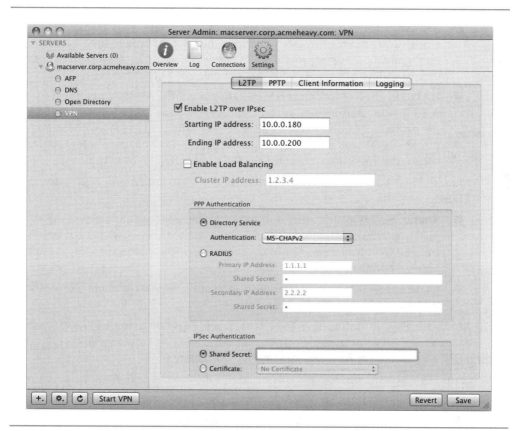

Figure 11-2.   Use the settings in the L2TP pane for the VPN service to set up an L2TP VPN.

4. Select the Enable L2TP Over IPSec check box to make the remaining controls in the pane available.

5. In the Starting IP Address text box, type the first IP address that you want to assign to clients that connect to the VPN.

CAUTION Give your VPN clients a block of IP addresses that you keep separate from the rest of your network. In particular, keep the VPN IP addresses separate from the block of IP addresses that your DHCP server assigns. This separation both helps avoid DHCP problems and lets you easily distinguish the VPN clients from local clients.

6. In the Ending IP Address text box, type the last IP address that you want to assign to VPN clients.

7. If you want to use load balancing on your VPN, select the Enable Load Balancing check box and then type the balancing IP address in the Cluster IP Address text box.

8. In the PPP Authentication box, choose the authentication method for PPP:

   ■ **Directory Service** Select this option button to have VPN clients authenticate via the directory service. Choose Kerberos in the Authentication pop-up menu if you've set up a Kerberos authentication server; choose MS-CHAPv2 if you haven't got Kerberos.

   ■ **RADIUS** Select this option button to have VPN clients authenticate via a Remote Authentication Dial-In User Service (RADIUS) server. Type the primary RADIUS server's IP address in the Primary IP Address text box and its shared secret in the Shared Secret text box, then enter the corresponding information for the secondary RADIUS server.

9. In the IPSec Authentication box, choose how to authenticate VPN clients via IPSec:

   ■ **Shared Secret** Select this option button to authenticate users via the password that you type in the text box. Make this password strong— 8 characters absolute minimum, 12 characters sensible minimum, including letters, numbers, and symbols.

   ■ **Certificate** Select this option button to authenticate users via the certificate that you pick from the pop-up menu.

10. Click the Save button to save the changes you've made to the VPN service.

Setting DNS, Search, and Routing Information for Clients

Now set up DNS, search, and routing information for the VPN's clients:

1. In Server Admin, with the VPN service selected in the Servers pane, click the Settings button on the toolbar to display the Settings pane.

2. Click the Client Information tab to display the Client Information pane (shown in Figure 11-3 with settings chosen).

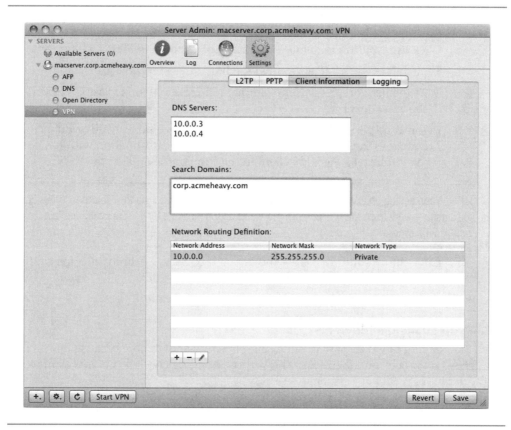

Figure 11-3.   In the Client Information pane for the VPN service, set the DNS server address, the search domains, and the network routing definitions.

3. In the DNS Servers text box, type the IP address of the DNS server the VPN clients should use for resolving DNS queries after connecting to the VPN. (For traffic that doesn't go to the VPN, the VPN client continues to use its usual DNS server—for example, one on the client's local network or at their ISP.) To enter multiple servers, put each on a new line.

4. In the Search Domains text box, enter any search domains that the client will need after connecting to the VPN. (You may not need to enter any search domains.)

NOTE   The entries in the Network Routing Definition box tell the VPN clients which addresses are on the network to which they've connected via the VPN. This lets a client know whether to send the request across the VPN connection or across its regular network or Internet connection. For example, when the client needs to connect to a server on the network, that request should go through the VPN; when the client wants to visit Google, that request should go straight to the Internet rather than to the VPN and then out to the Internet.

5. In the Network Routing Definition list box, set up the network routing definitions that the VPN clients need. Follow these steps:

   a. Click the + button to display the dialog box shown in Figure 11-4.

   b. Type the network's IP address in the IP Address text box.

   c. Type the network mask (for example, 255.255.255.0 for a Class C network) in the Mask text box.

   d. In the Type pop-up menu, choose the network's type: Private or Public. Private tells the VPN client to keep traffic for the destination within the VPN. Public tells the VPN client to send the traffic outside the VPN.

TIP   When setting up a VPN connection for clients who will connect via their Internet connection, you'll usually want to create one or more private routing definitions for your network and let all other traffic go elsewhere.

   e. Click the OK button to close the dialog box. Server Admin adds the routing definition to the Network Routing Definition list box.

6. Click the Save button to save the changes you've made.

Setting Up Logging for the VPN

Click the Logging tab to display the Logging pane (not shown here because there's only one check box to see), and then select the Verbose Logging check box if you want to see all the details of what happens on the VPN.

Verbose logging is usually helpful at first because it lets you tell exactly what's happening on the VPN, but when you're satisfied that things are working okay, you may want to drop back to regular logging by clearing the Verbose Logging check box.

Click the Save button to save the changes you've made.

IP Address:	10.0.0.0
Mask:	255.255.255.0
Type:	Private

Cancel   OK

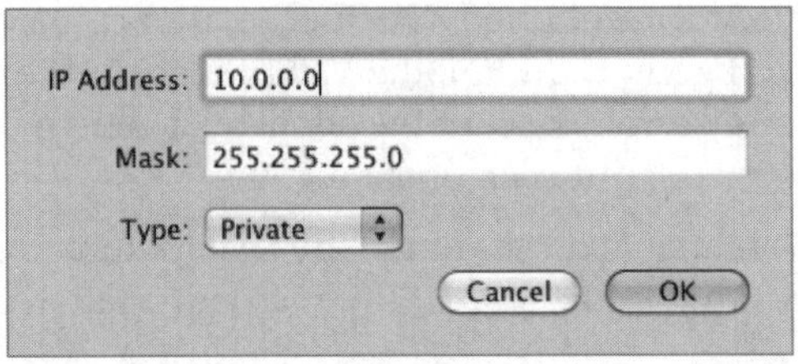

Figure 11-4.   Use this dialog box to create network routing definitions that tell the VPN clients which traffic belongs on the VPN and which doesn't.

Starting the VPN

With all the settings in place, you can now start the VPN by clicking the Start VPN button at the bottom of the Server Admin window.

Server Admin shows a green light next to the VPN item in the services list to show that the VPN service is up and running.

Setting Up the VPN Connection on the Macs

Now that the server is ready to accept VPN connections, you can set up the client Macs and connect them to the VPN.

Setting a Client Mac to Connect to the VPN

To set up a client Mac to connect to the VPN, follow these steps on the Mac:

1. Open the System Preferences window. For example, click the System Preferences icon in the Dock or choose Apple | System Preferences.

2. In the Internet & Wireless area, click the Network icon to display the Network pane.

3. Click the + button below the list of networks in the left pane to display the dialog box shown in Figure 11-5 (with VPN settings already chosen).

4. Open the Interface pop-up menu and choose VPN. The dialog box adds the VPN Type pop-up menu.

5. In the VPN Type pop-up menu, select the VPN type you need: L2TP Over IPSec, PPTP, or Cisco IPSec. This example uses L2TP Over IPSec. System Preferences enters a generic name derived from the VPN type in the Service Name text box—for example, VPN (L2TP).

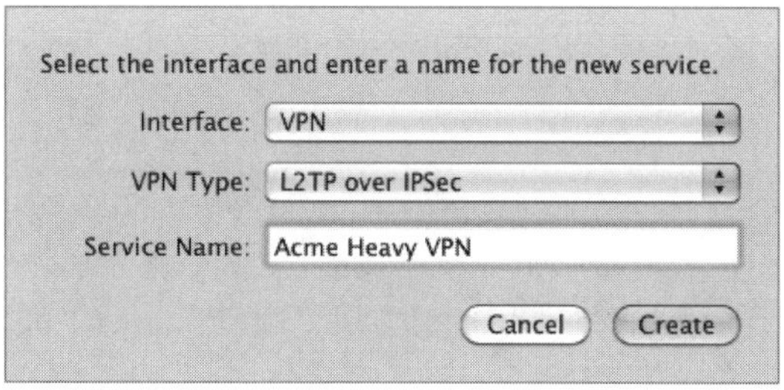

Figure 11-5.   In this dialog box, choose VPN in the Interface pop-up menu to start setting up a VPN connection.

6. In the Service Name text box, type a descriptive name that the user will easily recognize in place of the default name—for example, Acme Heavy Corporation VPN rather than VPN (L2TP).

7. Click the Create button to close the dialog box. System Preferences adds the VPN entry to the list of network interfaces. Click it to display its configuration screen (see Figure 11-6).

NOTE   You can create multiple configurations for the VPN. This section assumes you're creating just a single configuration. To create another configuration, open the Configuration pop-up menu and choose Add Configuration. In the Create A New Configuration Called dialog box, type the name for the configuration and then click the Create button. You can then set the details of the new configuration.

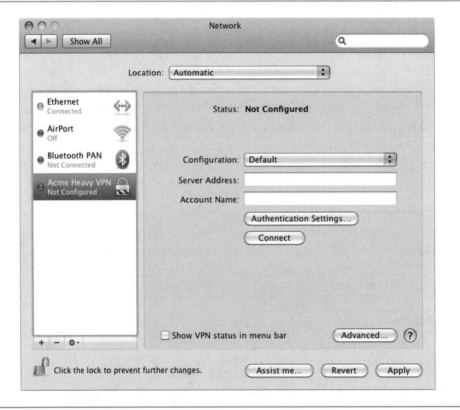

Figure 11-6.   The VPN entry shows up in the network interfaces list as "Not Configured," so your next move is to configure it.

8. Leave the Default item selected in the Configuration pop-up menu for now.

9. In the Server Address text box, type the IP address of the server.

10. In the Account Name text box, type the user's account name for the VPN connection.

11. Click the Authentication Settings button to display the Authentication Settings dialog box (see Figure 11-7).

12. In the User Authentication area, select the appropriate option button: Password, RSA SecurID, Certificate, Kerberos, or CryptoCard. For a password, type it in the text box. For a certificate, click the Select button, click the certificate in the Choose An Identity dialog box that opens, and then click the Continue button.

13. In the Machine Authentication area, select the option button for the means of authenticating the computer:

    ■ **Shared Secret**   If you select this option button, type the password in the text box.

    ■ **Certificate**   If you select this option button, click the Select button and then choose the certificate.

14. If this Mac is part of a group, type the group name in the Group Name text box.

15. Click the OK button to close the Authentication Settings dialog box.

Figure 11-7.   In the Authentication Settings dialog box, choose the means of authenticating the user and the computer.

16. Select the Show VPN Status In Menu Bar check box if you want to display the VPN status icon in the Mac OS X menu bar. This is handy if you (or the user) use the VPN often.

 NOTE The choices you've made in this section are all that you need for many VPN connections. If you need to choose further settings, see the next section, "Choosing Advanced VPN Settings".

17. Click the Apply button to apply the choices you've made.

Choosing Advanced VPN Settings

As well as the settings you've chosen so far, Mac OS X includes advanced VPN settings that you can set to control exactly how the VPN behaves. The default settings work well for many VPNs, but if you find you need to choose advanced VPN settings, click the Advanced button in the VPN pane to display the Advanced Settings dialog box and then work through the following subsections.

Choosing Settings in the Options Pane of Advanced Settings

Start by clicking the Options tab in the Advanced Settings dialog box to display the Options pane (see Figure 11-8). You can then choose settings for the following options:

- **Disconnect When Switching User Accounts** Select this check box if you want Mac OS X to disconnect from the VPN when you switch user accounts. Normally, this behavior is useful, so that you don't leave the VPN connection open when you're not there to use it, but you may need to clear this check box if you work from multiple accounts on your Mac.

- **Disconnect When User Logs Out** Select this check box if you want Mac OS X to disconnect from the VPN when you log out. This behavior, too, is usually what you want, but you can clear the check box if you need to maintain the VPN connection even when you log out.

- **Send All Traffic Over VPN Connection** Select this check box if you want your Mac to direct all your network traffic over the VPN rather than just that traffic sent to addresses on the VPN. Normally, you would select this check box when using a VPN to protect traffic on a wireless or wired network rather than when using a VPN to connect remotely across the Internet.

- **Disconnect If Idle For _N_ Minutes** Select this check box if you want Mac OS X to disconnect you from the VPN automatically after a period of inactivity. Type the number of minutes in the text box.

- **Use Verbose Logging** Select this check box if you want to log all the details of your VPN connections instead of just errors. Verbose logging is useful when you need to troubleshoot problems with the VPN, but regular logging is fine most of the time.

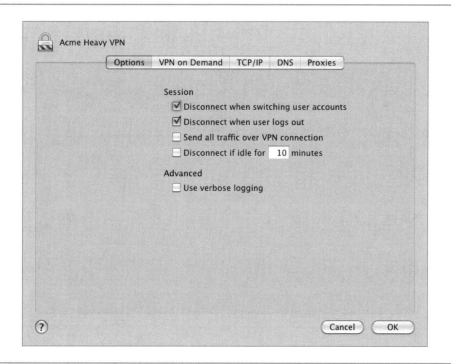

Figure 11-8.   The Options pane of the Advanced Settings dialog box lets you choose whether to disconnect automatically from the VPN and whether to use verbose logging.

Choosing VPN On Demand Settings

Next, click the VPN On Demand tab to display the VPN On Demand pane (see Figure 11-9). Here, you can create a list of any domains for which you want to use the VPN, so that when you enter that domain in your web browser, Mac OS X automatically uses the VPN. If you have multiple VPN configurations, you can choose which VPN configuration a particular domain fires up.

To add a domain, click the + button below the list box. In the entry that Mac OS X adds to the list box, type the domain name and then choose the configuration from the pop-up menu in the Configuration column. (If you've created only a Default configuration so far, that will be your only choice here.)

To remove a domain from the list, click it and then click the – button.

Configuring TCP/IP for the VPN Manually

In many cases, you can let Mac OS X handle the details of TCP/IP for the VPN connection, but sometimes you may need to choose settings manually. To do so,

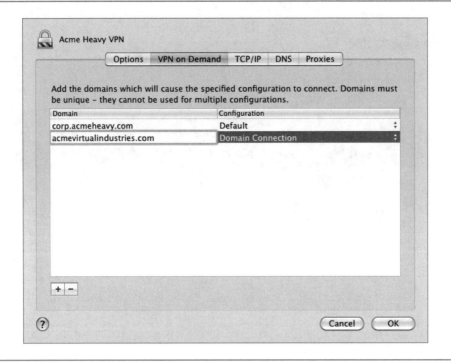

Figure 11-9. In the VPN On Demand pane of the Advanced Settings dialog box, you can specify domains for which Mac OS X should automatically use the VPN.

click the TCP/IP tab of the Advanced Settings dialog box and then work in the TCP/IP pane (see Figure 11-10).

If you're using IPv4, as most of us still are, open the Configure IPv4 pop-up menu and choose Manually instead of Using PPP. The TCP/IP pane displays the IPv4 Address text box, the Subnet Mask text box, and the Router text box, in which you can enter the details of the connection. Make sure the Configure IPv6 pop-up menu is set to Off.

If you're using IPv6, set the Configure IPv4 pop-up menu to Off and then choose Manually in the Configure IPv6 pop-up menu. You can then fill in the details in the Router text box, the IPv6 Address text box, and the Prefix Length text box that the TCP/IP pane displays.

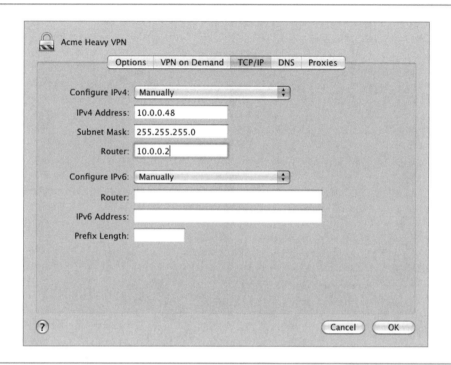

Figure 11-10.   You can configure TCP/IP settings manually for a VPN connection.

Configuring DNS Servers and Search Domains for the VPN

If you need to set DNS servers or search domains for the VPN, click the DNS tab in the Advanced Settings dialog box and then work in the DNS pane (see Figure 11-11). To add an item, click the + button below the DNS Servers list box or the Search Domains list box, and then type in the details. To delete an item, click it and then click the – button.

Choosing Proxy Servers for the VPN

The final pane of the Advanced Settings dialog box, the Proxies pane (see Figure 11-12), enables you to set up proxy servers for the VPN.

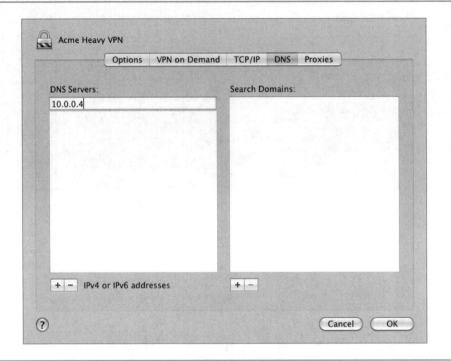

Figure 11-11. The DNS pane of the Advanced Settings dialog box lets you specify DNS servers and search domains for a VPN connection.

Follow these steps to set up proxying:

1. In the Select A Protocol To Configure list box, click the protocol for which you want to configure the proxy server. The pane displays text boxes to the right of the Select A Protocol To Configure list box.

2. Enter the details of the proxy server in these text boxes. For example, for a web proxy server, type the server's address in the Web Proxy Server text box and the port number in the second text box.

3. If the user needs to provide a password to use the proxy server, select the Proxy Server Requires Password check box. Type the username in the Username text box and the password in the Password text box.

4. In the Select A Protocol To Configure list box, select the check box for the protocol to activate the proxying.

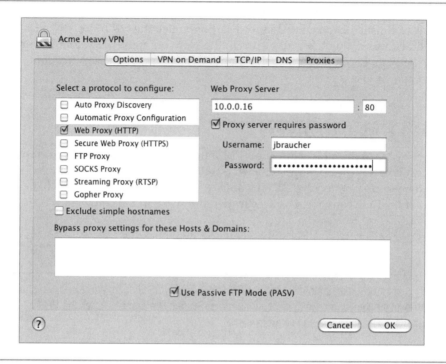

Figure 11-12.   If your VPN connection needs proxy servers, set them up in the Proxies pane of the Advanced Settings dialog box.

5. Repeat the previous four steps to configure the other protocols for which the VPN needs proxying.

6. Select the Exclude Simple Hostnames check box if you want to avoid using proxying for simple hostnames.

7. In the Bypass Proxy Settings For These Hosts And Domains text box, type the addresses of hosts and domains that the Mac should connect to directly, rather than going through the proxy. You can enter a target server's name (such as server2.corp.acmeheavy.com), an IP address (such as 10.0.0.27), or a domain name (such as acmeheavy.com); put an asterisk before the domain if you want to include all its subdomains (for example, *.acmeheavy.com).

8. Select the Use Passive FTP Mode (PASV) check box if you want the Mac to use passive FTP mode for FTP.

Applying the Changes You've Made

When you've finished choosing advanced settings, click the OK button to close the Advanced Settings dialog box and return to the Network pane of System Preferences.

Click the Apply button to apply the changes you've made to the VPN connection. It's now ready for use.

Connecting a Mac to a VPN

To connect a Mac to the VPN, click the VPN status icon on the menu bar and then click the Connect item for the appropriate VPN (see Figure 11-13). The VPN status icon displays the word "Connecting" as it establishes the connection, and then it shows a readout of the time connected as a delicate reminder that the connection is up and running.

To disconnect, click the VPN status icon and then click the Disconnect item on the menu.

NOTE If you choose not to display the VPN status icon, you can connect to and disconnect from the VPN using the controls in the Network pane of System Preferences. Click the VPN interface in the interfaces list to display the controls.

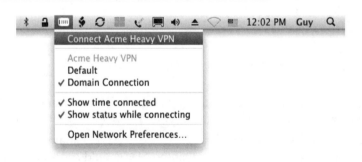

Figure 11-13. Use the VPN status icon on the menu bar to quickly connect to the VPN and disconnect from it.

Allowing Remote Access to Macs on the Network

You've now set up remote Mac users to connect to the network using their Macs, but you may also need to allow remote access to particular Macs on the network for special needs. For example, you may need to give yourself remote access to your über-Mac or your Mac server so that you can continue to run the roost or the network even when you're encamped on the beach rather than in your command bunker. Or key knowledge workers may need to access their Macs so that they can tap into their projects when inspiration strikes when they're at home.

There are three main ways of allowing remote access to particular Macs on the network.

- Give the Mac a public IP address.
- Set your router to direct packets on the appropriate ports to the Mac.
- Use the Back To My Mac feature that comes with Mac OS X and a MobileMe subscription.

Giving a Mac a Public IP Address

By giving a Mac a public IP address, you can put it directly on the Internet rather than keeping it on the internal part of the network. This means that you can connect to it directly across the Internet without needing to go through your network's router and address translation.

If you control your network's IP addresses, you can give a Mac a public IP address simply enough. But putting a Mac directly on the Internet raises serious security issues because it is directly exposed to any threat that's out there. That means you must lock down the Mac as tightly as possible with the Mac OS X firewall and perhaps its own hardware firewall to protect it from attacks. If the reason you're putting the Mac directly on the Internet is to expose sharing services such as Screen Sharing and File Sharing, you may be putting the Mac at risk—so this may not be the best solution to providing remote access to the Mac.

Routing Particular Ports to a Mac

Instead of putting a Mac directly on the Internet, you can keep it inside the network, but set your router to direct data it receives on particular ports to the Mac. For example, Apple's Screen Sharing uses port 5900, so you could route data on this port to the Mac you want to control via Screen Sharing.

Routing one or more ports to the Mac gives the Mac the protection the rest of the network enjoys except for this one kind of traffic. But it means that you can only send traffic to a single Mac, which may prove too limiting for your needs.

Connecting Using Back To My Mac

If you need to connect remotely to a particular Mac within the network, in many cases the easiest solution is Mac OS X's Back To My Mac feature, which uses Apple's MobileMe service to establish a path between the remote Mac and the Mac on your network.

In Back To My Mac, each Mac logs in to the same MobileMe user account, which lets the MobileMe servers reach the Mac without running aground on a firewall. You don't need to set up port forwarding on the firewall or give the network Mac a public IP address; instead, Back To My Mac establishes the path between the two Macs.

To use Back To My Mac, you first need to turn on the feature on both the network Mac and the remote Mac. You then need to set up sharing on the network Mac.

Turning On Back To My Mac

To turn on Back To My Mac, follow these steps on both the network Mac and the remote Mac:

1. Open System Preferences. For example, click the System Preferences icon on the Dock.

2. Click the MobileMe icon in the Internet & Wireless section to open the MobileMe pane.

3. If you're not already signed in to the MobileMe service, click the Sign In button.

4. In the tab bar, click the Back To My Mac tab to display the Back To My Mac pane (see Figure 11-14).

5. Click the Start button to start Back To My Mac. A Stop button replaces the Start button.

6. On the network Mac, click the Open Sharing button to display the Sharing pane and then set up the sharing you want to use—for example, Screen Sharing or File Sharing.

7. Quit System Preferences. For example, press ⌘-Q.

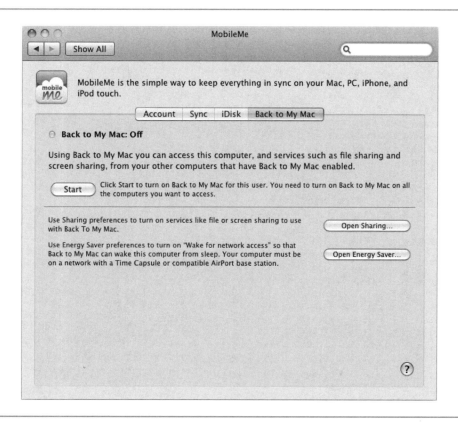

Figure 11-14.   Click the Start button in the Back To My Mac pane to turn on the Back To My Mac feature.

Making the Connection via Back To My Mac

To connect via Back To My Mac, open a Finder window. If the other Mac is available, it appears in the Shared category in the sidebar. Click the Mac, and then click the Connect button (to connect to it for file sharing) or the Share Screen button (three guesses).

CHAPTER 12 | Backing Up and Restoring Macs

Like plumbing, backup is a dirty and thankless job most of the time—but someone's got to do it, and I'm betting that someone is you. And when the pipes burst or vital files disappear, you can be sure of being the center of attention for as long as it takes to get the water working again or to restore the missing files from your capacious backup pocket.

If you're adding Macs to your Windows network, you'll need to back up the Mac users' files just as you back up the Windows users' files. In fact, if you've trained your Mac users to save their files in network home folders, you may be able to snap your Mac users' files straight into your existing backup strategy with no more effort beyond making more storage space available. If this is the case, I'll leave you in peace.

Life's seldom that easy, though, and you'll probably have Mac users who store their files in local home folders rather than on the network—for example, because they spend their days in coffee shops surfing the web on MacBooks or because they work offsite on desktop Macs.

For such users, you will probably want to implement a separate backup solution to keep their files safe. The easiest way to do so is to use Mac OS X's built-in Time Machine application, which you can set to back up data automatically to either a local drive or to a network drive.

The bulk of this chapter shows you how to set up Time Machine and how to use it to recover files that have gone astray. We'll also briefly consider choosing third-party software to back up Macs.

 NOTE Both the client and server versions of Mac OS X include Time Machine. So if you have a Mac server, you can use Time Machine to back it up to an external drive or to a network location.

Planning How You Will Back Up Mac Users' Files

Assuming you don't ritually wash your hands of responsibility for Mac users' files, you can back up these files in three main ways:

- *Back up the Mac users' network home folders along with the Windows users' folders.* If you've set your Mac users to use network home folders on a Windows server, you can simply back up these folders using the same backup solution as you're using for Windows users' folders. You can skip the rest of this chapter. But if you allow Mac users to store files in local home folders, or if you've put network home folders on an Mac OS X server, you'll need to back them up using one of the next two methods.

- *Use Time Machine.* Mac OS X includes the Time Machine backup application, so this is the natural place to start. We'll look at Time Machine in detail in the next section.

■   *Buy and implement a third-party backup solution.* If Time Machine doesn't meet your needs, you can choose from various third-party backup solutions for the Mac. See the section at the end of this chapter for a short stack of suggestions.

Backing Up Your Macs with Time Machine

In this section, you'll learn how to back up your network's Macs with Time Machine. We'll explore two main possibilities:

■   **Using Time Machine to back up a standalone Mac**   If you manage Macs that either operate on their own or connect to the network so seldom that network-based backup isn't a sensible choice, you can set up Time Machine to back up each Mac to an external drive.

Understanding How Time Machine Backups Work

Time Machine automatically backs up the data from a Mac (client or server) to a designated drive so that, when files go missing, you can dig into the past, grab the backed-up versions of those files, and bring them back to the future.

The first time you run Time Machine, it creates a full backup of the folders you've set it to protect. (You can exclude particular drives and folders from the backup, as you'll see later in this chapter.) The full backup contains a copy of every file in those folders, so it takes up roughly the same amount of space as those folders (with minor differences depending on the allocation units used for the disks involved).

The full backup necessarily takes a while, but after that Time Machine creates incremental backups that include only the files that have changed since the last backup. Here are the details of the incremental backups:

■   **Hourly backups**   Time Machine makes hourly backups of files that have changed since the last backup. On a normal system, most files won't have changed, so the hourly backup runs quickly.

■   **Daily backups**   Each day, Time Machine makes an incremental daily backup, consolidating the day's hourly backups into a daily backup. Time Machine keeps a month's worth of daily backups.

■   **Weekly backups**   Once you get further than a month in the past, it becomes less likely that you will need the daily backups. So Time Machine keeps weekly incremental backups after a month.

Time Machine automatically monitors the amount of space left on the backup disk and deletes the oldest backups when space runs short. You can choose whether Time Machine asks your permission before carrying out the hit or proceeds on its own initiative.

- **Using Time Machine to back up Macs to a server and then back up the server** If you have multiple Macs and a Mac OS X server, you can back up the Macs to the server and then use Time Machine to back the server up to an external drive. There are three steps:
  1. Set up the server as a Time Machine backup destination.
  2. Set up Time Machine on the Macs to use the server as the backup destination.
  3. Set up Time Machine on the server to back up the server itself.

Backing Up a Standalone Mac with Time Machine

To back up a standalone Mac with Time Machine, or to configure Time Machine to back up your Mac OS X server, set it up like this:

1. Open System Preferences. For example, click the System Preferences icon in the Dock or choose Apple | System Preferences.

2. In the System area, click the Time Machine icon to display the Time Machine pane (see Figure 12-1).

3. Click the Select Backup Disk button to display the dialog box shown in Figure 12-2.

Figure 12-1.   Use the Time Machine pane in System Preferences to set up Time Machine backups on a standalone Mac or on your server.

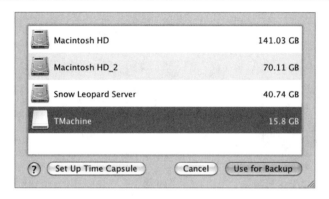

Figure 12-2. In this dialog box, select the drive to use for Time Machine.

 NOTE If you see the message "Reformat required (incompatible filesystem)" next to a drive in the dialog box for choosing the Time Machine backup disk, the problem is usually that the disk uses the FAT32 file system, which Time Machine can't use for backups. If you select such a drive for Time Machine, Mac OS X prompts you to erase its existing contents so that you can use it. Click the Erase button if you want to go ahead and get rid of everything on the drive. Mac OS X reformats it using the Mac OS X Extended file system.

4. Click the disk you want to use for Time Machine, and then click the Use For Backup button. Mac OS X closes the dialog box, displays the drive in the Time Machine pane, and starts counting down to the next backup (see Figure 12-3).

5. Click the × button to the right of the Next Backup readout if you want to stop the next backup from running immediately.

6. Click the Options button to display the Options dialog box (see Figure 12-4).

 NOTE On a MacBook, the Options dialog box also includes a Back Up While On Battery Power check box. Clear this check box if you want Time Machine to wait until you're back on power from a socket before it runs.

7. Add to the Exclude These Items From Backups list box each drive or folder you do not want to include in Time Machine backups:

    a. Your Time Machine drive appears here from the start, and you cannot remove it. (Nor should you want to.)

    b. To add a drive or folder, click the + button. Select the drive or folder in the dialog box that opens; select the Show Invisible Items check box if you need to select a hidden folder. After making your selection, click the Exclude button.

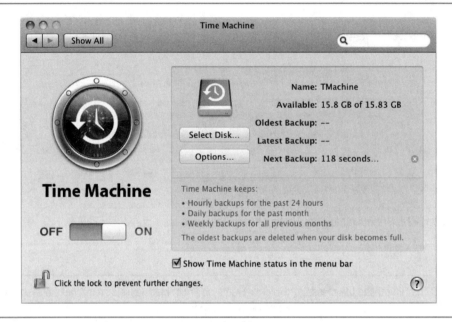

Figure 12-3. Click the x button if you want to stop the first backup from running immediately. Click the Options button to configure options for Time Machine.

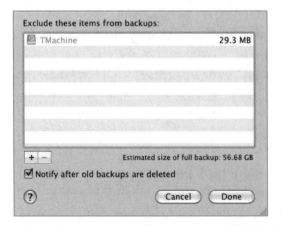

Figure 12-4. In the Options dialog box, choose which items to exclude from backups.

   c. To remove an item from the list, click it and then click the – button.

   d. Select the Notify After Old Backups Are Deleted check box if you want Time Machine to alert you after it has deleted older backups (to make space for new ones).

   e. When you've finished creating the list, click the Done button to close the dialog box and return to the Time Machine pane.

8. Select the Show Time Machine Status In The Menu Bar check box if you want to display a Time Machine icon in the menu bar. This icon spins when Time Machine is working; it also provides commands for starting and stopping backups, entering Time Machine, and opening Time Machine preferences. Displaying this icon is usually helpful.

9. Quit System Preferences. For example, press ⌘-Q.

Designating a Time Machine Disk the Quick Way

To help you get Time Machine set up, Mac OS X prompts you to use an external drive for Time Machine when you connect it to your Mac for the first time. This works for both the client and server versions of Mac OS X.

In the dialog box that appears (shown here), click the Use As Backup Disk button. Mac OS X displays the Time Machine pane in System Preferences so that you can choose options, together with a two-minute countdown to the first backup. You can click the × button to the right of the countdown timer to postpone the first backup if you want.

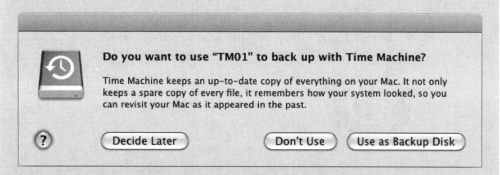

Do you want to use "TM01" to back up with Time Machine?

Time Machine keeps an up-to-date copy of everything on your Mac. It not only keeps a spare copy of every file, it remembers how your system looked, so you can revisit your Mac as it appeared in the past.

(Decide Later)   (Don't Use) (Use as Backup Disk)

If you don't want to use the external drive for Time Machine, click the Don't Use button instead. The dialog box also contains a Decide Later button that lets you postpone the decision.

Backing Up Macs and a Mac Server with Time Machine

In this section, you'll learn to use Time Machine to back up multiple Macs to a server, and then to use Time Machine to back up the server as well. This section assumes you're using Mac OS X Server in a magic triangle arrangement.

The first move is to set up Time Machine in Server Preferences on the Mac OS X server. You then set up the Macs to use the server as the Time Machine destination. Last, you set up the server's own Time Machine arrangement.

Setting Up Time Machine in Server Preferences

On your Mac OS X server, use Server Preferences to set up Time Machine like this:

1. Open Server Preferences. For example, click the Server Preferences icon in the Dock.

2. In the System area, click the Time Machine icon to display the Time Machine pane (see Figure 12-5).

3. Click the Select Backup Disk button to display the Choose Destination Volume For Client Time Machine Backups dialog box (see Figure 12-6).

4. Click the disk you want to use.

NOTE   If you have a Time Capsule (Apple's wireless network backup drive), click the Set Up Time Capsule button in the Time Machine Backups dialog box and then use AirPort Utility to set up the Time Capsule.

Figure 12-5.   The Time Machine pane in Server Preferences looks like this when Time Machine is not yet turned on.

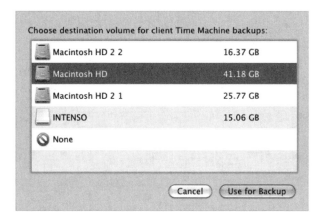

Choose destination volume for client Time Machine backups:

Macintosh HD 2 2	16.37 GB	
Macintosh HD	41.18 GB	
Macintosh HD 2 1	25.77 GB	
INTENSO	15.06 GB	
None		

Cancel · Use for Backup

Figure 12-6. Choose the disk on which to store the Time Machine backups for your client Macs.

5. Click the Use For Backup button. Server Preferences closes the dialog box, displays the disk in the Time Machine pane, and slides the Time Machine master switch from Off to On (see Figure 12-7).

6. To choose which users can back up using Time Machine, follow these steps:

   a. Click the arrow button to the right of Configure User Access to display the Users pane.

NOTE   To open the folder in which Time Machine stores the backups on the drive you chose, click the lower arrow button in the Time Machine pane.

   b. Click the Services button to display the Services pane (see Figure 12-8).

   c. Click the user you want to affect.

   d. Select or clear the Time Machine check box, as appropriate.

   e. When you've finished choosing the users, click the Back button in the upper-left corner of the Server Preferences window if you want to return to the Time Machine pane, or simply press ⌘-Q if you're ready to quit Server Preferences.

Figure 12-7. The Time Machine pane adds the disk you chose and turns on the master switch.

Figure 12-8. Use the Services pane in Server Preferences to control whether a user may back up to the server using Time Machine.

Moving Time Machine Backups to Another Disk

However capacious your backup disk, it'll fill up sooner or later. To buy time, you can delete older backups manually or let Time Machine delete them automatically, but sooner or later you'll probably want to replace the backup disk with another disk instead.

To switch to another backup disk, all you need to do is open the Time Machine pane in Server Preferences and use the Choose Destination Volume For Client Time Machine Backups dialog box to tell Time Machine which disk to use, just as you did when setting up Time Machine at first.

This is easy enough, but there's a complication: When you switch to another disk, Time Machine doesn't copy your old backups to the new disk. It just leaves them where they were.

This means two things:

- First, when users run their next backup, Time Machine will be making a full backup rather than an incremental backup. The backup will take that much longer—so you should warn them ahead of time.

- Second, if you want to keep some of those backups, you may want to copy them from the old disk to somewhere safe.

Setting Time Machine to Back Up a Client's Data

Now that you've set up the Time Machine disk on the server and chosen which user accounts to enable, you need to make the client Macs use the Time Machine disk as their backup location.

When a user who does not yet have Time Machine set up logs in to the network, Mac OS X automatically prompts them to use the Time Machine disk you've designated as their backup location. If the user accepts the invitation (and you should encourage them to do so), Mac OS X sets up Time Machine to use that disk and starts creating backups.

 NOTE   If a user is unable to set up Time Machine using the automated process, you can set up Time Machine manually by using System Preferences, as described earlier in this chapter.

Preventing Users from Changing Time Machine Settings

When Time Machine is set up, you may want to prevent users from turning it off or pointing it to another drive. To do so, remove Time Machine from System Preferences like this:

1. Open Workgroup Manager. For example, click the Workgroup Manager icon in the Dock.

2. In the Workgroup Manager Connect dialog box, enter the server's address, your username and password, and then click the Connect button.

3. Click the lock icon at the right end of the authentication bar to open the Authenticate To Directory dialog box, type your administrator name and password, and then click the Authenticate button.

4. Click the user you want to affect.

5. Click the Preferences button to display the Preferences pane.

6. Click the System Preferences icon to display the System Preferences screen (shown in Figure 12-9 with settings chosen).

7. In the Manage bar, select the Always option button.

8. Clear the Time Machine check box.

9. Click the Apply Now button to apply the change.

10. Click the Done button to close the System Preferences pane.

11. Quit Workgroup Manager. For example, press ⌘-Q.

Figure 12-9.   Workgroup Manager lets you remove Time Machine from System Preferences to prevent users from messing with its settings.

Running a Backup Manually

Usually, it's most convenient to leave Time Machine in peace to back up your systems at regular intervals. But sometimes it's useful to force a backup at a particular time—for example, before putting a MacBook through your local airport's security system.

To run a backup now, click the Time Machine status icon on the menu bar and choose Back Up Now from the menu. The backup runs immediately. If necessary, you can stop it by clicking the Time Machine status icon on the menu bar and then choosing Stop Backing Up from the menu.

NOTE   It's fine to stop a backup if you need to. Time Machine simply delays the backup until the next scheduled time. Or you can short-circuit the wait by opening the Time Machine status menu and choosing Back Up Now.

Setting the Server to Back Up with Time Machine

After setting your network's Mac clients to back up to your Mac server, you need to back up the server itself so that you can restore it if things go wrong.

Again, Time Machine can do this—and in fact it works in just the same way as setting up a standalone Mac to back up to an external drive. So to set the server to back up with Time Machine, follow the instructions in the section "Backing Up a Standalone Mac with Time Machine," earlier in this chapter.

Recovering Data Using Time Machine

When files go missing on either a client Mac or the server, recover them like this:

1. Open a Finder window to the folder that contains the files you want to recover. For example, click the Finder button in the Dock and then navigate to the folder.

2. Launch Time Machine. Click the Time Machine icon in the menu bar and choose Enter Time Machine from the menu, or click the Time Machine icon in the dock. (If the Mac has neither the menu bar icon nor the Dock icon, open the Applications folder and then double-click the Time Machine icon.)

3. On the star-field screen that Time Machine displays, click the Finder window you opened. Time Machine displays a stack of available versions of that folder, stretching back into the past (see Figure 12-10).

4. Navigate to the version you want to recover:

   - Click the title bar of a window down the stack to bring it to the front.

   - Click the upward arrow in the lower-right corner of the screen to display the next older window, or click the downward arrow to display the next newer window.

   - Move the mouse pointer over the timeline on the right side of the screen to display the dates and times of available backups, and then click the line for the backup you want.

Figure 12-10.   Time Machine displays the available versions of the folder in date order, with the latest at the front.

5. Click the files or folders you want to recover.

6. Click the Restore button to restore them to their previous location.

7. If the items you are restoring will overwrite existing files with the same name, Time Machine displays the Copy dialog box (see Figure 12-11) to check whether you want to do this. Make the appropriate choice:

- **Keep Original**   Click this button to cancel the restore operation. You can then check out the current version of the file, see if it's worth keeping, and run Time Machine again if it's not.

- **Keep Both**   Click this button to have Time Machine rename the current version of the file by adding "(original)" to its name, and then restore the older version without changing its name.

- **Replace**   Click this button to have Time Machine replace the current version with the older version.

- **Apply To All**   Select this check box if you want to take the same action with each of the items you're restoring that causes a file conflict.

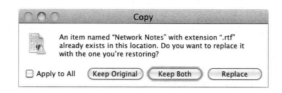

Figure 12-11. When restoring files, you may need to tell Time Machine how to resolve file conflicts.

After restoring the items, Time Machine automatically closes, leaving you to work with the restored items.

Recovering the Server Using Installer

If things go drastically wrong with the server, you may need to restore the whole thing from a Time Machine backup. Here's how to do that:

1. Insert your Mac OS X Server DVD in the optical drive, and then restart the server.

2. Hold down c at the startup sound to boot the server from the DVD.

3. On the first screen, choose the installation language and then click the arrow button.

4. On the Install Mac OS X Server screen, choose Utilities | Restore System From Backup to display the Restore Your System screen.

5. Click the Continue button to display the Select A Backup Source screen.

6. In the Backups list box, click the disk that contains the backup.

7. Click the Continue button, and then follow through the prompts to perform the restoration.

Backing Up Macs with Third-Party Backup Software

If you find that Time Machine doesn't meet your backup needs, there are plenty of third-party backup applications for the Mac. Here are three of the leading contenders you may want to examine:

■ **EMC Retrospect for Mac** EMC Retrospect (www.retrospect.com/products/software/retroformac/) is full-powered backup software for Mac OS X. EMC Retrospect comes in both client and server editions. Pricing starts at $129 for a three-user package, with a server plus 20 clients costing $479.

- **ChronoSync**   ChronoSync (www.econtechnologies.com) is a comprehensive backup package for Mac OS X. ChronoSync's strong points include backing up to many different types of devices and creating bootable backups—backups that you can boot directly into rather than having to restore them first. ChronoSync's basic pricing is $40 per Mac, but you can get volume discounts.

- **QRecall**   QRecall (www.qrecall.com) is a backup application that can handle anything from a single file to an entire volume. QRecall specializes in keeping down the size of backups, which is handy if you're pushed for space. QRecall does this by analyzing the data each file contains and backing up only the data that has changed, not the whole file—incremental backup within files, as it were. QRecall costs $40 per Mac.

NOTE   If you need to back up individual Macs to online destinations, look at CrashPlan (www .crashplan.com). If you need to create bootable complete backups of Macs in case their hard disks fail, try Carbon Copy Cloner (www.bombich.com).

CHAPTER 13 | Recovering from Disasters on Macs

M acs have gained their enviable reputation among Mac lovers not just for their sleek and shiny hardware and the ease of use of their operating system, but also because the combination of hardware and software is usually highly reliable.

Even so, you'll need to know how to recover when disaster strikes one of the Macs in your stewardship. At the most basic level, you'll want your network's Mac users to deal with software hangs and lockups so that you don't have to bring your wisdom to bear on fleeting problems. But beyond that, you'll need to repair permissions errors and disk errors, use Safe mode to force a disk check and repair, fix problems manually with the fsck command, and reinstall Mac OS X when nothing else can bring a Mac back from the lip of the grave.

Dealing with Hangs and Lockups

To save yourself unnecessary support calls, make sure all your network's Mac users are familiar with how to deal with hangs and lockups. This section covers the essential techniques you should teach the users.

Dealing with Application Hangs

When an application hangs, you can usually *force quit* it—force it to quit its antisocial behavior. Mac OS X provides a couple of ways of force quitting an application.

The easiest way to start is to click the application's icon in the Dock and keep holding down the mouse button while steam issues from your nostrils. Mac OS X hides all the other applications and displays a pop-up menu of essential commands for the application. If Mac OS X thinks the application is working fine, this pop-up menu includes the Quit command; if Mac OS X has noticed that the application is dead in the water, the Force Quit command appears on the pop-up menu.

If this pop-up menu contains the Force Quit command (see Figure 13-1), click it. If not, press OPTION to change the Quit command to a Force Quit command, then hit the mouse button.

NOTE   If the Mac you're succoring is running an earlier version of Mac OS X than 10.6, the pop-up menu will look substantially different. But you should have no trouble locating the Force Quit command.

If Mac OS X keeps displaying the Spinning Beachball of Death (SBOD) so that you're not sure which application has hung, choose Apple | Force Quit or press ⌘-OPTION-ESC. In the Force Quit Applications dialog box that Mac OS X displays (see Figure 13-2), click the application and then click the Force Quit button. If Mac OS X has identified the application's delinquency, the Force Quit Applications dialog box will show "Not responding" alongside it—but this cue doesn't always appear.

Figure 13-1.   The easiest way to force quit an application is to use the Force Quit command on the pop-up menu from the application's icon in the Dock.

Either way, Mac OS X double-checks that you really want to quit the application, as shown here. Click the Force Quit button to shut the application down forcibly.

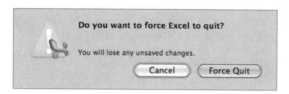

TIP   If you often need to sandbag applications with the Force Quit commands, here's a keyboard shortcut to learn: Press ⌘-OPTION-SHIFT-ESC to force quit the front application without confirmation. Press and hold this quadruple-bucky for three seconds to make it take effect. It doesn't always work, so you may need to fall back on the Force Quit Applications dialog box.

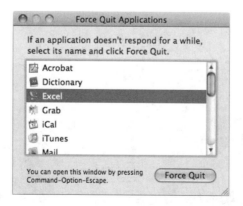

Figure 13-2.   Use the Force Quit Applications dialog box to identify the application that's gone into a death spin. Click the application, and then click the Force Quit button.

Dealing with Lockups

On the Mac, lockups generally come in two flavors:

- **Detected lockups** Sometimes Mac OS X traps the error, darkens the screen to convey the full gravity of the situation, and displays a message telling you that you need to restart the computer (see Figure 13-3).

- **Undetected lockups** Sometimes Mac OS X simply stops responding to the keyboard and mouse. If moving the mouse produces neither the Spinning Beachball of Death nor the regular mouse pointer, and the Mac doesn't respond to the keyboard, you'll need to turn the Mac off.

In either case, hold down the power button for four or five seconds, until you hear the Mac turn off. Give the Mac ten seconds to calm its mind while you curse or take deep breaths (I can combine the two), and then press the power button as normal to start the Mac again.

If a Mac gives you hangs, freezes, or generally excitable performance consistently, there's probably an underlying problem that you need to deal with. The most likely candidates are permissions problems (discussed next) and hard disk errors (discussed after that).

Repairing Permissions Errors

One of the things that most often goes wrong on Macs is permissions. Each file and folder has permissions that control who can view it (read permission), change it (write permission), or otherwise work with it. If the permissions get scrambled, you may not be able to run applications or open files as you should be able to.

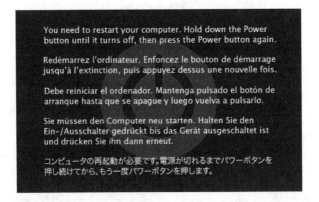

Figure 13-3. If you see this error message, you can brush up on your European languages or Japanese before holding down the Power button to turn off the Mac.

To repair problems with permissions, you use Disk Utility. Your first step is to verify the permissions to see if there's a problem you need to fix. If so, you repair the problem.

Verifying Disk Permissions to See If There's an Error

To verify the permissions on a disk, use Disk Utility like this:

1. Click the Finder button on the toolbar to open a Finder window or to activate a window that's currently open.

2. Choose Go | Utilities to open the Utilities folder in that window.

3. Double-click the Disk Utility icon to open Disk Utility (see Figure 13-4).

4. In the left pane, click the hard disk you want to verify permissions on.

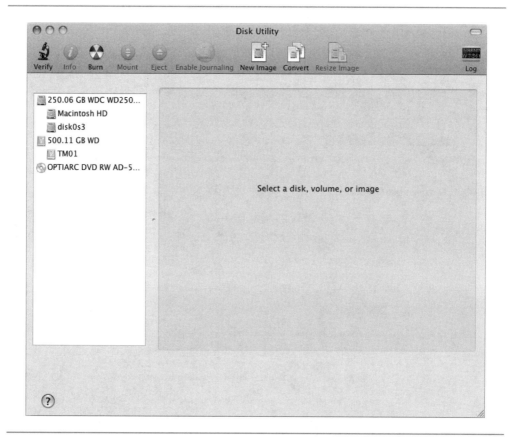

Figure 13-4. Disk Utility is the tool you use to verify and repair disk permissions and to eliminate disk errors.

5. Click the First Aid tab to display the First Aid pane.

6. Select the Show Details check box to make Disk Utility display all the gory details as it works.

7. Click the Verify Disk Permissions button. Disk Utility starts verifying the permissions, displaying its progress as it does so (see Figure 13-5).

NOTE You can keep working on the Mac while verifying disk permissions, but the Mac will be less responsive than usual, and your interference will make the verification process take longer. So it's usually better to leave the Mac alone while Disk Utility runs.

8. When the Permissions Verification Complete message appears (see Figure 13-6), see whether Disk Utility has found problems. If so, leave Disk Utility open so that you can repair them as described next. Otherwise, you can either verify the disk (as described later in this chapter) or simply quit Disk Utility (press ⌘-Q).

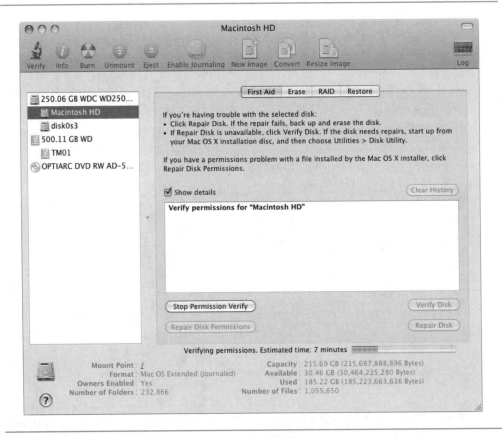

Figure 13-5. Verifying disk permissions with Disk Utility.

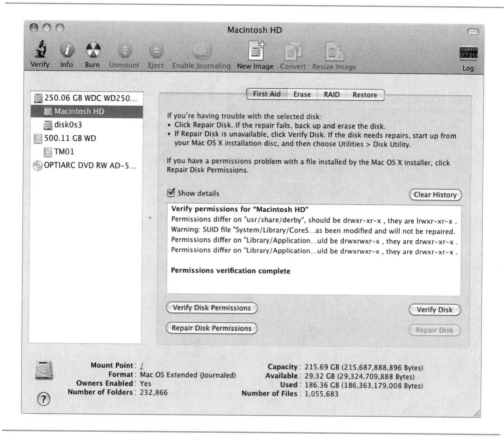

Figure 13-6.   Disk Utility shows the details of any permissions problems it has uncovered.

Repair Errors in Disk Permissions

To repair problems in disk permissions, follow these steps:

1. Open Disk Utility from the /Applications/Utilities/ folder. If you already have Disk Utility open from the previous section, you're all set. Skip ahead to step 4.

2. In the left pane, click the hard disk you want to verify permissions on.

3. Click the First Aid tab to display the First Aid pane.

4. Select the Show Details check box to make Disk Utility display full details of what it's doing.

5. Click the Repair Disk Permissions button. Disk Utility starts checking the permissions, displaying a readout of its progress as it does so (see Figure 13-7).

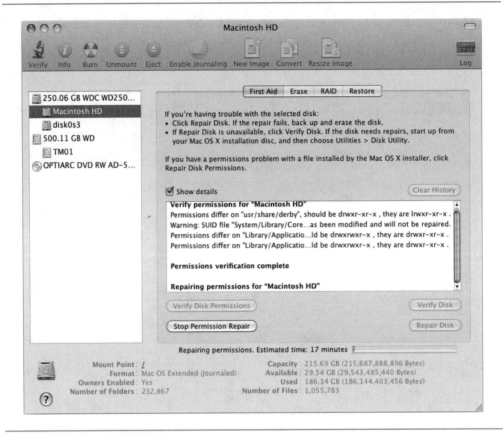

Figure 13-7. Repairing disk permission errors with Disk Utility can take a while.

 NOTE As with verifying disk permissions, you can continue to work on the Mac while repairing disk permissions, but it's better—and (perhaps more persuasively) quicker—to leave Disk Utility in peace to complete the process.

6. When the Permissions Repair Complete message appears, quit Disk Utility by pressing ⌘-Q or choosing Disk Utility | Quit Disk Utility.

Repairing Disk Errors

Disk permission errors are usually pretty easy to recover from—and they may not cause too much grief in the first place. Disk errors tend to be a different kettle of catfish and a much greater cause for concern, because they not only can cost you data but can even prevent a Mac from booting. So if a Mac starts acting seriously squirrelly, check the hard disk for disk errors and fix any that show up.

What's tricky about repairing disk errors is that the disk they tend to occur on is the Mac's startup disk—especially if the Mac's hard drive has only a single partition, the way most Macs come set up (unless and until you repartition them). To repair any errors Disk Utility finds, you must boot from a different disk so that Disk Utility has elbow room to fix the problems. Otherwise, Disk Utility needs to saw off the branch it's sitting on, and Apple has made it smart enough to refuse to do that.

Verifying a Disk to See If It Contains Errors

The first step is to verify the disk for errors. You can do this part without restarting from a different disk—at least, assuming that the Mac is still running rather than booting to an existential question mark on a sad gray screen.

To verify a disk to see if it contains errors, follow these steps:

1. Quit any applications you're running. Don't use the Mac while you're verifying the disk.

2. Open Disk Utility in your preferred way. For example, press ⌘-SPACEBAR, type **disk** in the Spotlight field, select the Disk Utility result, and then press RETURN.

3. In the left pane, click the hard disk. In most cases, this will be the startup disk.

4. Click the First Aid tab to display the First Aid pane.

5. Select the Show Details check box to make Disk Utility display full details of what it's doing. This time, you may not actually get the details, because Disk Utility tends to update its interface only in fits and starts while verifying a disk—but select the check box anyway. We demand entertainment, even if the action is slow.

6. Click the Verify Disk button. If the disk you chose is indeed the startup disk, Disk Utility warns you that the Mac may act slow and surly while being verified, as shown here. This is a natural enough reaction to being stopped and cavity-searched by the authorities, so click the Verify Disk button, raise your hands, and step back from the keyboard or mouse.

7. Disk Utility checks the disk. Depending on what it finds, Disk Utility may not display updates in the list box, and other applications may give you the Spinning Beachball of Death (this is why I suggested quitting them first). Leave Disk Utility to get on with the scan, and eventually it will give you the verdict. In Figure 13-8, the last line in the list box is green rather than gray and says "The volume Macintosh HD appears to be OK."

8. If Disk Utility has found a problem on the disk, you'll need to repair it. If the problem is on your startup disk, you'll need to restart your Mac using another disk as described in the next section. If the problem is on another disk, you have the option of going ahead and clicking the Repair Disk button. Before you do, though, it's a good idea to back up the Mac if it contains any data whose loss would sting; see Chapter 12 for suggestions.

9. Quit Disk Utility. For example, choose Disk Utility | Quit Disk Utility.

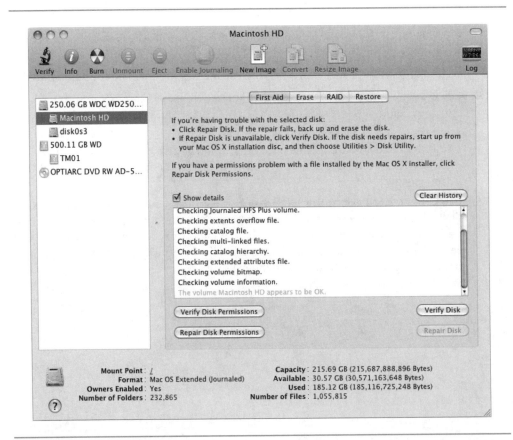

Figure 13-8. When Disk Utility returns its verdict on the Mac's hard disk, you'll know whether you need to repair the disk or not.

Repairing Disk Errors

If Disk Utility tells you that the Mac's disk contains errors, you'll need to repair the disk. Again, you use Disk Utility—but with a couple of complications.

First, be sure to back up from the Mac any files that you—or, more specifically, the Mac's users—care about. That may sound flippant, but if you've set your network's Macs to use network home folders, the Mac may not contain any files that you need to back up. (If you're saying "Dream on"—yes, I understand. Break out a capacious FireWire-800 external drive and get on with the backup.)

Second, as I mentioned earlier in this chapter, if the disk that contains the errors is the Mac's startup disk, you'll need to boot the Mac from another disk to give Disk Utility room to work. Normally the best disk to use is a Mac OS X installation DVD, but if you've cloned Mac OS X using a backup utility such as those mentioned in Chapter 12, you can also boot from an external drive.

To repair disk errors, follow these steps:

1. Insert a Mac OS X installation DVD in the Mac's optical drive.

2. Restart the Mac as usual. For example, click the Apple menu, hold down OPTION, and then click the Restart item.

3. Press and hold down c when the startup chime rings out. Keep holding c down until you can hear or see that the Mac is starting from the DVD.

4. On the first screen that Installer displays, choose your language and then click the right-arrow button to proceed.

5. When Installer displays the Install screen, choose Utilities | Disk Utility from the menu bar (see Figure 13-9, which shows Mac OS X Server) to open Disk Utility.

6. In the left pane, click the Mac's startup disk.

7. Click the First Aid tab to display the First Aid pane.

8. Select the Show Details check box to make Disk Utility display information as it works. Because Mac OS X is running from a different disk, Disk Utility should be able to keep you updated regularly rather than in fits and starts.

9. Click the Repair Disk button. Disk Utility fixes the problems it finds.

NOTE   If Disk Utility tells you to repair disk permissions and then run the repair again, do so. Sometimes fixing one problem uncovers another can of worms that Disk Utility needs to step on.

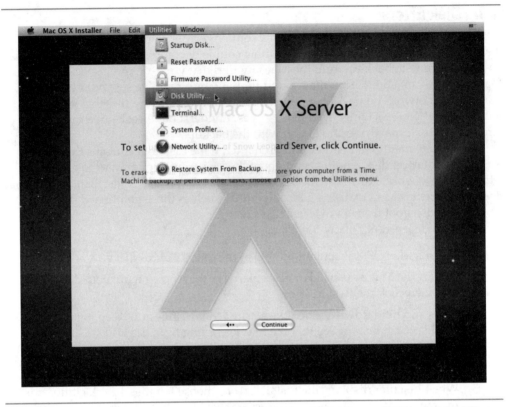

Figure 13-9. After booting from a Mac OS X installation DVD, choose Utilities | Disk Utility to launch Disk Utility so that you can repair the Mac's startup disk.

10. When Disk Utility tells you that the disk appears to be OK, quit Disk Utility by pressing ⌘-Q. This brings you back to the Install screen.

11. Choose Utilities | Startup Disk to display the Choose Startup Disk dialog box (see Figure 13-10).

12. Click the Restart button. Mac OS X displays a confirmation message box.

13. Click the Restart button in this message box too.

The Mac then starts up from its hard disk—and with any luck, you will have restored it to health.

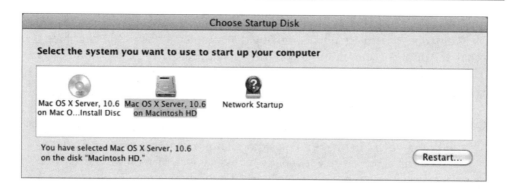

Figure 13-10. In the Choose Startup Disk dialog box, click the Mac's startup disk, and then click the Restart button.

Forcing a Disk Check and Repair with Safe Mode

If a Mac fails to boot, you can try booting into Safe mode to fix the problem. When you boot into Safe mode, Mac OS X automatically checks the startup disk and repairs any problems it finds.

NOTE Safe mode is also called Safe Boot.

To start a Mac in Safe mode, either restart it (if Mac OS X was running) or power it on from a standstill. Press SHIFT for a few seconds at the startup chime.

Startup will seem to take forever and a day, because Mac OS X is poking at the disk like a careful dentist and fixing any problems it finds. While this goes on, the Mac's screen displays the Apple logo and the Flickering Circle of Terminal Indecision that's supposed to symbolize the general advance of technology. Below these, a progress bar appears for a while at first, but then disappears without explanation or apology and leaves you to endure the wait alone.

When the checks are finished, you see the logon screen as usual, except that the words Safe Boot appear at the top (see Figure 13-11) to make sure you remember how you started the Mac.

You can now log on as usual to check if things seem to be working better. If they are, restart the Mac normally, and put it on a sensible diet and light exercise for a couple of days while you keep it under professional observation.

Repairing Disk Problems That Disk Utility Can't Fix

Disk Utility does a pretty good job at fixing disk problems—as well it ought to, given that Apple provides it. But if you run into a problem that Disk Utility can't fix, look at these three tools:

- **DiskWarrior** DiskWarrior (www.alsoft.com) focuses on fixing disk problems, and it's pretty good at it.

- **Drive Genius** Drive Genius (www.prosofteng.com) repairs directories and clones disks. Perhaps its most popular use is defragmenting hard drives—an action that isn't usually necessary on a Mac unless the hard drive becomes too full, contains huge files, or (bonus points) both.

- **TechTool Pro** TechTool Pro (www.micromat.com) fixes disk problems, but it also deals with other issues, such as problems with the parameter RAM (PRAM) on Macs.

Each of these utilities costs $100 or a shade under. If you're dealing strictly with disk problems, you'll probably want to try them in the order in which they appear here.

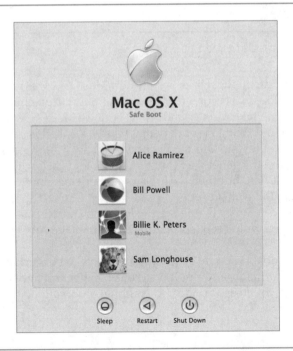

Figure 13-11.   Booting into Safe mode forces Mac OS X to check the startup disk and repair any problems.

Fixing Problems with fsck

If you can't get the Mac to start up in Safe mode by pressing SHIFT at the startup chime, you may have to resort to the fsck command. The same goes if you need to repair the disk but you don't have a Mac OS X installation DVD on hand, or if your toolkit is groaning with such DVDs but the Mac doesn't have an optical drive.

NOTE fsck is short—kinda—for *file system consistency check*. It's also used by techies as an acceptable written version of the classic Anglo-Saxon invective term that we can't print in a family-friendly book like this. If you feel funny reading it, that's okay—I feel funny typing it.

To use fsck, you need to start up the Mac in single-user mode. Follow these steps:

1. Shut down the Mac. Shut it down completely—a restart isn't good enough this time.

2. Turn the Mac on by pressing its power button.

3. Hold down ⌘-S to start the Mac in single-user mode. You can release the keys as soon as you see white text start to scroll down the screen at NASCAR speeds.

4. When you see the **:/ root#** prompt, type the following command:

   `/sbin/fsck -fy`

5. Press RETURN to run the command. You'll see a dozen or so lines of text as fsck works, and then you'll see the **:/ root#** prompt when it has finished.

6. Check the output. If it says "** The volume Macintosh HD appears to be OK," all is well. If it shouts "***** FILE SYSTEM WAS MODIFIED *****" in capitals like that, run the fsck command again as in step 4 to check whether any other repairs are necessary. (Those asterisks are just fsck trying to get your attention, not hard-to-guess five-letter expletives.)

7. When the Mac's disk seems to be okay, type the **reboot** command at the prompt and press RETURN. The Mac then boots normally.

NOTE Before you ask, that **-fy** tacked on to the fsck command is two *flags* or parameters (or, less pretentiously, options). The **f** flag makes fsck check the file system even if it appears *clean*, or okay. The **y** flag says you want to say yes to any questions fsck has about repairing the disk or salvaging files.

Reinstalling Mac OS X

If straightening out corrupt permissions, hammering down disk errors, and starting in Safe mode doesn't restore a Mac to health, you may need to reinstall Mac OS X.

You have a choice of three main ways to install Mac OS X:

- *Perform a straightforward installation from a Mac OS X installation DVD.* The process is easy enough, but you need to be physically present, though your mind is allowed to wander as the installation meanders along. Just insert the DVD in the Mac's optical drive, hold down c at the startup chime, and you're away. Choose the Archive And Install installation type if you want to keep the old installation so that you can retrieve files from it if necessary.

- *Pick up a copy of a NetInstall image you've prepared and put on the server.* See Chapter 9 for coverage of NetInstall and the wonders it can work.

- *Restore a cloned image from an external hard drive or from another Mac that you connect in Target Disk mode.* For example, if you have used SuperDuper! or Carbon Copy Cloner to create a bootable backup of the Mac, you can restore that image to the Mac.

CHAPTER 14 | Adding Macs to Small Windows Networks

U p till now, we've been looking at how to integrate Macs into Windows networks built around servers running Windows Server—perhaps just one of the beasts, perhaps a whole ravening pack of them that you keep firmly locked in a darkened room.

But you may also need to integrate Macs into small Windows networks—ones that don't use a server but instead have a peer-to-peer arrangement in which various computers provide services to other computers as needed.

The good news is that you can slot Macs into peer-to-peer Windows networks pretty easily and make them play nice with Windows. The bad news is that you don't get to use centralized management tools on a peer-to-peer network, so you will need to configure the computers individually. But given that you're presumably already doing this for the Windows boxes on such a network, having to configure the Macs individually as well should come neither as a shock nor as a gross inconvenience.

There are three main things you'll probably want to share in a peer-to-peer network: your Internet connection, your printers, and folders. This chapter shows you how to share these items from Macs and with Macs—after you've connected the Macs to the network first.

Connecting the Macs to the Network

First, you'll need to connect the Macs to the network. As with bigger networks, you have two main choices:

- **Wired connection**   Connect each Mac's Ethernet port to a network cable connected to a network switch (or, if you must, a network hub).

- **Wireless connection**   Connect each Mac's AirPort to your wireless access point.

 NOTE   For small and intimate networks, you can use FireWire connections among the computers. This is worth considering only for a handful of computers that you keep in the same room (FireWire cables are limited to 4.5 meters, but you can achieve longer distances by using FireWire hubs) and for which you have no satisfactory Ethernet or wireless connection. Many PCs don't have FireWire ports, so a FireWire network tends to be a better bet when you're using only Macs, almost all of which do have FireWire. FireWire cables are more expensive than Ethernet cables, and much more expensive than wireless networks that use built-in wireless adapters, but FireWire can be a good solution for very small networks.

Configuring an Ethernet Connection

If your network includes a router that provides DHCP service, the Mac will normally acquire an IP address, subnet mask, router address, and DNS server address automatically as soon as you connect it.

After connecting the Mac, you can test connectivity like this:

1. Open a Finder window and check that any computers that are sharing folders or devices appear in the Shared category in the sidebar.

2. Open Safari and see if it can connect to the Internet. If not, Safari displays a Network Diagnostics button that you can click to launch the Network Diagnostics tool and probe the connection problems.

If you need to configure the network connection manually, follow these steps:

1. Open System Preferences. Either click the System Preferences icon on the Dock or choose Apple | System Preferences.

2. Click the Network icon in the Internet & Wireless section to open the Network pane (see Figure 14-1).

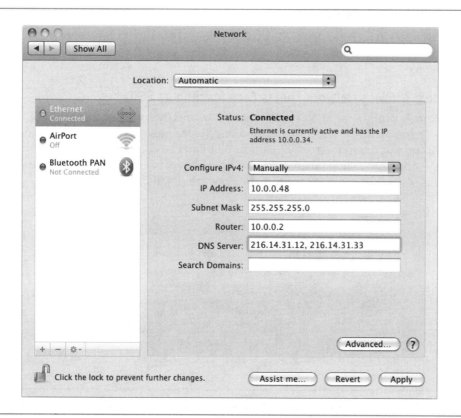

Figure 14-1.   If your network doesn't have a DHCP server, choose Manually in the Configure IPv4 pop-up menu and then type in the settings your network needs.

3. Open the Configure IPv4 pop-up menu and choose Manually.

4. Type the IP address in the IP Address text box—for example, 10.0.0.48 or 192.168.1.12.

5. Type the subnet mask in the Subnet Mask text box—for example, 255.255.255.0.

6. Type the IP address of the router or gateway in the Router text box—for example, 10.0.0.2 or 192.168.1.1.

7. Type the DNS server address in the DNS Server text box. In a small network, the DNS server addresses will typically be at your ISP rather than on your network. If you have two or more addresses, put the primary one first and separate each pair of addresses with commas.

8. Click the Apply button to apply the settings you've chosen.

Test the Mac's connectivity as described earlier.

Configuring a Wireless Connection

If your wireless network is running and is broadcasting its SSID, you can connect a Mac to it in seconds. If the network is closed (not broadcasting the SSID), it takes a moment longer.

Connecting to a Wireless Network That Is Broadcasting Its SSID

Click the AirPort icon at the right end of the menu bar, and then choose the network from the pop-up menu. (If the AirPort is turned off, choose Turn AirPort On from the pop-up menu, and then open the menu again so that you can choose the network.) Type the password in the dialog box that Mac OS X displays (shown here), select the Remember This Network check box to store the network details, and then click the OK button.

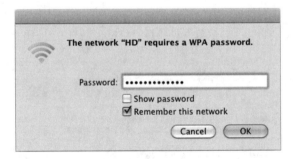

 NOTE If the AirPort icon doesn't appear on the menu bar, open System Preferences and click the Network icon in the Internet & Wireless section. In the Network preferences pane, click AirPort in the list box on the left, and then select the Show AirPort Status In Menu Bar check box. Quit System Preferences.

Connecting to a Closed Wireless Network

If your wireless network is closed (not broadcasting its SSID), you will need to know the network's name before you can connect the Mac to it, because the network name will not show up in the AirPort pop-up menu. Follow these steps to tell AirPort the network name:

1. Click the AirPort icon on the menu bar and choose Join Other Network to display the Enter The Name Of The Network dialog box (shown in Figure 14-2 with all its controls displayed).

2. Type the network name (the SSID) in the Network Name text box.

3. Open the Security pop-up menu, and then click the security type the network uses—for example, WPA2 Personal. The Enter The Name Of The Network dialog box displays the Password text box and the Show Password check box.

4. Type the password in the Password text box. Select the Show Password check box if you find it helpful to see the characters you're typing.

5. Select the Remember This Network check box to store the network's details.

6. Click the Join button to join the network.

Configuring TCP/IP and DNS Settings for a Wireless Network

Normally, when you connect a Mac to a wireless network, the Mac picks up the TCP/IP details its needs automatically. But in some cases, you may need to configure them manually to get everything working the right way.

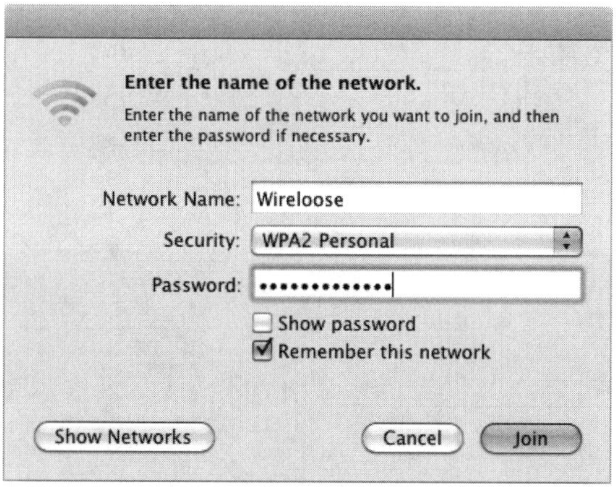

Figure 14-2.   Use the Enter The Name Of The Network dialog box to join a closed network.

To configure TCP/IP and DNS settings for a wireless network, follow these steps:

1. Click the AirPort icon on the menu bar and choose Open Network Preferences to go directly to the AirPort pane in Network Preferences.

2. Click the Advanced button to display the Advanced dialog box.

3. To configure TCP/IP settings, click the TCP/IP tab to display the TCP/IP pane (see Figure 14-3). You can then open the Configure IPv4 pop-up menu and choose Using DHCP, Using DHCP With Manual Address, or Manually; for either of the last two, enter the settings needed.

4. To specify which DNS servers to use, click the DNS tab and work in the DNS pane (see Figure 14-4). To add an entry, click the Add (+) button below the DNS Servers list box and then type the server's IP address. To remove an entry, click it in the DNS Servers list box and then click the Remove (–) button.

5. Click the OK button to close the Advanced dialog box. Mac OS X returns you to the Network Preferences pane.

6. Quit System Preferences. For example, press ⌘-Q.

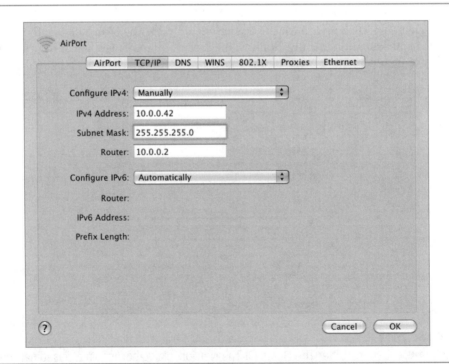

Figure 14-3. You can configure TCP/IP for a wireless connection manually in the TCP/IP pane in the Advanced dialog box of Network Preferences.

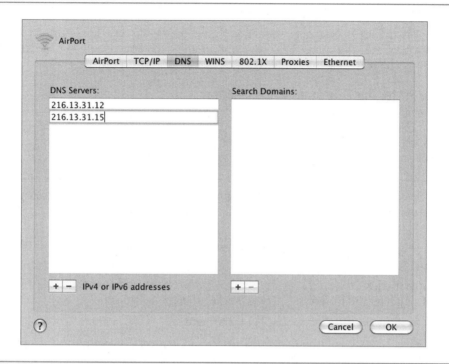

Figure 14-4.   Use the DNS pane in the Advanced dialog box of Network Preferences to tell the Mac which DNS servers to use for the wireless network.

Sharing an Internet Connection

Few people can do without an Internet connection these days, so the odds are good you'll need to share an Internet connection on your peer-to-peer network. To get your colleagues off your back, set up the Internet sharing before you tackle sharing folders and printers.

Sharing an Internet Connection via a Router Connected to the Network

If your network shares an Internet connection using a DSL router or cable router that's connected to the network, you've most likely connected the Mac to the shared Internet connection by simply connecting it to the network.

To confirm that the Internet connection is working, open Safari and check that it can display a website of your choice. Celebrate discreetly, and then allow one of your colleagues to access their essential sports sites.

Sharing an Internet Connection Connected Directly to a Computer

If your network has an Internet connection that connects directly to a PC or Mac rather than to a router that can share the connection on the network, you need to set the PC or Mac to share the Internet connection with other computers on the network.

Setting a PC to Share Its Internet Connection

To set a PC to share its Internet connection, follow these steps:

1. Click the Start button, right-click the Network item on the Start menu, and then choose Properties to open a Network And Sharing Center window.

NOTE   If the Network item doesn't appear on the Start menu, choose Start | Control Panel, and then open Network And Sharing Center from the Control Panel window.

2. In the left pane, click the Change Adapter Settings link to display the Network Connections window.

3. Right-click the connection that you want to share, and then choose Properties to display the Properties dialog box for the connection.

4. Click the Sharing tab to display its contents.

5. Select the Allow Other Network Users To Connect Through This Computer's Internet Connection check box.

6. If you want other users to be able to launch or stop the Internet connection, select the Allow Other Network Users To Control Or Disable The Shared Internet Connection check box.

7. Click the OK button to close the Properties dialog box. Windows sets the Internet connection for sharing.

8. Click the Close button (the × button) to close the Network Connections window.

Setting a Mac to Share Its Internet Connection

To set a Mac to share its Internet connection, follow these steps:

1. Open System Preferences. For example, click the System Preferences icon in the Dock or choose Apple | System Preferences.

2. In the Internet & Wireless area, click the Sharing icon to display the Sharing pane.

3. In the services list on the left, click the Internet Sharing item to display the controls for Internet sharing (shown in Figure 14-5 with settings chosen). Don't select the Internet Sharing check box yet.

4. In the Share Your Ethernet Connection From pop-up menu, choose the network interface that's connected to the Internet—for example, Ethernet.

5. In the To Computers Using list box, select the interface or interfaces on which you want to share the Internet connection—for example, AirPort or FireWire.

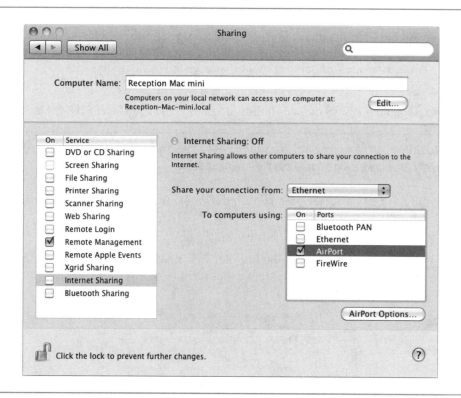

Figure 14-5.   Turn on Internet sharing in the Sharing pane of System Preferences.

6. If you selected the AirPort check box, set up the network like this:

a. Click the AirPort Options button to display the dialog box shown here.

b. Type the network name in the Network Name text box.

c. Set the Channel menu to Automatic for now. If the network seems to run slowly, try different channels to reduce interference from other wireless networks and other equipment that uses the same frequencies.

d. Select the Enable Encryption (Using WEP) check box.

e. Open the WEP Key Length pop-up menu, and then select 128-Bit in it.

CAUTION   Don't even dream of using 40-bit WEP—it is so grotesquely unsafe as to set computer security experts weeping steadily into their overpriced ale.

f. Type a 13-character password in the Password text box and the Confirm Password text box.

g. Click the OK button to close the dialog box.

7. In the Sharing pane, select the Internet Sharing check box. Mac OS X makes sure you know what you're doing, as shown here.

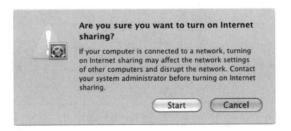

8. Click the Start button to start the sharing.

9. Quit System Preferences. For example, choose System Preferences | Quit System Preferences.

Connecting a PC or Mac to the Shared Internet Connection

Once you have shared an Internet connection on either a PC or a Mac, you can get your other computers to use the shared connection by simply connecting them to the same network. Each PC or Mac then automatically picks up the DHCP information for the network and starts using the shared connection.

If a PC is unable to connect to the Internet, open the Network Connections screen, click the connection used for the Internet, and then click the Diagnose This Connection button on the toolbar. Follow through the Windows Network Diagnostics screens and try the remedies it suggests.

If a Mac is unable to connect to the Internet, open Safari (for example, click the Safari icon in the Dock). When Safari bemoans the fact that your Mac isn't connected to the Internet, click the Network Diagnostics button and then follow through the Network Diagnostics screens, which automatically detect and apply the right settings to use the Internet connection.

Sharing Printers

Unless you've achieved the dream of the paperless office or you simply give each computer a printer, you'll want to share printers on your network. To do so, you first set up the PC or Mac to which you've connected the printer to share the printer on the network, then add the printer to the other PCs or Macs that need to use it.

 NOTE   Another option is to get a printer that connects directly to the network via Ethernet or wireless. You can then set up your network's computers to use the printer without one computer having to share it with the others.

Setting a Windows PC to Share a Printer

To set a Windows PC to share printers with Macs, you must set Windows to run the Line Printer Daemon (LPD) service. Once you've done that, you can share the printers from the Devices And Printers window.

Adding the Line Printer Daemon (LPD) Service to Windows

To add the Line Printer Daemon (LPD) service to Windows, follow these steps:

1. Choose Start | Control Panel to open a Control Panel window.

2. In the Programs category, click the Uninstall A Program link to open the Programs And Features window.

3. In the left column, click the Turn Windows Features On Or Off link to open the Windows Features dialog box (see Figure 14-6).

Figure 14-6.   Use the Windows Features dialog box to turn on the LPD Print Service feature.

4. Double-click the Print And Document Services category to expand its contents.

5. Select the LPD Print Service check box.

6. Click the OK button to close the Windows Features dialog box, and then tap your fingers in complex rhythms while Windows regurgitates the LPD print service and installs it.

7. Click the Close button (the × button) to close the Programs And Features window.

Sharing a Printer

To share a printer connected to a Windows 7 PC, follow these steps:

1. Install the printer on the PC if you haven't already done so.

 NOTE To share a printer connected to a Windows XP PC, choose Start | Printers And Faxes. In the Printers And Faxes window, right-click the printer and then choose Properties from the context menu. Click the Sharing tab to display its contents, select the Share This Printer option button, and then edit the name in the Share Name text box as needed. Click the OK button.

2. Choose Start | Devices And Printers to open a Devices And Printers window.

 NOTE To share a printer connected to a Windows Vista PC, choose Start | Control Panel. In the Control Panel window, click the Classic View link in the upper-left corner and then double-click the Printers icon. In the Printers window, click the printer and then click Share on the toolbar to display the Sharing tab of the Properties dialog box. Click the Change Sharing Options button, click the Continue button in the User Account Control dialog box, and then select the Share This Printer check box. Edit the name in the Share Name text box as needed, select the Render Print Jobs On Client Computers check box, and then click the OK button.

3. Right-click the printer and choose Printer Properties from the shortcut menu to display the Properties dialog box for the printer. The General tab (see Figure 14-7) should be at the front; if it's not, click it.

4. Click the Change Properties button to release Windows' iron grip on the printer properties.

5. Type the printer's location in the Location text box so that network users will know where to find the printer.

6. Type any comment about the printer in the Comment text box. For example, note that it's the high-quality black-and-white laser printer, or that this is the printer to use for color photos.

7. Click the Sharing tab to display its contents (see Figure 14-8).

8. Select the Share This Printer check box.

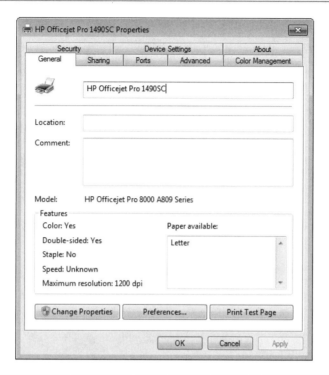

Figure 14-7.   On the General tab of the Properties dialog box for the printer, click the Change Properties button to make the properties editable. You can then enter the printer's location and any comment needed.

9. Edit the name in the Share Name text box as needed. Windows suggests the printer's model name, but you may want to substitute something descriptive such as "High-Quality Laser."

10. Select the Render Print Jobs On Client Computers check box to make the computer sending each print job do the grunt work of translating the print job into printer language. If you clear this check box, your Windows PC has to render the print jobs, which can slow it down at unexpected moments.

NOTE   If you want to limit the times of day the printer is available, click the Advanced tab, select the Available From option button, and use the two spin boxes to set the times.

11. Click the OK button to close the Properties dialog box for the printer.

Figure 14-8. Click the Change Sharing Options button on the Sharing tab of the Properties dialog box for the printer. You can then turn on sharing and set the shared name.

Connecting a Windows PC to a Printer Shared by a PC

To connect a Windows PC to a printer shared by a PC, follow these steps:

1. Choose Start | Devices And Printers to open a Devices And Printers window.

2. Click the Add A Printer button on the toolbar to launch the Add Printer Wizard. The wizard displays the What Type Of Printer Do You Want To Install? screen (see Figure 14-9).

3. The wizard then searches for shared printers and displays a list of the ones it finds (see Figure 14-10). If the printer you want is on the list, click it. Then click the Next button and go to step 10. Otherwise, click the button named The Printer That I Want Isn't Listed to display the Find A Printer By Name Or TCP/IP Address screen (see Figure 14-11).

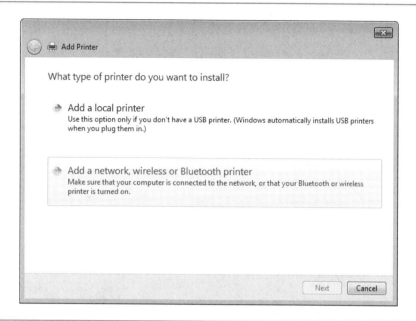

Figure 14-9.   Click the Add A Network, Wireless, Or Bluetooth Printer button on the What Type Of Printer Do You Want To Install? screen of the Add Printer Wizard.

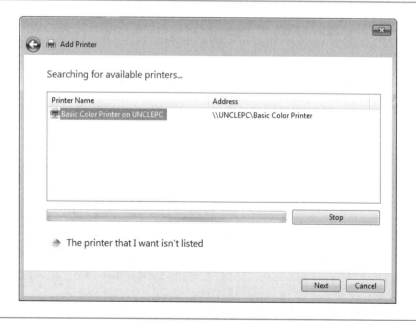

Figure 14-10.   If the Add Printer Wizard finds the printer you want, click it; if not, click the button called The Printer That I Want Isn't Listed.

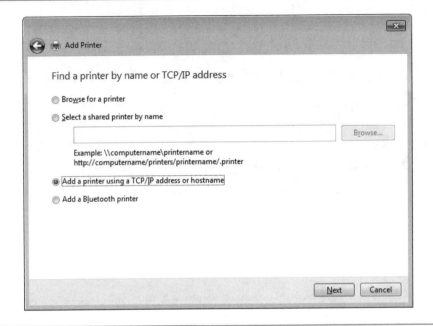

Figure 14-11. On the Find A Printer By Name Or TCP/IP Address screen of the Add Printer Wizard, select the Add A Printer Using A TCP/IP Address Or Hostname option button.

4. Select the Add A Printer Using A TCP/IP Address Or Hostname option button, and then click the Next button to display the Type A Printer Hostname Or IP Address screen (see Figure 14-12).

5. Open the Device Type drop-down list and choose TCP/IP Device.

6. Type the sharing computer's IP address in the Hostname Or IP Address text box.

7. If you know the port name, enter it in the Port Name text box. If not, just leave the IP address (which the wizard automatically picks up from the Hostname Or IP Address text box).

8. Select the Query The Printer And Automatically Select The Driver To Use check box.

9. Click the Next button to display the first You've Successfully Added page.

10. If you want to change the printer's default name, type the change in the Printer Name text box.

11. Click the Next button to move along to the final screen of the wizard.

12. Select the Set As The Default Printer check box if you want to use this printer as the default.

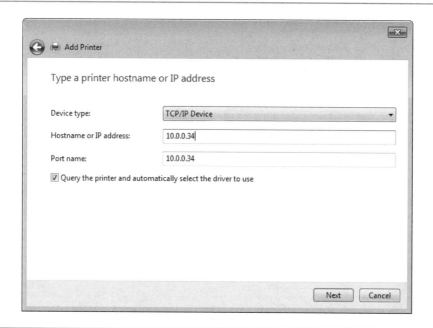

Figure 14-12.   Enter the details of the printer on the Type A Printer Hostname Or IP Address screen of the Add Printer Wizard.

13.   Click the Print A Test Page button to verify that the printer is working correctly.

14.   Click the Finish button to close the Add Printer Wizard.

Connecting a Windows PC to a Printer Shared by a Mac

It's possible to connect a Windows PC to a printer shared by a Mac by using the technique described in the previous section, but there's an easier alternative: Install Apple's Bonjour Print Services For Windows zero-configuration networking tool, and then use the Bonjour Printer Wizard to connect the Windows PC to the network.

Download the latest version of Bonjour Print Services For Windows from the Downloads page on the Apple website (www.apple.com/downloads/macosx/apple/application_updates/bonjourprintservicesforwindows.html) and install it. You can then choose Start | All Programs | Bonjour | Bonjour Printer Wizard to launch the Bonjour Printer Wizard (see Figure 14-13), which walks you through the process of setting the printer up on Windows.

NOTE   You can also use the Bonjour Printer Wizard to set up a PC to print to a standalone network printer running Bonjour. Many recent models of printer support Bonjour; if you're looking for a printer, consider adding Bonjour to your requirements.

Figure 14-13. Apple's Bonjour Printer Wizard is the easiest way to set up a Windows PC to print using a printer shared by a Mac.

Setting a Mac to Share a Printer

To set a Mac to share a printer with other computers on the network, follow these steps:

1. Install the printer on the Mac that will make the printer available for sharing. For example, connect the printer to the Mac via a USB cable, and let Mac OS X automatically choose and load the driver to use for the printer.

2. Open System Preferences. For example, click the System Preferences icon in the Dock or choose Apple | System Preferences.

3. In the Hardware section, click the Print & Fax icon to display the Print & Fax pane (see Figure 14-14).

4. Look at the Location readout and the Kind readout below the printer, and see if they make clear which printer this is, where it's located, and what it's for. If you want to improve the information, click the Options & Supplies button, enter more informative details in the General pane of the dialog box that opens (see Figure 14-15), and then click the OK button.

5. Select the Share This Printer On The Network check box to turn on sharing.

 NOTE When you select the Share This Printer On The Network check box, the Print & Fax pane may display a warning icon and the message "Printer sharing is turned off." This is fine, because you'll turn on printer sharing in a moment.

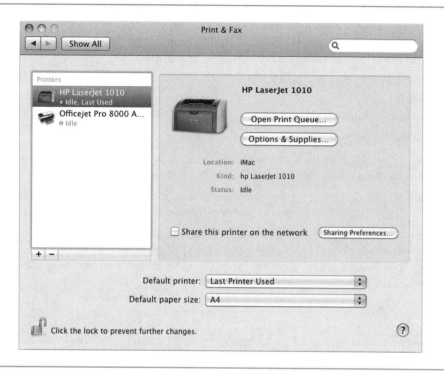

Figure 14-14. To share a printer, select the Share This Printer On The Network check box in the Print & Fax pane in System Preferences.

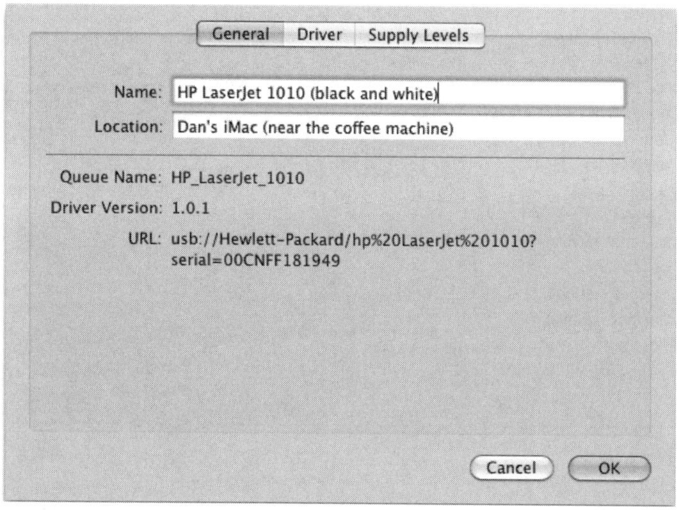

Figure 14-15. Use the Name text box and Location text box in this dialog box to make clear which printer this is and where your colleagues will find it.

6. Click the Sharing Preferences button to display the Sharing pane of System Preferences (shown in Figure 14-16 with settings chosen). System Preferences automatically selects the Printer Sharing item in the Sharing list box so that you can see which printers you're currently sharing.

7. If the Printer Sharing check box is currently cleared, select it to turn on printer sharing.

8. In the Printers list box, click the printer for which you want to set permissions.

9. In the Users list box, build the list of users:

   ■ If you want to allow every user to print, click the Everyone entry that appears by default and then choose Can Print from the pop-up menu next to it.

   ■ Similarly, to block everyone from printing, click the Everyone entry and then choose No Access in the pop-up menu.

   ■ To add another user who may use the printer, click the + button below the Users list box. In the dialog box that appears, select the user and then click the Select button. You can also add multiple users or groups of users in the same way.

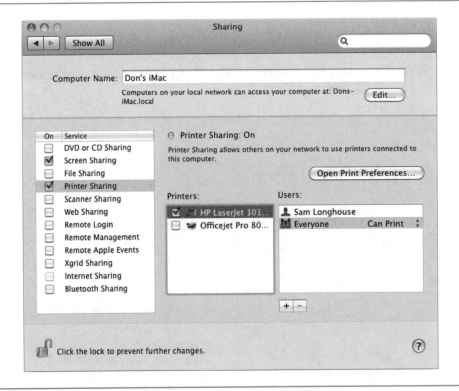

Figure 14-16.   In the Sharing pane of System Preferences, choose which users may use which printer.

NOTE   To share another printer from the Sharing pane, select the printer's check box in the Printers list box. You can then set permissions for printing on the printer.

10. When you've finished setting up printer sharing, quit System Preferences. For example, press ⌘-Q.

Connecting a Mac to a Shared Printer

To connect a Mac to a shared printer, follow these steps:

1. Choose Apple | System Preferences to open the System Preferences window.

2. In the Hardware category, click the Print & Fax icon to display the Print & Fax preferences pane (see Figure 14-17).

3. Click the + button below the printers pane on the left to display the Add Printer dialog box.

4. If the Default pane (see Figure 14-18) isn't already displayed, click the Default button on the toolbar to display it.

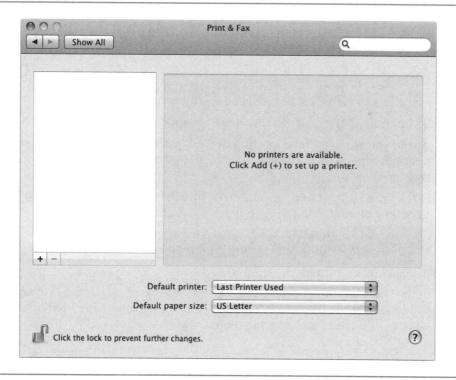

Figure 14-17.   Click the + button in the Print & Fax preferences pane to start adding a shared printer to a Mac.

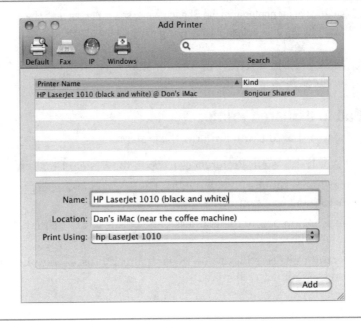

Figure 14-18. Use the Default pane of the Add Printer dialog box to add a shared printer on another Mac on your peer-to-peer network.

5. In the Printer Name list box, select the printer you want to add.

6. If you want, change the default name that appears in the Name text box.

7. Also if you want, edit the location in the Location text box. If you've set a clear description of the location on the shared printer, you shouldn't need to change it.

8. In the Print Using pop-up menu, make sure that Mac OS X has selected the right type of printer. If not, open the menu and choose it yourself.

9. Click the Add button. Mac OS X installs the software needed for the printer and then displays the printer in the Print & Fax pane in System Preferences.

10. Add any other printers you need to add now.

11. In the Default Printer pop-up menu (see Figure 14-19), select the printer you want to use as the default. You can select the Last Printer Used item to use whichever printer you last printed on.

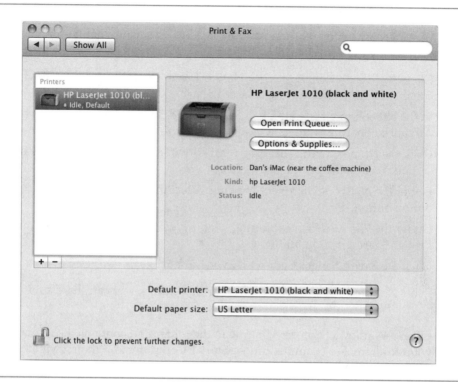

Figure 14-19. After adding one or more printers, choose the user's default printer. You can also set the default paper size.

12. In the Default Paper Size pop-up menu, choose the default paper size to use for printing—for example, US Letter or US Legal.

13. Quit System Preferences. For example, press ⌘-Q or choose System Preferences | Quit System Preferences.

Sharing a Folder

When you've dealt with sharing the Internet connection and printers, you'll probably want to share some folders as well. This section shows you how to set both Windows PCs and Macs to share folders and to connect to folders that other computers on the network are sharing.

Setting a Windows PC to Share a Folder

To set a Windows PC up for sharing, you first need to make sure that your advanced sharing settings are right. Follow these steps:

1. Click the Start button, right-click Network, and then choose Properties from the context menu to open a Network And Sharing Center window.

2. In the left column, click the Change Advanced Sharing Settings link to open the Advanced Sharing Settings window (see Figure 14-20).

3. Click the Home Or Work heading (or its down-arrow button) to reveal the settings it contains (see Figure 14-21).

4. Under the Network Discovery heading, select the Turn On Network Discovery option button.

5. Under the File And Printer Sharing heading, select the Turn On File And Printer Sharing option button.

6. Click the Save Changes button to save your changes.

Once you've sorted out your advanced sharing settings, you can share a folder like this:

1. Open a Windows Explorer window to the folder that contains the folder you want to share. For example, choose Start | Computer and then navigate to the enclosing folder.

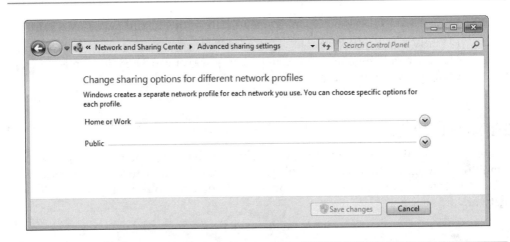

Figure 14-20.   In the Advanced Sharing Settings window, expand the network profile for which you want to set sharing. Normally, this is the Home Or Work profile.

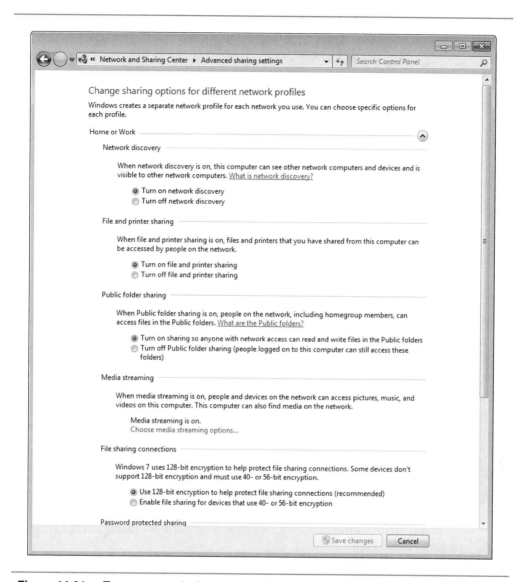

Figure 14-21.   Turn on network discovery and file and printer sharing in the Advanced Sharing Settings for your Home Or Work network profile.

2. Right-click the folder, click or highlight Share With on the context menu, and then click Specific People to display the File Sharing dialog box (see Figure 14-22).

3. Add the appropriate names to the main list box. To add a name, either type it in the text box or open the drop-down list and choose the name from the list. Then click the Add button.

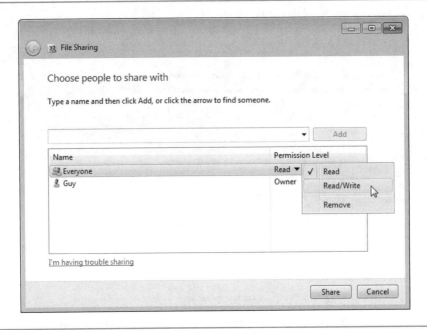

Figure 14-22. In the File Sharing dialog box, build the list of people with whom you want to share the folder, and assign each person or group the appropriate level of permissions.

NOTE If you're simply sharing the folder freely with all the users of the network, choose Everyone in the drop-down list, click the Add button, and then set the permission level to Read/Write.

4. Set the permission level for each user or group. Click the user or group in the list box, then open the Permission Level pop-up menu and choose the Read permission level (for anyone who needs to view files but not change them) or the Read/Write permission level (for anyone who needs to change the files or create new ones in the folder).

5. Click the Share button to share the folder.

6. Click the Done button to close the File Sharing dialog box.

Setting a Mac to Share a Folder

To set a Mac to share a folder, follow these steps:

1. Open System Preferences. For example, click the System Preferences icon in the Dock or choose Apple | System Preferences.

2. In the Internet & Wireless area, click the Sharing icon to display the Sharing pane.

3. In the list of services, click the File Sharing item to display the options for it (shown in Figure 14-23 with settings chosen).

NOTE Don't select the File Sharing check box just yet—wait until you've set up the folders you want to share and the colleagues with whom you want to share them.

4. Now choose the protocols you'll use to share the folder. Follow these steps:

   a. Click the Options button to display the dialog box shown in Figure 14-24.

   b. Select the Share Files And Folders Using AFP check box. AFP is Apple Filing Protocol, the best protocol for sharing folders among Macs.

CAUTION The dialog box for choosing file-sharing protocols lets you share folders using FTP as well as AFP and SMB. FTP is not secure, so avoid using it unless you must provide file transfer across Internet connections.

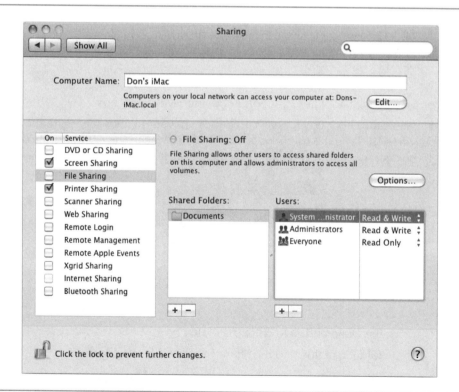

Figure 14-23. To share files, set up File Sharing in the Sharing pane in System Preferences.

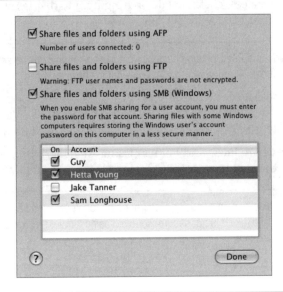

Figure 14-24.   Choose your file-sharing protocol in this dialog box. Normally, you'll want to use AFP to share files with your Macs and SMB to share with Windows.

    c. Select the Share Files And Folders Using SMB check box.

    d. Select the check box for each account you want to allow access to the folder via SMB. Type the user's password for this Mac in the Authenticate dialog box (shown here), and then click the OK button.

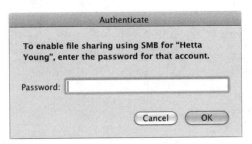

    e. Click the Done button to close the dialog box.

  5. Add the folder or folders to the Shared Folders list box like this:

    a. Click the + button below the Shared Folders list box to display a dialog box.

    b. Select the folder you want to share.

    c. Click the Add button.

6. Set up the users who are allowed (or denied) access to the folder like this:

■ If the user or group appears in the Users list box, choose the permission level in the pop-up menu: Read Only (which lets the user open files but not save changes to them), Read & Write (which lets them open files and save changes), or No Access (which blocks the user or group completely).

NOTE The fourth option on the permissions pop-up menu, Write Only (Drop Box), lets users add files to a folder but not see its contents. Use Write Only permission when setting up a folder in which some users can leave files for other people. This is the permission Mac OS X uses for each user's / Public/Drop Box/ folder.

■ If the user or group doesn't appear, click the + button below the Users list box to display the dialog box shown here.

■ If the user or group appears in this list box, click it and then click the Select button. You can change the category in the left column as needed, or use the search box to search for a user or group by name.

■ Otherwise, click the New Person button and then enter the person's name and password in the New Person dialog box (shown here). Click the Create Account button to close the dialog box and create the person's account, then click the new person in the dialog box, and click the Select button.

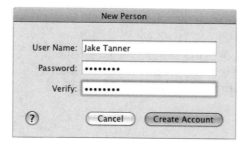

■ After adding the user or group to the Users list box, open the permissions pop-up menu and set the level of permissions—for example, Read & Write or Read Only.

NOTE Each user who accesses folders that a Mac is sharing must have either a regular user account (Administrator, Standard, or Managed) or a Sharing user account on that Mac. The New Person dialog box automatically creates a Sharing user account with the details you enter. You can also create Sharing user accounts in the Accounts pane in System Preferences.

7. In the Services list box, select the File Sharing check box. Mac OS X turns on file sharing.

Connecting a PC to a Shared Folder

After you've set up your shared folders, you can connect a PC to a shared folder like this:

1. Choose Start | Computer to open a Windows Explorer window to the Computer folder.

NOTE If you need to connect to a shared folder only once, you can simply browse the network and open the folder. But for folders that you use regularly, map a drive to the shared folder.

2. Click the Map Network Drive button on the toolbar to display the Map Network Drive dialog box (see Figure 14-25).

3. In the Drive drop-down list, select the drive letter you want to assign to the drive. Windows suggests Z: or the first unused letter from the end of the alphabet, but you can choose any other unused letter.

4. Enter the address of the shared folder in the Folder text box, using the format *server**share*, where *server* is the hostname or IP address of the server and *share* is the folder name—for example, \\10.0.0.34\Templates. You can type in the address or click the Browse button and use the Browse For Folder dialog box to pick the folder.

5. Select the Reconnect At Logon check box if you want Windows to automatically connect this drive each time you log on. As long as the shared folder is always there, this option is a good idea.

6. Select the Connect Using Different Credentials check box if you need to supply a different username and password for the shared folder than those of the account you're currently using.

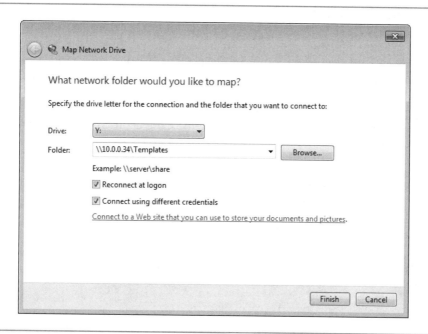

Figure 14-25. Use the Map Network Drive dialog box to map a network drive to a shared folder on another computer.

7. Click the Finish button. If you selected the Connect Using Different Credentials check box, Windows displays the Windows Security: Enter Network Password dialog box (shown here). Type your username and password for the shared folder, select the Remember My Credentials check box if you want to store them, and then click the OK button.

Windows automatically opens a Windows Explorer window showing the contents of the shared folder, so you can start working with them.

Connecting a Mac to a Shared Folder

To connect a Mac to a shared folder, follow these steps:

1. Open a Finder window. For example, click the Finder icon in the Dock.

2. In the sidebar, expand the Shared category if it's currently collapsed.

3. Click the Mac that's sharing the folder.

4. Click the Connect As button to display the Connect As dialog box, shown here.

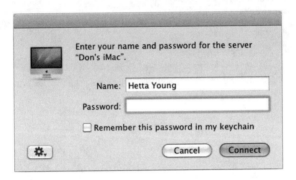

5. Make sure the Name text box contains the username for the shared folder (which may be different from the account you're using).

6. Type the corresponding password in the Password text box.

7. Select the Remember This Password In My Keychain check box if you want to store the password. This is normally a good idea for regular connections.

8. Click the Connect button. The Connect As dialog box closes, and Mac OS X establishes the connection.

The Mac can then work with files and folders as usual in the folder to which you have connected it.

NOTE To disconnect from a shared folder, open a Finder window and then click the Eject icon next to the shared folder in the sidebar. Usually, though, you'll probably want to simply leave the shared folder connected until you log out from your Mac or shut it down.

To make the Mac connect to the shared folder automatically at login, follow these steps:

1. Connect to the shared folder as described previously.

2. Open System Preferences. For example, click the System Preferences icon in the Dock or choose Apple | System Preferences.

3. In the System section, click the Accounts icon to display the Accounts pane.

4. Click your account if it's not already selected.

5. Click the Login Items tab to display the Login Items pane (see Figure 14-26).

6. Drag the shared folder from your desktop (if it appears there) or from a Finder window to the These Items Will Open Automatically When You Log In list box. It appears there as a volume (rather than as an application).

7. Quit System Preferences. For example, press ⌘-Q.

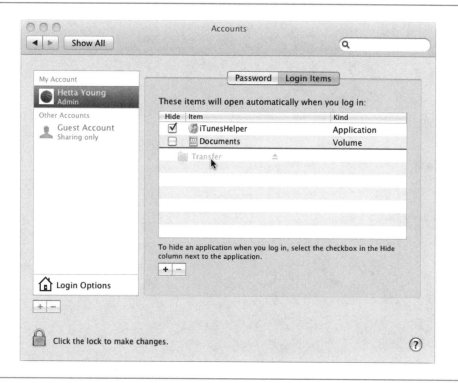

Figure 14-26. To make your Mac automatically open a shared folder when you log in, add the folder to your Login Items list in the Accounts pane of System Preferences.

Index